LIBERTY FROM ALL MASTERS

THE NEW AMERICAN AUTOCRACY VS. THE WILL OF THE PEOPLE

BARRY C. LYNN

St. Martin's Press
New York

First published in the United States by St. Martin's Press, an imprint of St. Martin's Publishing Group

www.stmartins.com

Design by Meryl Sussman Levavi

Library of Congress Cataloging-in-Publication Data

Names: Lynn, Barry C., author.
Title: Liberty from all masters : the new American autocracy vs. the will of the people / Barry C. Lynn.
Description: First edition. | New York : St. Martin's Press, 2020. | Includes bibliographical references and index. | Identifiers: LCCN 2020021884 | ISBN 9781250240620 (hardcover) | ISBN 9781250240637 (ebook)
Subjects: LCSH: United States—Economic conditions—21st century. | Liberty—United States. | Monopolies—United States.
Classification: LCC HC106.84 .L96 2020 | DDC 306.20973—dc23
LC record available at https://lccn.loc.gov/2020021884

Our books may be purchased in bulk for promotional, educational, or business use. Please contact your local bookseller or the Macmillan Corporate and Premium Sales Department at 1-800-221-7945, extension 5442, or by email at MacmillanSpecialMarkets@macmillan.com.

First Edition: 2020

10 9 8 7 6 5 4 3 2 1

Your people will rebuild the ancient ruins . . .
and will raise up the age-old foundations.

ISAIAH 58:6–7, 11–12

CONTENTS

THE MONOPOLISTS AND THE PANDEMIC

On the evening of March 11, 2020, I found myself in midtown Manhattan at Joe Allen, which has a good bar for a late dinner alone. Earlier that day I'd taken the train from Washington to New York for meetings. I had planned to eat downtown with a friend, but she had a cough and did not want to leave her apartment. I settled onto a stool and ordered a bourbon and a small steak.

As the bartender set down my plate, the world suddenly seemed to tilt. The television near the front door was muted, but President Trump was on the screen and the news ticker told us he planned to stop all travel from Europe. I looked at the bartender as he stared at the TV, his half smile of disbelief slowly tensing. At the other end of the bar, three waiters stood, mouths agape. It wasn't hard to imagine their thoughts; about their jobs, their homes, their way of life. For a few moments the bar burst into nervous chatter. Then another flash of news: the NBA planned to suspend all games. Folks began to close out their tabs and hurry into the night.

Many years ago I worked as a warehouse carpenter and truck driver in the Garment District. Ever since, Midtown has felt like a second home. Many New Yorkers despise the area. But I love the energy of so many people, from all around the world, just trying to make a buck or have some fun. The piles of schlock, the hawkers and posers, the sea of faces glowing blankly in the pulsing light beneath looming dark towers of stone. Life, on the avenue.

But on this night, as I walked out of the bar and under the marquees, the wolfish or buzzed looks of the performers and partiers had been replaced by nervousness and fear. At the hour when bars normally fill, people instead rushed to trains or into cabs or to hotels, their eyes flaring if anyone came too close, the dull sheen of chemicals or simple happy human ignorance gone.

The next morning, New York's theater owners announced that, for the foreseeable future, Broadway was closed. In the weeks that followed, more than 15,000 New Yorkers would die of Covid-19, and more than 30 million Americans would lose their jobs. Nations fought over facemasks, states fought over ventilators, people fought for rolls of toilet paper.

I didn't expect to be walking on Broadway when the lights went out, but I have thought a lot about how societies break down. From 20 years of close study of human systems I have long believed that it was only a matter of time till some event triggered a cascading collapse of our most important assembly lines, including those for medical facemasks and essential drugs. That's why I also knew that we could have easily avoided much of the chaos and confusion and pain and death of the first months of the pandemic.

Covid-19 is a hard disease. It spreads fast and can kill swiftly. But the effects of Covid-19 were made far worse by stupid decisions that allowed monopolists to ruin and wreck many of our most vital industrial systems, in ways that endanger us as individuals and as a nation.

I know this issue well. I have written two books about the economic and political threats posed by the ways monopolists have reorganized American and international industry over the last generation. Just this spring, the Open Markets Institute that I head launched a partnership with the Organisation for Economic Co-operation and Development, in Paris, to study these dangers and recommend fixes.

In *Liberty from All Masters* I don't address these dangers in depth, though I do touch on them. Instead I focus on something even more fundamental—the tools that will help us build not merely a far safer world in the days to come, but also a more fair and just world.

The idea that there are basic flaws in how we have engineered our assembly lines may seem shocking. After all, Americans mastered mass manufacturing more than a century ago, and have benefited enormously from the prosperity it made possible.

But the basic problem is not hard to understand.

Monopolists, to gain money and power, routinely concentrate control over some vital activity, such as the production of a semiconductor, or chemical, or component in N95 facemasks. In the process, they also often concentrate the capacity to make these goods. This means that rather than manufacture an important product in, say, five factories around the world, they centralize production in a single factory. The most obvious result of such monopolization is that we end up with fewer of the things we need—such as facemasks and syringes—and what we do get costs more.

A second result, in some respects more dangerous than the first, is that when a shock such as an earthquake or a pandemic cuts off access to one of these keystone factories, it can trigger a cascading crash of entire systems of production.

Every one of us knows not to put all our eggs in one basket. Yet when it comes to many of the products and foods and drugs that keep us alive, monopolists have put most or even all the machines that produce these goods in a single city, often in a single factory, often on the other side of the world.

I first learned of this flaw in September 1999, after an earthquake in Taiwan resulted in an almost immediate shutdown of computer factories in the United States. At the time I was running a magazine called *Global Business*, and I had spent years studying how corporations were reengineering their assembly lines to take advantage of the radical new rules of trade put into place after the collapse of the Soviet Union.

Even so, the fact that our government had allowed two foreign corporations to concentrate most of the world's capacity to build an essential semiconductor in one city in Taiwan surprised me. So I set out to learn how this happened and what it meant.

I first wrote about the problem in *Harper's* in June 2002, in an article titled "Unmade in America: The True Cost of a Global Supply Chain." I provided more detail in my first book, *End of the Line: The Rise and Coming Fall of the Global Corporation*, in 2005. In that book I also explained how such concentration can create dangerous political dependencies, especially on China.

I returned to the subject in my second book, *Cornered: The New Monopoly Capitalism and the Economics of Destruction*, in early 2010. My main goal in *Cornered* was to explain how monopolization threatens our democracy. But I also devoted large sections to showing how the one-two punch of monopolization and shareholder governance of corporations results almost inevitably in the destruction of the machines and skills we rely on to feed and clothe ourselves and keep ourselves healthy and safe.

Ever since, I have walked these warnings around Washington, Silicon Valley, Wall Street, and world capitals. I have met with top officials in the Treasury and Commerce departments, in the Pentagon and the CIA, in manufacturing and banking and insurance corporations.

In October 2005, in the *Financial Times*, I distilled the warning into two sentences. "We now live in a world where an isolated political or natural disaster on the far side of the globe can disrupt basic systems on which we all depend. Consider what would happen in the event of war on the Korean peninsula . . . or an avian flu pandemic in industrial Asia."

Most of the officials and executives I met easily understood my arguments about the dangers of concentration. But almost every one said they lacked the ability to do anything about it.

I finished *Liberty from All Masters* just before the lockdown. My editor and I spent a few days debating whether to change the text to address the lessons of Covid-19. In the end we decided to leave the book largely as I first wrote it—as the culminating work of a trilogy.

This makes sense on two levels. Technically, *Liberty from All Masters* builds on the reporting of *End of the Line* and *Cornered* by clarifying the specific nature of the political and economic threats posed by Google, Facebook, and Amazon. Even before the pandemic, these three corporations were vastly more dangerous than the dominant monopolists I covered a decade ago, and it is of vital importance to understand the nature of their power. Further, each has grown only more powerful since the beginning of the Covid-19 crisis.

More fundamentally, in *Liberty from All Masters* I detail the commonsense philosophy of competition that Americans used during the first 200 years of our nation to master all dangerous concentrations of power, control, and capacity.

A generation ago the monopolists blinded us to the thinking that lies at the heart of this philosophy, precisely to free themselves to put so many of our most important eggs in single baskets.

If we are ever again to make ourselves physically and politically safe, we must first relearn how to use this philosophy. That in turn will empower us to deal not only with the monopolists, but with the people they hired to blind us.

As I write these words in mid-May the sun is out, the roses are in full bloom, and people are venturing into the streets and parks. But on any day, most of us still bounce moment by moment from terror to confusion to disillusionment to despair.

Probably the single dominant feeling now is sadness.

We feel sad for all the people who lost someone, and were not able to say goodbye.

We feel sad for all the children. Already bracing for radical changes in the world's climate, many have lost what little remained of their sense of freedom and future.

We feel sad for the people who do the jobs that must be done, in warehouses and slaughterhouses and jails and nursing homes and hospitals, without proper protection, and for wages that barely cover lunch.

We feel sad for all the people who built the businesses that help to hold our communities together, and all the people who dedicated their lives to crafting the music and films and food and clothing that help to make our lives fresh and fun.

We feel sad for ourselves. So many of the little joys, of gathering with friends and family, of sitting in a bar, of feeling alive and human, are gone.

Yet as bad as this pandemic is, almost all of us should count ourselves very lucky.

We are lucky because the collapse of systems could have been far more devastating. Thanks to a few good breaks, most keystone factories were able to keep running, allowing us to avoid cascading industrial crashes.

We are lucky because this disease has reminded us that we are still subject to a natural world we don't fully understand. Which in turn makes it more clear why we must stop our suicidal spewing of waste and poison into our air and water.

We are lucky because the devastating shortages of even such basic items as facemasks and swabs illuminate the role of the monopolist in creating this crisis. This helps us understand that the only way to fix the problem is to break the power of the monopolist, here at home and around the world.

For a generation now, we have allowed a few men to exploit their control over our corporations and banks to force us to compete with one another, by nation, by race, by class, by gender, as individual against individual.

This fight of all against all threatens our freedom and democracy, and led us to break the machines we depend on.

Covid-19 is our last warning. Our last opportunity to understand that, acting together, we have the power to master the monopolist and to rebuild, from the bottom up, our lives, our communities, our nations, our world.

In *Liberty from All Masters* I hope you find the guide you were looking for.

MAY 24, 2020, WASHINGTON, D.C.

INTRODUCTION

THE CRISIS OF LIBERTY

AMERICANS ARE OBSESSED WITH LIBERTY, MAD ABOUT LIBERTY. ON any day, we can tune into arguments about how much liberty we need to buy a gun or get an abortion, to marry who we want or fully embrace the gender or genders we feel. We argue endlessly about liberty from regulation and observation by the state and proudly rebel against the tyranny of the course syllabus and Spotify playlist. Redesign the penny today and the motto would read, "You ain't the boss of me."

And yet, somehow, we as a people missed the most radical revolution in political economic thinking in our history, and consequently, the rise of the greatest domestic threat to many of our fundamental liberties since the Civil War.

It's not President Trump who poses this danger. Subversive, often destructive, and gleefully so, Donald Trump is but a symptom of the problem, and sweeping him from office will do little to solve it. Nor is it nationalism, or tribalism, or a generalized loss of faith in liberal democracy that poses the danger. These too are but signs of what lies beneath.

The crisis is monopolization on a scale that far surpasses even that of the days of the plutocrats. It is extreme concentration of power and control that has disrupted our political systems, our social systems, our economic systems, our ability to communicate with one another, our ability to build our communities and families, even our ability to make our own selves and our own futures.

Until the Covid-19 lockdown, the economy was in very good shape, at least on the surface. Roads were jammed, the stock market was soaring, and restaurant windows were filled with hiring signs. But even before the pandemic, the American people knew that something was wrong with the fundamental structure of our political economy and our society. And so they despaired and sometimes raged.

Yet because people didn't fully understand the nature of the threat, their search for answers led them often in terribly wrong directions, toward answers that made the problem only worse. Like blaming other victims of power. Or blaming the "nature" of "capitalism." Or embracing romantic and naïve ideas about what the "state" can do. Or blaming "identity politics," as if Americans must sacrifice one form of liberty for another.

The simple fact is that no liberty is safe among a people who have forgotten what it takes to prevent the concentration of extreme power and control within their own political economy. Who have forgotten how to protect the markets where, to a very great degree, they and their children make their society and their lives and their selves. Who have forgotten, in short, that power is a zero-sum game, and in the end there are only two types of liberty: liberty for the master, to exercise power over the rest of us, and liberty for all of us, from all masters.

Ultimately this is a book not only about power but also about identity. It is about who you are within today's political economy, and who you might become in a world in which power and control are less concentrated. It is about whether you are in charge of your own destiny or an object shaped and directed by distant bosses. It is about whether you are a grower, maker, creator, thinker, dreamer—or a blinking, brooding, bleating bundle of appetites, lured by cheap aromas down a concrete corridor toward a kill room.

The gravest crisis we face today? The rise of autocracy in America and around the world. The most intimate of subjects? Your own sense of who you are, and how you fit into an ever-changing world. In the pages that follow, I hope you will come to understand how these two stories are one.

MONOPOLIES EVERYWHERE

By now you have probably read somewhere that America faces a monopoly crisis. Polls show most Americans fret about some form of monopoly every day—at home, at work, while sitting at school or driving to church. We worry that giant corporations rip us off and tie us down, that they have too much power over our community and our politics. But generally, Americans tend to view monopoly as merely one in a long list of problems in our lives, yet another threat to keep us awake at night.

It's vital to understand that monopoly is not *one* of many economic problems but rather *the* political economic problem of our time. In America today, just about every grave problem we face was created by, or made worse by, monopolists. Consider:

Why were there fewer good jobs than in the past, even before Covid-19? And why do almost all jobs pay less? It's because monopolists use their power over our markets to cut the total number of jobs, to restrict your liberty to trade one job for another, and thereby to drive down wages.

Why must you drive farther to get to a hospital? And why does routine care cost so much more than a few years ago? It's because monopolists buy up all the hospitals in a region, then cut the total number of beds and the total number of doctors, nurses, and aides.

Why is your rent so high? And why will your mortgage debt never go away? It's because monopolists use their massive piles of cash to drive up the price of the land right under your home, so they can charge you more just to sleep.

Why do drugs and medical devices cost so much? And why are there so many shortages, even of basic items like facemasks? It's because monopolists use their power to cut supply, to eliminate investment in research, and to block rival manufacturers, even when the result is to kill people. Nowhere was this more obvious than with facemasks during the early months of the Covid-19 pandemic.

Why are so many farmers leaving the land? And why are so many rural towns dying? It's because monopolists have captured control over almost all the markets designed to connect the farmer to the eater, and monopolists use their power to charge us more for less and to pay the farmer less for more.

Why did the stores on Main Street close, even before the pandemic? And why are your public schools out of money? It's because corporations like Walmart and Amazon and Wells Fargo bankrupted your neighbors' businesses, then transferred the money they took from you to Wall Street or London or Shanghai, rather than into your town's treasury.

Why is your commute so long? And why is air travel so awful? It's because monopolists like Koch Industries use their power to block mass transit. And because monopolists have cut not only the size of airline seats but the total supply available.

Why is it so hard to get simple justice in today's America? It's because monopolists use the arbitration requirements they impose in the fine print of their contracts to lock people out of the people's own courts.

Whatever you are angry about, somewhere in the chain of blame you will almost always find a monopolist.

We blame the Chinese for stealing American factories. We should also blame the monopolists, who used their influence to change our trade laws and then shipped our factories to China.

We blame the Russians for disrupting our elections with "fake news." We should also blame Google and Facebook and other monopolists who built systems to manipulate us, then rented those systems out to any autocrat or anarchist with a wallet full of bitcoin.

We rail at poor folks for crossing our borders to take our jobs. But what about the monopolists who looted the economies of Mexico, Honduras, and El Salvador and drove those citizens in desperation from their own homes?

We read terrifying reports about the speed of global warming and blame hardscrabble frackers and miners for pulling gas and coal from the earth. But what of the monopoly utility corporations that block us from installing solar panels on our roofs or recharging stations on our streets?

We blame our neighbors for their diabetes and overdoses and cirrhosis and psychoses. Yet what of the monopolists who all but freely push opium and booze and pot and sugar on us, to a point where soon half of all adults will be obese and where for the first time in our nation's history, many of us will live shorter lives than our parents?[1]

We bemoan "inequality" and the "1 percent," and threaten to tax billionaires so we can spend the money on college or some basic income scheme. But what about taking from the billionaires their actual tools of control? What about breaking their chokehold on our future?

Never have Americans seen so much control in so few hands. In our country today it is the monopolist who feeds you, bathes you, warms you, entertains you, even sings you to sleep at night, all while carefully cataloging your dreams and silently pilfering your pockets.

Little wonder so many Americans today felt so disconnected and anxious and angry, even before Covid-19 settled in. Driven from the marketplace and the town hall, made subservient and servile, what is left but to retreat into one's own bedroom, one's own despairing soul?

THE NEW AUTOCRACY

The crisis is getting worse fast. In the 1980s and 1990s, the Reagan and Clinton administrations, under the thrall of radical right-wing and left-wing philosophies, overthrew America's antimonopoly regime. Since then, the process of monopolization in America has moved forward in two stages. In the first, corporations like Walmart, Microsoft, Citibank, Goldman Sachs, Monsanto, News Corp, Comcast, and Koch Industries were each able to amass great reach and sway over one or a few sectors of the American economy. This concentration posed many economic and political problems, as we will see. But well into the twenty-first century, real power in America was still distributed among a few hundred of these corporate and financial lords. Which meant there was still plenty of room in our society for something like democracy, something like open debate.

Today, however, we are far along in a second and far more

dangerous stage of monopolization, in which Google, Amazon, Facebook, and a few other platform monopolists have captured control over the gateways that connect those of us who have something to sell or say with those of us who want to buy what's for sale or hear what's being said. And these corporations increasingly use their control over these chokepoints to determine how we communicate with one another and how we do business with one another.

Some have termed this business model "surveillance capitalism." But what we see here has nothing to do with capitalism as we have known it, or as we can reasonably imagine it. And the surveillance itself, the spying on the individual citizen and individual business, is not the fundamental problem. The problem is not even the size of those three corporations, or the fact that they have become so essential to our lives and businesses.

The most fundamental problem is that we have left those three corporations—and similar middlemen corporations of the digital age—with a *license* to treat each citizen, and each business, uniquely. That we have left these corporations with a *license* to deliver to each of us different information, different prices, different services.

Over the first 200 years of our nation's history, Americans applied various types of a "common carrier" law to every provider of essential services, including all transportation and communications networks. We used such laws to ensure that any corporation that controlled access to a vital service treated every person who depended on that monopoly the same.

Absent such rules, Google, Facebook, and Amazon are now free to treat each of us differently. They use all the personal information they gather and store on each of us individually to manipulate *how* we sell and buy, *what* we speak and read, *where* we go and *what* we view, even *how* we vote and *what* we think, to a degree that no previous private power, in any nation, has ever come close to achieving.

The actual business models of these three corporations differ slightly.

In the case of Google and Facebook, the corporations sell their ability to manipulate us to almost anyone who wants to do so. Google and Facebook make almost all their money from renting out such services, under the guise of "selling advertising," and in 2019 the corporations carted home roughly $120 billion and $70 billion respectively by doing so.

Amazon, by contrast, is designed to make money by charging fees for the "services" it provides to the people who sell on its platforms. This includes the warehousing and packing and shipping of other people's goods. The corporation also makes money by exploiting its control of the market to steer buyers away from other people's products toward items manufactured for Amazon itself.[2]

The most immediate danger posed by these corporations is to free speech and the free press. Google and Facebook, as already mentioned, routinely and eagerly rent their manipulation machines not only to consumer goods retailers like Procter & Gamble and Coca-Cola but to just about any demagogue or anarchist with a desire to peddle propaganda and misinformation to disrupt our democracies and societies.

Even more dangerously, Google and Facebook every year divert many billions of dollars in advertising away from both traditional newspapers and magazines and pure digital publishers. This means—compared with only a few years ago—thousands fewer journalists walk the halls of our governments and markets and report on the deeds and misdeeds of our politicians and businesspeople.

In short, not only do these corporations spread bad information, they also choke off our ability to gather trustworthy and useful information.

As bad as this is for our democracy, these three corporations increasingly wield an even more dangerous power. Their monopolization of key marketplaces, combined with their license to open and close the gate to these markets according to no rule other than their own interest or whim, gives them the ability to engage in a sort of routinized extortion of any person or corporation who depends on them to get to market.

And Google, Facebook, and Amazon extort more than money in exchange for permission to pass through their gates. As we will see in the following pages, these three corporations also increasingly extort various forms of political favors from the corporations in their thrall, the most important of which is simply silence about the nature and extent of their power.

The result is a fast-accelerating collapse of the rule of law, as even the biggest of businesses and properties are no longer safe from the predations of Google, Facebook, and Amazon. Put another way, the result is an unprecedented pyramiding of power, as even many of the most potent corporate masters of the last generation increasingly live to serve the vastly more wide-reaching masters of this generation.

THE AMERICAN SYSTEM OF LIBERTY

My goal in *Liberty from All Masters* is not to identify and survey the monopolists or the specific dangers posed by the corporate structures and piles of capital that they control. I did that in my last book, *Cornered*, in 2010. And recent books by Sally Hubbard, Christopher Leonard, Zephyr Teachout, Thomas Philippon, Jonathan Tepper, David Dayen, and others all do a good job of catching today's readers up on how today's monopolists are strip-mining your family, your community, and your nation.

Instead, I will use *Liberty from All Masters* to build on that base, in three main ways.

First, I will detail the rise of the new autocracy we face today in America. In chapter one, I will describe the first of the two stages in the concentration of power and control in our nation, by detailing how the "neoliberal" revolution of the 1980s and 1990s cleared the way for the rise of a new oligarchy of corporate and banking lords. Then in chapter two I will expand on this description and detail how Google, Facebook, and Amazon are concentrating dangerous degrees of power over the oligarchs of the last generation by choke-pointing their path to the marketplace and by building immensely powerful mechanisms precisely to manipulate the flow of information and commerce in our society.

Second, in the heart of the book, I will reintroduce you to what I call the American System of Liberty. This was the complex network of concepts, laws, and policies that Americans designed with great care over the first two centuries of our nation to protect the liberties of the individual and the democratic institutions of the community by breaking and harnessing the power of the monopolist. In chapters three and four, I will detail how Americans first envisioned and established this system in the eighteenth and early nineteenth centuries. Then in chapters five and six, I will detail how Americans updated and adapted the system to address the challenges posed by then-revolutionary technologies such as the cotton gin, railroad, and telegraph, as well as electrical power and mass broadcast communications, and such existential threats as industrialized war.

Innumerable books have focused on the U.S. Constitution's system of political checks and balances. But *Liberty from All Masters* is the first in decades to look at how Americans intentionally extended the system of checks and balances into every corner of the American political economy to regulate competition among individuals in their private relations as well as in their public ones. Along the way, I will show how Americans structured this system not merely to protect liberty and democracy but also to ensure that competition was mainly constructive in nature and would achieve certain fundamental social, moral, and intellectual ends.

This section will, I hope, also be of immediate use in understanding how to address the threat posed by Google, Facebook, and Amazon. In recent years, writers and researchers including Rana Foroohar, Lina Khan, Stacy Mitchell, Roger McNamee, Marc Rotenberg, Tim Wu, Frank Pasquale, Maurice Stucke, Franklin Foer, Cathy O'Neil, Jonathan Taplin, Ariel Ezrachi, Bruce Schneier, Shoshana Zuboff, and others have published a wide range of incredibly useful work on the threats posed by these corporations. Yet with a few exceptions—including former senator Al Franken, law professors Sabeel Rahman and Ganesh Sitaraman, the historian Richard John, and Phillip Longman, my close colleague at the Open Markets Institute—almost no one has focused closely on our failure to apply common carrier rules to the platform monopolists. Nor has anyone investigated in depth how such non-discrimination rules can be brought to bear today.

Liberty from All Masters will, I hope, help to fill this gap by identifying useful analogies and lessons from our long and ultimately successful struggle to master the railroads and other network monopolists of the nineteenth century and by detailing how nondiscrimination law and regulation actually function. This book will also study the terrifying political and economic effects that result when we fail to pry these tools from the hands of the private monopolist.

Third, I will describe how particular ideas and language systems can help us to understand how power is concentrated and used within the political economy, and how to structure and direct power in ways that promote democracy and the liberty of the individual.

We will first see, in the central chapters of the book, how for 200 years Americans used a particular vision of the individual as a *citizen* to teach one generation after another to view all economic relationships through a lens of power. And to teach one generation after another to seek individual liberty foremost, to make and build and think and speak and sell, free from control by any master. Then in chapters seven and eight, we will see how, over the last generation, the powerful have used the conception of the individual as a *consumer*—along with other forms of ideological and rhetorical trickery—to hide the role of power in political economic relationships, and thereby to revolutionize how we see the world around us, and our place in it, in ways that have made it far harder for us to understand how today's masters exercise power over us.

In recent years Thomas Frank, Angus Burgin, Nancy MacLean, Quinn Slobodian, Kim Phillips-Fein, Lawrence Glickman, and others have published excellent books on the rise and use of the reactionary, antidemocratic philosophy widely known as "neoliberalism" or "libertarianism." They have detailed how the patrons of neoliberalism aimed to undermine the power of unions, to cut taxes on the rich, and to rewire corporate governance laws to favor the already powerful. Unfortunately, none of these scholars focused on the single most important act of neoliberal sabotage, which was the rewriting and ultimate overthrow of America's system of antimonopoly law.

In *Liberty from All Masters* I will detail how, through the manipulation of ideas and language systems, the neoliberals managed to make antimonopoly law mean the exact opposite of what it had meant for two centuries. In other words, how they managed to take a body of law and policy designed to protect the individual and the community from dangerous concentrations of power and turn it into a system that gives the monopolist an almost complete license to do with us, and our world, as he wishes.

A HISTORY RESURRECTED

For a writer, it's always tempting to present your work as entirely new and fresh. And as you read this book, it may seem I am indeed presenting a unique history of America, and an alternative interpretation of the Constitution. Yet I see my task more as resurrecting one of the original histories of America.

Liberty from All Masters presents a story of our nation as seen through the lens of antimonopoly philosophy and policy. It's a story that, in one form or another, the American people repeated to one another for the nation's first two centuries; a story of trying to structure power in ways that enable citizens to build a truly democratic community. Indeed, I believe the story I tell in these pages would have seemed familiar, even natural, to any reasonably educated, reasonably observant American voter, white or black, in 1965 or 1936 or 1912 or 1896 or 1860 or 1832 or 1800.

It's a history that has been largely wiped from our textbooks and our discourse over the last generation.[3] As we will see, this is mainly the result of efforts by the same people who supported the overthrow of America's antimonopoly laws in the 1980s and the 1990s. To a lesser extent, it is also an unintended byproduct of the long-overdue reckoning by America's historians with the ways in which members of dominant cultures have traditionally exercised power over other groups of people, such as people of color, women, and members of the LGBTQ community. For instance, in *These Truths*, her admirable history of various forms of oppression of one group by another, Jill Lepore almost entirely ignores private corporate power.[4] It's a history I am now able to resurrect precisely because I have devoted the last two decades to studying not only America's foundational antimonopoly laws and policies but the political and social philosophies that underlie them.[5]

To the extent that any particular spirits have guided my work in *Liberty from All Masters*, it is those of the historians W. E. B. Du Bois and Gordon Wood.

It was from Wood's book *The Radicalism of the American Revolution* that I first learned of the extent to which the early debates in our nation focused on the distribution of political economic power, and especially the role that common people played in driving that early radicalism, even when those people happened to be outside the actual rooms where elected and unelected leaders debated and drafted the nation's early documents and institutions. *Radicalism* is a flawed book. As the historian Leslie Harris has written, while he "discusses the Founders' ability to eliminate other forms of hierarchy, Wood has no explanation for why they were unable to eliminate slavery." But it was precisely Wood's discussion of efforts to destroy hierarchy, and to create a new form of citizen, that led me to take my exploration of the origins of America's monopoly crisis today back to the Founding.[6]

From Du Bois, I learned something even more important. In 1935, he published *Black Reconstruction in America*, a book in which he overthrew the lie that the period of Reconstruction of southern societies and economies after the Civil War had been a time of mismanagement and misgovernment by poorly educated and inept blacks and working-class whites. Du Bois demonstrated that, on the contrary, Reconstruction was often a time of highly progressive and effective popular government, a time when black and white citizens established modern and democratic constitutions and built the region's first public school systems and other forward-looking institutions.

I found *Black Reconstruction* to be especially important for this book in two ways. First, it is one of the most powerful paeans to American democracy and liberty ever written. Or as Du Bois himself put it, a paean to America as a "vision of democratic self-government," which he then defined as "the domination of political life by the intelligent decision of free and self sustaining men."[7]

Equally important, Du Bois left for all future writers of history a simple description of the role that concentrated power can play in distorting how a people remember and tell their own stories. After five years struggling to gather the facts and arguments necessary to overcome a cartoonish libel of black rule that had been solidified into hard consensus history, not only among segregationists in the South but also among "professional" historians of the North, Du Bois warned of the precariousness of truth and common sense in any world where we allow avarice and racism to rule.

"With sufficient general agreement and determination among the dominant classes," Du Bois wrote near the end of his book, "the truth of history may be utterly distorted and contradicted and changed to any convenient fairy tale that the masters of men wish."[8]

As is true with any history that runs contrary to a recent consensus, some of our favorite historical figures will come out looking somewhat tarnished. If you are an admirer of Ronald Reagan, it's likely the Reagan we meet on these pages will disturb you, due to his role in overthrowing America's traditional system of capitalism. The same is true if you admire Bill Clinton. Not only did the Clinton we will meet here fail to oppose the Reagan administration's overthrow of the American System of Liberty, he worked energetically to complete the effort.

For similar reasons, we also may find ourselves embracing some of the writings and actions of people we have widely vilified in recent years, such as Thomas Jefferson and Woodrow Wilson. To be clear, my goal here is not to get you to like these people as people, or to embrace all or even most of their actions and statements while on this earth. Rather, it is simply to relearn how to use the immensely powerful modes of analysis, language systems, institutions, and legal tools these deeply flawed men developed to understand and disperse dangerous concentrations of private economic power.

No history of American liberty can avoid the issue of slavery and Jim Crow, and of other forms of discrimination based on gender and religion. American liberty was marred from the first by fundamental hypocrisies, and my own take is that the American people did not even come close to realizing the promise of the Declaration of Independence until the Voting Rights Act of 1965. If anything, I believe the discussions of race and class in *Liberty from All Masters* provide ample evidence that even in the absolute best moments of the last half century, we never realized true liberty for all.

Ultimately, my argument about the intersection of American liberty and American racism can be distilled into a simple, two-point thesis. Along with Du Bois and other writers, I hold that the American quest for individual liberty provided the spiritual foundation for what people today think of as civil and human rights. Somewhat more originally, I argue that the American System of Liberty that Jefferson and others originally devised to make and protect these liberties also provided many of the practical tools that generation after generation of Americans—of all colors and genders—used to make and keep these and other liberties for themselves and their children.

Yes, the American System of Liberty was at times shaped by the interests and motives of the slaveholder and the racist, not only in the earliest days of the nation but right through the heart of the twentieth century. But the slaveholder and racist were not the only ones in the room and certainly not the only ones in the street. The American people, white, black, and brown, were also there from the first. And for long periods of time many of us succeeded—through the populist and civil rights movements—at making this system ours too, as individuals, as communities, and sometimes even as a community. Our challenge today is, for the first time in our history, to make the system truly work for everyone.

AN HONEST RECKONING WITH POWER?

In the spring of 2015 the political economist and former labor secretary Robert Reich published a long article in the twenty-fifth anniversary edition of *The American Prospect*. "For the past quarter-century," he wrote, "I've offered . . . an explanation for why average working people . . . have failed to gain ground and are under increasing economic stress: Put simply, globalization and technological change have made most of us less competitive."

But, Reich continued, this explanation was wrong, or at least very incomplete. "I've come to believe it overlooks a critically important phenomenon: the increasing concentration of political power in a corporate and financial elite that has been able to influence the rules by which the economy runs. And the governmental solutions I have propounded, while I believe them still useful, are in some ways beside the point because they take insufficient account of the government's more basic role in setting the rules of the economic game."[9]

It's rare for any public intellectual to admit error, and Reich deserves real credit for doing so, especially in such an eloquent, graceful, and useful way.

Unfortunately, few others among our nation's intellectual elites have joined Reich in acknowledging that—for the last generation—they failed to see how the U.S. political economy was geared to concentrate enormous amounts of power in the hands of the few. On the contrary, many have opted instead to focus their work on some of the more superficial effects of that concentration of power and to do so in increasingly apocalyptic terms.

It's been widely documented that public debate in America is more polarized than at any other time since the Civil War, as ever more people take in information along entirely partisan lines, from entirely partisan sources of news and views. Less well explored is how another form of polarization has come to warp our conversations about politics and the future. This is the increasing division of the American people into nihilists and utopians, with hardly a space between for practical action.

Perhaps most maddening are the nihilists, who hold that liberal democracy has largely failed, and there's little we can do but retreat into monasteries and huts in the woods, where for a few years we can watch from afar as civilization collapses and the earth burns. The one consolation? If we carry their books into our sad little lairs, we can at least feel smug in our superior insight and wisdom, even as we choke on the smoke of flaming farm and forest and the ravening mob closes upon our door.

If you are a "progressive," you may have come across such arguments in the works of Yascha Mounk, especially in his book *The People vs. Democracy*, or perhaps William Galston, in his book

Anti-Pluralism. The ultimate lesson of such writers, as they stare bewildered at Donald Trump and his supporters, is that the institutions and norms of democracy have been too corrupted to save, hence we must find ways around them, though we probably won't. If you are "conservative" you may have come across similarly pessimistic musings in books by Patrick Deneen, Rod Dreher, and Yuval Levin, who set out to explain the supposed failures of liberalism, of democracy, of the open society, in terms not of the corruption of democracy but of a corruption of morals and a general decline in religiousness.

The utopians, by contrast, at least seek to keep hope aglow in our souls. They hold that a good future is not only possible but perhaps even imminent. There are three main strains of utopianism, each with its own map to Canaan. All three include a fundamentally material promise: if we do a better job of bringing new technologies to maturity we might be able to save our society and our world.

The most simple of these utopianisms holds that there's nothing fundamentally wrong with America at all and that if we only relax, things will work out fine; this in essence is the message of Steven Pinker in *Enlightenment Now,* and of Pinker fans like Bill Gates. The second and perhaps fastest-growing utopianism holds that there is in fact a lot wrong with how wealth and power are distributed in America today, but ultimately there's nothing the "government" can't fix, if we can only get "the market" and "capital" and "profit" out of the way. This is, in essence, the message of Bernie Sanders. The third utopianism, libertarian utopianism, is much the same as it's been for the last 50 years. It holds there's nothing fundamentally wrong with America that "the market" can't fix, if only we can get "government" out of the way.

Despite their focus on a better future, these visions are almost as sterile, almost as practically useless, as the visions of the nihilists. Without an analysis of power, they similarly offer no lessons about how we actually got into this problem in the first place or how to get out of it now. The utopians know in their gut that humans have the capacity to build a better economy and society. They just have no idea how to liberate people to do so.

There are many reasons this last generation of intellectuals simply stopped thinking coherently about the concentration of political economic power over the individual. There are also many reasons why today—despite overwhelming evidence, despite challenges from within their ranks such as Robert Reich's—they still refuse to address this single most important political fact of our time.

In a few instances, as we will discuss in chapters seven and eight, it's because they were funded by interested sponsors of their universities and think tanks specifically to hide this concentration of power. These intellectuals then took an active part in the writing of false narratives and the distribution of false economic sciences.

For most, however, the answer is less a matter of such intellectual corruption and more a matter of a naïve, romantic, sentimental belief that is especially common among progressives, liberals, and libertarians. This holds that human beings are fundamentally good and well-meaning, and that if only you can get into a position where you can reason with your opponents you will be able to persuade them of the wisdom of your beliefs.

One of our most important challenges in the days to come will be to build a new intellectual and moral culture, one that is bluntly realistic about the actual nature of human beings and that forces us to reckon honestly with the limits of simple persuasion and reason.

Yes, human beings are social animals, and yes, we are often very good at working together toward a common good. Yes, human beings are also often able to act rationally and to respond to reasonable economic arguments and rewards. But human beings are also selfish. And sometimes we are thugs and brutes who take wicked joy in bullying and beating others.

It was such desires that drove many of today's monopolists to concentrate power in the first place. Their goal, often, is not only or even mainly to get rich. It is to control others, to impose their will on others. Some of these monopolists, certainly a large enough number to matter, will do so even if the result is to kill people, even if the result is to kill the world in which they and their own children live.

There are certainly exceptions. Some people do change their minds in response to a reasoned presentation of facts, and it's vitally important always to assume every individual has this capacity. But in the aggregate, such evangelizing of the benighted will not solve our problems. As Ibram Kendi put it in *Stamped from the Beginning*, his excellent and important book on the history of racist ideas: "Power will never self-sacrifice away from its self-interest. Power cannot be persuaded away from its self-interest. Power cannot be educated away from its self-interest."[10]

The good news? As soon as we see power, as soon as we begin to think in terms of the need to concentrate and wield public power in ways that allow us to protect ourselves and our society from concentrated private power, we may well find that we are also able to begin to build something like true utopia.

As I wrote earlier, it was antimonopoly law—with its close focus on the structuring of markets and corporations to distribute and check private power—that for 200 years enabled Americans to make our liberty, our democracy, and our prosperity. The men and women who established antimonopoly law and refined it over those two centuries did so based on a highly realistic understanding of human nature, on an honest admission that there is a limit to the power of simple persuasion and that sometimes we must use power to break power.

What I hope you also come to understand in *Liberty from All Masters* is that when we allow others to concentrate power over us, it affects not only our economic well-being, but also our sense of self and community, our sense of personal and human possibility, in ways that can make us passive or, even worse, destructive. What I hope you also come to understand is that it was antimonopoly that for 200 years empowered the American people—to a very great degree—to think freely, to dream freely, to build freely. And that only by bridling and breaking today's masters can we truly liberate the constructive spirit in all the rest of us.

I believe something like the better future envisioned by the utopians is indeed possible. But we will get there not by fixating on the making of new technologies; indeed, we already have most of the basic ideas we need. We will get there by breaking the power of those who stand in the way of actually using these better technologies, thereby empowering ourselves not merely to imagine what is impossible but to make what is impossible, possible.

THE WILL OF THE PEOPLE

I wrote the first words of this book in Paris in late December 2018, watching the rain roll down the cold panes of my hotel windows, sirens shrilling in the streets below. Christmas was a week away, but stores were boarded with plywood to protect against crowbars and cobblestones. The working people of France, pushed to the wall by shrinking salaries, enraged by the prerogatives of the rich, were increasingly hearkening to New Right politicians murmuring old fascist folktales. And they were not alone. In my travels in the previous days and months, I'd seen similar dramas playing out in Germany, Italy, Britain, America.

I began the final edits on this book in London, in December 2019. In many ways the world seemed in worse shape than the year before. I arrived just in time to see Boris Johnson wield a stiff concoction of racism and nationalism to win power for a Tory party that for a decade, with a joyful maliciousness, had cut the salaries and services of working people, students, retirees, and the poor. In Washington? The government was paralyzed by impeachment. In France, strikers had shut down much of the economy and day-to-day life. And still fresh in mind were the shattering heat waves and fires of the summer, blazing proof that our climate is changing in ever more terrifying ways.

And yet I knew that the people of the United States, and of the world's democracies, had made major advances in those 12 months. Before arriving in London I spoke at a conference in Brussels on the crisis of monopoly and the state of antitrust law in Europe and America. There I saw a new generation of attorneys general from individual U.S. states, as well as enforcers from Paris, London, and Cologne, share lessons with one another of the many new investigations they had launched of the platform monopolies and of their new thinking on the dangers posed by concentrated private power.

Enforcers from the U.S. Justice Department and from the European Commission were also there. But something important had changed over the previous year. The interpretation of antimonopoly law was no longer the prerogative of a tiny cohort of "experts" stationed in Brussels and Washington. It was now a sword in the hands of the people of Texas and Nebraska and Iowa. And as events elsewhere in the world had shown, also in the hands of citizens in Johannesburg and New Delhi and Mexico City.

More encouraging yet, the monopoly crisis had become a topic of main-stage debate in American politics. This was true of the Democratic presidential candidates, all of whom were asked to address the issue in depth. It was true in the House of Representatives, where Congressman David Cicilline of Rhode Island had launched the most far-reaching set of investigations of monopoly in a half century. And it was also increasingly true in the Senate, where both Democrats and Republicans increasingly recognized the dangers posed at least by the biggest of the monopolists, Google, Facebook, and Amazon.

It takes a while for the people of America to think through a problem and to set our will. We are still early in that effort. I am confident we will learn and move swiftly. And that in the end we shall succeed.

If for no other reason, the stakes are simply too clear. Fail and it all comes down—our democracy, our families, our world. Prevail, and we establish a new political economy, one that greatly expands the realm of human liberty. One in which a free people will be able to devise technologies and techniques fit for the particular challenges we face today and the particular hopes and dreams of this generation.

The next steps are up to us. No savior will drop from behind the proscenium to set things right. The world is ours to remake. And we shall. As soon as we again declare our individual liberty from all masters.

ONE

THE OLIGARCHS IN THE GARDEN

CORNERING THE CHECKERBOARD

IN THE SPRING OF 1950 SAM WALTON AND HIS FATHER-IN-LAW drove across the greening hills of northwest Arkansas into the little town of Bentonville. Sam later wrote that Bentonville appealed to him because it was close to his wife Helen's hometown in Oklahoma, and it was a good place to hunt birds. At the time the area was home to many apple orchards and chicken farms, and bobwhite quail thrived in the brush that grew between the farm fields and woods.[1]

Walton had recently sold his first store, a Ben Franklin franchise in Newport, Arkansas, and he now used the $50,000 he had cleared to buy Luther Harrison's variety store on Bentonville's town square. Walton's father-in-law, Leland Stanford Robson, loaned him another $20,000 to buy the barbershop next door. After knocking down that wall, Walton opened a 4,000-square-foot "five-and-dime" variety store.

"At the age of thirty-two, I was a full-fledged merchant," Walton wrote in his autobiography. "I love competition, and [Bentonville] just struck me as the right place to prove I could do it all over again."[2] And Walton would indeed have to compete. Although Bentonville's population was only 2,900, the town already had three other variety stores.

America in 1950 was a land of independent farms, independent stores, independent businesses, and independent communities ruled to a very large degree by the people who lived in them. It was a world in which almost any citizen who wanted to get ahead had real opportunity to do so (or, at least, any white male citizen with access to the generous government programs and bank credit of the time). One way Sam Walton got ahead was through simple hard work. This included extensive travel to the small clothing factories of western Tennessee and the Garment District of Manhattan, to save a few pennies by buying straight from the manufacturer.[3] He also closely studied how powerful suppliers of branded goods, like Procter & Gamble, manipulated the little guy, in order to figure out ways to escape from their sway.[4]

The Walmart museum in Bentonville today describes Walton's five-and-dime as a "huge success."[5] Yet at 80 feet by 50 feet, Walton's original store was anything but huge. Nor was the chain of 24 stores Walton built over the coming two decades in any way huge. By 1967 yearly sales per store still barely topped $500,000.[6]

Most people reading these words were probably taught that the independent stores and independent farms of midcentury America were nothing more than artifacts of an earlier time, inefficient businesses in an inefficient backwater of the world waiting to be modernized and rationalized. Yet such a story could not be more wrong. As we will see over the course of this book, the political economy of Bentonville in 1950 was very much by design. Not only the outlines of the fields and the size of the stores, but even how its citizens thought and acted were to some degree the result of two centuries of hard political struggle by the American people, expressed in thousands of laws and policies designed to protect the liberty of the citizen and democratic institutions.

The America of the 1950s was very much also a land of the "organization man" in the "gray flannel suit," and of giant unions at corporations like General Motors and U.S. Steel.[7] And it was very much a land of intricate, nation-spanning networks—of communications and transportation, of finance and industry—networks more advanced than anywhere else in the world. These systems, taken as a whole, had helped to empower Americans to fight and win a two-front war against Germany and Japan. But the fact that, five years after the end of the war, America was still home to millions of prosperous, family-owned farms and stores—and family-owned trucking companies, and family-owned insurance agencies, and family-owned bakeries, and family-owned icehouses and slaughterhouses—was the result of millions of American families rising up, time and again, to keep the financier and corporate lord out of their business. So, too, was the fact that millions of American working people could count on strong unions to protect them in their work.[8]

As we will see, it was a design that consciously elevated the protection of individual liberty and democracy above certain forms of efficiency. As we will also see, it was a design that in many respects proved to be far more efficient than many of the systems imposed by the monopolists.

In the case of small general merchandise stores like Sam Walton's, men wielding concentrated capital had tried many times to roll up control. By 1912, for instance, F. W. Woolworth had assembled nearly 600 stores into a single chain, gone public, and put his name on the tallest skyscraper in the world just a few blocks north of the Wall Street bankers who gave him the money. In the case of farming, powerful men—land barons in the North, plantation owners in the South—had been attempting to roll up control over America's farmlands since the beginning of the nation. But the American people had repeatedly fought back with various forms of antimonopoly law, consciously tracing their actions back to what they understood to be the true promise of the American Revolution.[9]

Today the Walmart corporation runs nearly 5,000 stores across America. Together these hold as much merchandise as at least 150,000 stores the size of Sam Walton's first.[10] To serve these stores, Walmart runs 42 distribution centers and employs 1.5 million people. The corporation completely dominates retail in America, often capturing more than 30 percent of sales for particular items, and increasingly controlling markets across entire regions. For instance, in 43 metropolitan areas in the United States, Walmart has captured more than half of all grocery sales.[11]

To put this into political terms, the Walmart corporation today is the still-largely-undisputed commercial master of thousands of towns and suburbs, and it sets the standard for wages and working conditions in many parts of the country. The corporation's control of the gate to the market also enables it to essentially dictate terms to thousands of companies, including some of the biggest manufacturers in America. Walmart can make or break communities, corporations, careers, and candidates.

But it is not merely the corporation that has amassed power. So too has the Walton family. The six sons and daughters of Sam Walton together hold as much wealth as nearly 150 million Americans, making them the richest family in the history of the world.

These children of Sam Walton do many good things with their wealth. They build museums and schools and protect rivers and wetlands. But here at the start of our book, let's make sure we understand the full implications of this concentration of wealth and power in the hands of one family. What we see reflected in their rise is a whole array of political and social revolutions that have remade just about every aspect of American life. The stripping out of our towns? The collapse of American entrepreneurship? The collapse of American manufacturing? The shift from competition in markets to corporate systems of command and control? The rise of China as a world power? The dysfunction in American politics? Every one of these radical changes is largely a function of the same changes that cleared the way for the rise of Walmart, and the Waltons, and a few other superpowerful families and individuals like them.

Sam Walton and his family bulldozed much of the America that gave him his start. But Sam Walton didn't build that bulldozer. Someone else did, and it's important to understand who that was, how they did it, and who else helped to drive it. That's why my aim in this first chapter is simply to provide a brief history of what we can call "Stage One" in the monopolization in America, from the election of Ronald Reagan in 1981 up through the Wall Street crash of 2008.

It's also important to understand who's driving that bulldozer now. Because as awesomely powerful as Walmart and the Waltons remain, in today's world they look more and more like bit players.

That's why in the next chapter I will describe "Stage Two" in the monopolization of America: I will detail how powers like Amazon and Google have taken advantage of new technologies and online platforms to seize the initiative from the giants that so dominated the U.S. political economy only a few years ago. And why I will provide some description of exactly how Google and Amazon are supercharging the bulldozer in ways that are vastly accelerating the smashing of social and political balances exemplified by Walmart and its power.

Taking the time to understand the similarities and differences between these two stages of monopolization is a vital first step to understanding our discussion—at the center of *Liberty from All Masters*—of how citizens made, protected, and expanded the American System of Liberty over our nation's first two centuries. And to understanding why it's so important to relearn these ideas and this language as we seek to master Google, Amazon, Walmart, and the other powers that so threaten our democracy and our most basic liberties today.

LIBERTY FOR THE CAPITALIST

In August 1981, President Ronald Reagan fired 11,345 air traffic controllers for failing to heed his order to abandon a strike and return to work. To make sure such a strike never happened again, Reagan decertified the controllers union and banned every striker from working again for the government, for life.

For British prime minister Margaret Thatcher the opportunity to break the power of unionized working people came in 1984, when coal miners struck to protest the closing of smaller pits. Thatcher also aimed to ensure no such strike ever happened again. She directed police to arrest strikers, and ordered soldiers to deliver the coal. She also directed her government to block welfare payments to miners' families.

At the time, the actions by Reagan and Thatcher were widely depicted as the first shots in a coordinated transatlantic "libertarian" or "neoliberal" reaction against "government control" over the economy. In addition to their assault on unions, Reagan and Thatcher also sharply cut taxes on the wealthy, slashed regulation of corporations in order to provide greater liberty for business executives and financiers, and promoted the privatization of many activities that had been run by the public for the public.

The political and social effects of breaking the unions were far-reaching and profound. Working people in the United States first began to form modern unions early in the nineteenth century, and their victories had long inspired workers around the world. For most of the twentieth century the unions of working people had played a powerful and sometimes determinative role in American politics, with both parties vying for their support. But after Reagan's stroke against the controllers, it became much harder for working people to organize unions, not only in government service but in manufacturing, construction, transportation, and services.

For millions of workers both in the United States and Britain, the effect was traumatic. As one reporter put it later, "the unions . . . lost their power, influence, millions of members and a large swathe of their rights."[12]

Yet what almost every labor leader—as well as almost every policymaker and historian in the years since—missed or chose to ignore was that Ronald Reagan and Margaret Thatcher did not aim *just* to make it harder for working people to organize and cheaper for the rich to pay their taxes.

Antimonopoly law can be understood as a tool that citizens use to prevent the capitalist and corporate masters from organizing their own unions and consolidating their own overarching systems of power and control. And over the course of America's first 200 years, citizens had devised hundreds of different laws and policies to break any such concentration of power that threatened individual liberty and democracy. This was—as we saw in the introduction—the American System of Liberty.

Yet in the early 1980s, both Reagan and Thatcher aimed precisely to lift almost all such restrictions and limits on consolidation and coordination, thereby—in essence—liberating the capitalist and corporate masters to organize their own unions. In Reagan's case, his team came to power with a well-honed plan to overthrow America's entire antimonopoly system. Indeed, even before Reagan took office, the man he had chosen to run the Antitrust Division of the Justice Department, William Baxter, had already detailed the administration's thinking to the Senate. Baxter had said that from Reagan's inauguration on, the government planned to use the law to promote "efficiency" rather than liberty and democracy.

Then and over the course of the next year, a small group of senators, Republican and Democrat, assailed the changes. Ohio Democrat Howard Metzenbaum wrote that the Reagan administration "has a penchant for entrusting administration of our most important laws to those who believe they should not be enforced. Nowhere is this better illustrated than in the case of William F. Baxter, chief of the Justice Department's antitrust division." The Reagan White House, he said, shows "disdain [for] the entire political and social dimension of our antitrust laws."[13]

But few heeded the warnings. It was not only labor leaders who missed or misunderstood the radical nature of what the Reagan administration was doing. It was also most of the organizations that represented the interests of family businesses and family farms and of America's families and communities generally. To be sure, there were many crises in the early 1980s that helped distract Americans from this putsch, including a harsh recession and sharp tensions with the Soviet Union. But the key factor of its success was a lack of organized opposition in either party.

In chapters seven and eight, I will detail how Reagan administration officials, along with allies in the Democratic Party, planned and sold this revolutionary change in policy—after replacing the word "efficiency" with a yet more benign-sounding euphemism, "consumer welfare." In the rest of this chapter, and the next, my aim is simply to detail what happened after the traditional restraints on monopoly were eliminated.

The U.S. Justice Department did not publish the new pro-monopoly rules until June 1982. But the impact of the change began to be felt much earlier, almost as soon as it became clear that the grumbling senators lacked the ability to stop Baxter. By August 1981 financiers and CEOs had launched a frenzied remaking of the American economy, with deals among airlines and banks and oil companies on a pace nearly double that of 1980.[14] By December 1981, Jack Welch, the CEO of the industrial conglomerate General Electric, had clarified the thinking that would shape corporate America for the next generation. General Electric, he announced, planned to abandon all markets where the corporation was "not already number one or two."[15]

Of all the effects of this consolidation, the restructuring of retail—the world of Sam Walton—would prove to have some of the most extensive and radical effects. Through most of the twentieth century, Americans had staunchly opposed the concentration of power within giant middleman corporations. Their reasoning was simple: they did not want anyone to capture control over the marketplace and then use that control to dictate terms to sellers and buyers. It was this basic thinking that helped to inspire the Tea Party in Boston in 1773. Early in the twentieth century this way of thinking had inspired the American people's reaction against Woolworths, A&P, and the other new chain retailers.

Now, with the stroke of William Baxter's pen, all limits were off.

In the case of Walmart, the transformation could not have been more extreme. Although the corporation had gone public in 1970 and had purchased at least two small chains, by the late 1970s its operations were still limited to 125 midsize stores in five states.

As we have seen, the massive consolidation of power that resulted came at the expense of independent store owners. As we will discuss shortly, it also came at the expense of independent farmers. But before moving on, it's important to understand that this consolidation also affected workers in ways that had little to do with the Reagan administration's breaking of unions. Fewer new businesses also means fewer new jobs. It also means less competition for workers, which means lower wages and worse benefits. And indeed, as economists have finally begun to prove in recent years, the age of Walmart has witnessed sharp declines in real wages in America, with monopolists today wielding their new buyer power to drive down the average worker's pay by 20 percent or more, or one dollar out of every five, compared to a generation ago.[16]

Less competition for the labor of working people also plays out in more political ways. It also means, for instance, that the average employee is more stuck in their job, and more subject to the whims of their boss, whether they like the boss or not. And indeed, over the last generation we have seen a sharp decline in the ability of the average working person to move from one job to the next.

The political economic structure of Bentonville in 1950 was, as we will see in more detail in the coming chapters, very much by design. So too the concentration of wealth and power we see today in corporations like Walmart and in the hands of families like the Waltons. This unraveling of prosperity and of liberty was something that was done to you, your family, and your community intentionally. And it was done not only in the business of retail but in every other corner of the American economy as well.

BILL PICKS UP WHERE RONNIE LEFT OFF

In January 1961, in his last days as president, Dwight Eisenhower delivered one of the most important speeches in the history of the United States. Here was a man who during the Second World War had been the supreme allied commander in Europe. Eisenhower then served as president during the early years of the atomic era, one of most dangerous periods in human history. Yet Eisenhower during this time managed to engineer a new system of governance in post-war Europe, a system that would prove to be one of the true foundations of democracy in the modern world. And in his parting words to the American people, Eisenhower chose to emphasize one thing especially: concentration of industrial and political power right at home posed as grave a threat to democracy and peace as the power of the Soviet Union.

"We must guard against the acquisition of unwarranted influence, whether sought or unsought, by the military–industrial complex," Eisenhower said. "The potential for the disastrous rise of misplaced power exists, and will persist. We must never let the weight of this combination endanger our liberties or democratic processes. We should take nothing for granted."[1]

It was a fear that had long shaped Eisenhower's policies. At home, his administration enforced antimonopoly law as aggressively as had New Dealers Franklin Roosevelt and Harry Truman.[18] Overseas, his administration followed Truman's lead in imposing antimonopoly on both occupied Germany and occupied Japan, believing that the concentration of private power in these nations in the 1930s had helped to destroy civilian government and to unleash the horror of industrialized war.

In 1993, 32 years after Eisenhower's speech, President Clinton's deputy secretary of defense William Perry held a dinner for 15 defense industry chiefs at the Pentagon.[19] Perry said the Clinton administration wanted the number of big defense contractors in the United States cut by at least half within five years. To help, the government offered huge subsidies, theoretically to pay for the "cost" of the mergers. The dinner became known as the "last supper" and unleashed a massive consolidation among America's defense contractors. And it worked even better than hoped. By 1997, the number of top-tier contractors was down to four.

In retrospect, it's clear that this rationalization of the defense industry was a very bad idea. It resulted in skyrocketing costs, slower innovation, and a less secure America. It also means that today many civilian industries are less innovative and less safe; Boeing's purchase of McDonnell Douglas in 1997, for instance, eliminated not only a weapons maker but an independent rival in the manufacture of airliners, an absence acutely felt today in the aftermath of Boeing's grotesque failure to ensure the safety of the 737 MAX.

But in the mid 1990s, Perry's experiment was simply one in a long series of efforts by the Clinton administration to carry the Reagan administration's overthrow of antimonopoly law beyond the reach of the Justice Department and the Federal Trade Commission— whose enforcement of antitrust law affects only a portion of the overall economy—into innumerable business sectors regulated by other government departments and agencies.

At the time, most Democrats viewed Clinton as a savior. After years of union busting and tax cutting by Ronald Reagan and George H. W. Bush, Clinton promised to reverse course. Yet when it came to the most vital issue in a democracy—the engineering of corporate and market structures to guard liberty and democracy against politically dangerous concentrations of power—Clinton proved to be more radical than Reagan. Not only did Clinton's antitrust team do little to challenge the philosophy of efficiency introduced by the Reagan administration into the enforcement of antitrust law by the Justice Department and the Federal Trade Commission,[20] they also unleashed extreme consolidation across the political economy, including in:

The News Media. The Telecommunications Act of 1996 lifted key restrictions on corporate ownership of media, paving the way for giants like News Corp and Fox, which now have the power to control entire political parties and even nations.

Banking. The Interstate Banking and Branching Efficiency Act of 1994 removed limits on the horizontal size of banks. Approval of Citicorp's merger with Travelers in 1998 removed limits on the vertical structure of banks.

Finance. The Financial Services Modernization Act of 1999 repealed many of the barriers that had separated different forms of financial activity since the Glass-Steagall Act of 1933. Retroactively, it made the Citicorp-Travelers deal legal.[21]

Energy. The Clinton administration green-lighted Exxon's takeover of Mobil, Chevron's takeover of Texaco, and British Petroleum's takeover of Amoco and ARCO.

Farming. Not only did the administration approve megamergers in the railroad, grain handling, seed, and chemical industries, but it also merged the Packers and Stockyards Administration with the Federal Grain Inspection Service and changed their mission from protecting the markets that protect farmers to selling commodities.[22]

Commodities Markets. The Commodities Futures Modernization Act of 2000 sharply limited public regulation of financial instruments, including futures, options, and swaps, creating the foundation for both the Enron scandal of 2001 and the soaring prices for oil, grains, and metals that helped precipitate the crash of 2008 and the Great Recession.[23]

As president, Bill Clinton even took actions to concentrate power *within* the corporation, such as promoting changes in tax policy that led corporations to shift executive compensation from salary to stock, thereby aligning the interests of executives with the investor rather than the customer, employee, and community.[24]

To be clear, many other leading progressives had for years promoted various policies that aimed to undermine antimonopoly law and make it easier to consolidate power. Jimmy Carter, the Democrat who served one term as president just before Reagan, was the first to use the term "deregulation." Stephen Breyer, whom Clinton appointed to the Supreme Court in 1994, and Robert Reich, who served as Clinton's first secretary of labor, had both promoted similar changes since the mid-1970s, as we will discuss in more detail later.

But it's important to understand that once in power, Clinton and his main economic team—led by Robert Rubin and Larry Summers—embraced monopolism more firmly and gleefully than any previous Democratic president in history, going back to Thomas Jefferson in 1801. Indeed, they embraced monopolism more firmly and gleefully even than the Reagan administration, as their actions in the defense industry illustrate. If anything, when it came to the disassembly of New Deal–era thinking and institutional structures, Clinton and his team acted in ways far more feckless and reckless than the Reaganites dared imagine.

Through the full length of the twentieth century, the Democratic Party had been the party of the people. As we will see in chapter five, one of its great achievements—80 years before Bill Clinton's election—was precisely the overthrow of plutocracy and the restoration of America's antimonopoly regime. In the 1990s, however, Bill Clinton and his cronies sold the Democratic Party back to the plutocrats. Rather than serve as president of the American people and reverse the dangerous actions taken by Reagan, Clinton seemed instead to prefer the title of first butler to big business. Or perhaps more accurately, panderer in chief.

ONE WORLD UNDER MONOPOLY

Of all Bill Clinton's efforts to serve the monopolist, the most far-reaching in its effects was his administration's remaking of trade policy. Since the founding of the nation, Americans have used trade to promote many goals—including prosperity, innovation, and national security. Most importantly, at least until President Clinton, Americans always used trade policy foremost as a form of antimonopoly policy. And Americans understood that the way to achieve these other ends was through the intelligent regulation of international competition.

To understand this essential purpose of trade, we need merely consider the goals of America's two wars with Britain, in 1776 and 1812. In both the aim was to ensure the United States was not subject to Britain's trade monopoly and was free to diversify its imports and exports among many nations. A second aim was to ensure that the American people had the ability to arm themselves, in case of war. These twin goals of independence and industrial self-sufficiency shaped American thinking and policy right through the Second World War.[25]

In the years after the Second World War, the U.S. government adopted a very different approach to trade. Faced with a growing threat from the Soviet Union and the need to rebuild the devastated economies of Europe, America used the Marshall Plan and other policies to engineer a new industrial system in Europe and across the Atlantic that was much more highly integrated across borders. One goal was to bind all these nations to one another industrially, in ways that made it hard for one nation ever again to go to war against another. A second goal was to allow for greater specialization of labor among these nations, and thereby enable all the peoples within these nations to grow and prosper together in ways that supported democracy against the Soviet threat. The United States soon extended this system to Japan, Korea, Taiwan, and Southeast Asia.

Although these moves were sometimes viewed as an imperial project, the U.S. government time and again during this period refused to protect the interests of U.S. corporations and often traded away those interests in the name of promoting industrial integration among nations. American leaders applied abroad the same basic antimonopoly policies that Americans had adopted at home—and used their power to ensure that there would always be many corporations competing in any particular market, and that no corporation or group of corporations would ever have sufficient power to threaten public control over the state.

From the creation of the Bretton Woods system in 1944 until 1994, under every president from Franklin Roosevelt through George H. W. Bush, the U.S. government remained in firm control of this system, using various forms of antimonopoly and other policies to limit the power and direct the actions of private corporations, in America and around the world, toward the public good.[26] The United States worked out these relationships in direct public negotiations with other nations, through groups such as the Organisation for Economic Co-operation and Development. One result was that, at least within the democratic nations, the various compromises and trade-offs necessary to make the system work always had to accord ultimately with the will of the people.

By any fair measure this system worked phenomenally well, delivering a period of unprecedented prosperity and peace among the industrial nations of the world. Yes, the system served American interests. But what we see in this system is not a Trumpian "America First" interpretation of the national interest. Rather we see a far more sophisticated selfishness, in which the United States chose often to forgo immediate material benefits today for much greater benefits—both material and political—in years to come.

Even the Reagan administration, when it came to thinking about the international system, set aside its radical neoliberal philosophy and continued to use trade power to promote constructive competition. In the mid-1980s, for instance, when the Japanese government and Japanese manufacturers attempted to exploit liberal U.S. trade policy to concentrate control over computer components and car parts, the administration responded neither by ceding the U.S. market to Japan nor by implementing blunt protectionism designed to block Japan entirely from the U.S. market. Rather, it used sophisticated antimonopoly policies to promote the distribution of capacity from Japan to third-party nations, including South Korea, Taiwan, and Malaysia, in ways that increased competition and limited U.S. dependence on any one nation.

If a single year proved the wisdom of America's post-war system for governing international trade, it was 1989, the year of the Tiananmen democracy uprising in China and the collapse of communism in most of Eastern Europe. The world was treated to a perfect demonstration of the difference between the communist and American systems of economic governance. One, top down in nature, after long years of dysfunction, broke down suddenly and hard. The other, built from the bottom up—and in 1989, the re-monopolization of the United States was still in a relatively early stage—provided wealth, opportunity, and resiliency.

The Cold War had ended without hot war. The West's ability to build sophisticated weapons played a major role. Far more important had been the American people's ability to build a democratic economy not only at home but internationally.

Bill Clinton's defeat of George H. W. Bush in the 1992 election meant it was up to Clinton to determine how the United States would adjust the international trading system to account for the collapse of the Soviets. On taking office, Clinton faced two fundamental decisions.

First was whether he should tilt U.S. policy toward post-Soviet Russia, which was then struggling toward democracy. This would have been a direct continuation of the U.S. policy that had stabilized democracy in Western Europe and around the world. Or he could tilt policy to favor China, where recalcitrant Maoists had just ordered tanks to drive over protesting working people and college students.

Clinton's second decision was whether to continue to use trade policy to fight monopoly, in keeping with the fundamental traditions of the United States. Or he could carry the new neoliberal principles into trade policy as well, and here also clear the way for private monopolies to control and govern.

By mid-1993 Clinton had made up his mind. It was for China and its autocrats. And it was for private monopoly at home, which was achieved by structuring the North American Free Trade Agreement, the World Trade Organization, and America's bilateral trade agreements to make it vastly easier for foreign states and private corporations to concentrate power. In other words, at one and the same time, Bill Clinton's trade policy threw the door wide open to the exploitation of *both* the American people *and* the other peoples of the world by the exact same globe-spanning corporations.

THE LORDS OF PLUTOPIA

For a few years at the end of the 1990s, and then again around 2005, America's economy looked fabulous. Unemployment was at a low, the stock market boomed, and wages ticked up a bit. But the structure of the economy was radically different than before the overthrow of antimonopoly law. Instead of the wide distribution of property and power, which had long held in America, economic activity was now largely fenced into a few hundred or so domains, each ruled over by one or two corporate lords, their rights descending from some grant of privilege by Ronald Reagan or Bill Clinton.

It was a world that would have looked familiar to John D. Rockefeller or J. P. Morgan. Sure, the bowlers, canes, and ascots of those times were absent. But the egos, hierarchies, courtiers, and private estates made the new plutocratic era seem almost English in its splendor and Elizabethan in its power relationships.

In addition to the Walton clan from Longshelfington, there was Lord Gates of Dosminster and Viscount Koch of Carbonbourne. And Earl Ellison of Erpcester and Baron Dell of Wintelford. And Duke Buffett of Conglomerary and Lord Welch of Turbine Old Hall. And Earl Stonecipher of Airehaven and Baron Tyson of Nuggetshire. And Lord Malone of Settopboxsett and Viscount Dimon of Vaultingham.

There were lords of candy (the Mars family), sneakers (Phil Knight), casinos (Sheldon Adelson), pop music (David Geffen), brokerage services (Charles Schwab), glossy magazines (Si Newhouse), cruise ships (Micky Arison), real estate (Sam Zell), heavy construction (the Bechtel family), pipelines (Richard Kinder), bathrooms (the Kohler family), cosmetics (the Lauder family), hotels (the Hilton family), and financial data (Mike Bloomberg). Some domains, like Wrigley's gum, dated to the nineteenth century. Others, like the opium of the Sackler family, hearkened to the days of the old China trade, only now opium was a product pushed right here at home in America.

Some lords were more powerful than others; Rupert Murdoch, for a while, owned his own political party.[27] And the masters of funds like Blackstone and Renaissance—the Paulsons and Simonses and Dalios and Schwarzmans—often controlled many domains all at once.

A few pirates—like Carl Icahn and T. Boone Pickens—strode the halls. But the competitions—for precedence and power—had an almost chummy character. And indeed, the lords carefully reinforced their rule through ownership, governance, industrial, and financial structures that tied them to one another in a single community of property and power.

These lords formed, very much, a society, with the ability to identify and exclude the outlier. Some—think Dennis Kozlowski, a conglomerate maker who was convicted for buttressing his holdings through crude fraud—had been thrown in the tower. A few—think Dan DiMicco, the steel manufacturer, sworn enemy of Chinese imports, and ultimately one of the masterminds of the Trump campaign of 2016—had been locked outside the walls, to plot, angrily.

It was a world that was, in fact, almost fully internationalized or, to use Bill Clinton's favorite term, "globalized." In the mountain aerie of Davos, the American peers mingled with the grandees of Carrefour, ArcelorMittal, Gazprom, Samsung, Tata, SoftBank, and LVMH.

In 1998, the historian and business consultant Daniel Yergin wrote that "the decamping of the state from the commanding heights marks a great divide between the twentieth and twenty-first centuries." And indeed, these new lords, as they looked down from the peaks of the Alps, could rightly fancy themselves the rulers of all they surveyed.[28]

And yet, even so, those few years of fin de siècle plutopian triumphalism look now like an almost innocent time. There was still some coherence to the political and economic structures, still some ability to raise a sigh about the immorality of poverty. The news media was still largely intact. Congress was still largely intact. The power of the lords was truly awesome, yet it was still highly delimited in its nature.

Timing is important in books. In 2009 David Rothkopf published a work titled *Superclass: The Global Power Elite and the World They Are Making*. Discussing history and sociology, Rothkopf got a lot right. But he got one key word wrong. By the time his tome hit bookstores in March 2009, the world had fallen into the deepest financial crisis since the Great Depression. It was now very clear that Rothkopf's "power elite" had not been making the world but rather breaking it.

Underneath the glitz and tinsel, the industrial and financial systems over which these great men had captured control had become fantastically unstable. And after the collapse of Lehman Brothers in September 2008, it all came cascading down.

A more clear-sighted vision of the new power structure appeared almost simultaneous with that of Rothkopf. This was an article by Simon Johnson, who had served as the chief economist of the International Monetary Fund, titled "The Quiet Coup." In the piece, Johnson wrote not of a "power elite" but of "an American financial oligarchy."[29] And he made clear that he did not regard this gang as particularly deserving of their positions and responsibilities.

"Regulators, legislators, and academics almost all assumed that" these oligarchs "knew what they were doing," Johnson wrote. "In retrospect, they didn't."

Writing in the immediate aftermath of the crack-up, Johnson did not speculate in great detail as to why these experts had missed the warning signs. But he did offer one key piece of analysis that tied the crisis directly to the radical change in antimonopoly thinking a generation earlier. The largest U.S. banks, he wrote, had become "too big to fail." This in turn gave them "disproportionate influence" over public policy.

That, if anything, was Johnson's one major understatement in the article. Although the government did arrange for the shuttering of a few failed institutions, such as Lehman Brothers, in most other cases it simply used public funds to bail out these private actors. In some cases, the regulators all but demanded that the big get even bigger, and when institutions like JP Morgan Chase demurred, the officials tossed in yet more taxpayer monies to tempt the already glutted to eat more.

The Obama administration, newly in power, had in short chosen to socialize the risk that had been voluntarily assumed by these private corporations. It did so at a time when the recession was in the process of destroying nearly 10 million jobs and driving more than 9 million families from their homes.[30] Perhaps not surprisingly, regulators spent a lot of time thinking up ways to hide what they were doing. "As the crisis has deepened and financial institutions have needed more help," Johnson wrote, "the government has gotten more and more creative in figuring out ways to provide banks with subsidies that are too complex for the general public to understand."

In the end, the monopolists did something far worse than break the economy. They also broke American politics. Millions of Americans came to understand that the new lords had captured control over the state and were now able to use the state to serve their own private purposes, by shifting tax monies from working people to themselves, or by buttressing their own power over some particular industrial activity or other. Even when they broke the financial system, the new lords kept their control. Perhaps nowhere was this more clear than when the Obama administration responded to a crisis triggered by bigness by making banks and other corporations even bigger. Which is one of the main reasons why millions of Americans began to look for alternative ways to get justice, be it through the Tea Party, Occupy Wall Street, Bernie Sanders, or Donald Trump.

Perhaps most dangerous of all, the monopolists of this first generation—once they had profited so enormously from the overthrow of antimonopoly law—failed to close the door against a far more powerful set of actors who, as we will see in the next chapter, posed an even greater threat to American democracy and American liberty.

FROM RULE OF LAW TO LAW OF THE COCKPIT

In 2006, the business journalist Charles Fishman published *The Wal-Mart Effect*. In that book, he described Walmart's unprecedented power over America's markets—where it accounted for upward of 30 percent of total sales of many common goods. Given that very few companies can stand to suddenly lose 30 percent of their business without going bankrupt, this gave Walmart the ability, Fishman wrote, to use its "muscle" to "squeeze" suppliers, and often to "dictate" to them not only the price they could charge, but where and how to manufacture their own products. Walmart, Fishman wrote, had become a "quiet but irresistible force."[31]

We are accustomed to thinking about the ways that monopolists harm us as buyers by charging higher prices and by cutting quality and supply. But the ways that monopolists harm us as makers and sellers of things can be far more dangerous to us as individuals and as a society. As monopolists exploit their power to extract various forms of wealth from the businesses and people under their sway, one result can be a destruction of the technologies, machines, and skills on which our prosperity and security depend (such as the capacity to produce N95 facemasks).[32] There is also, as we will see, the bankrupting of family businesses and the destruction of entire communities. There is also the blunt political effect of being able to make even powerful people, and companies, afraid.

In the case of Walmart, the immediate effects of the corporation's relatively sudden concentration of power fell hardest on the makers of jeans, pickles, bicycles, pet food, coolers, and other consumer goods. But Walmart was merely one of many such consolidation plays by retailers and other middlemen, and the capitalists who backed them. Between the early 1980s and the early 2000s, America's economy was rebuilt on an entirely new plan. In place of open markets, with many buyers and sellers and many middlemen, including many retailers, one or a few supergiant retailers or trading companies now enjoyed the power to essentially govern the production and distribution of everything from medical devices to office supplies to fire safety equipment to car parts to industrial gauges.

This concentration of power harmed not only the businesses that made things but the people who worked for those businesses: in other words the actual scientists, engineers, and assembly-line workers who designed and built the products that kept us happy and alive, as well as the janitors who cleaned up afterward. As we've seen, recent studies have detailed how wages across America today are 20 percent or more lower, relative to the economy as a whole, than a generation ago. And further, that the main reason for this decline is that the monopolists who captured control over our markets have exploited their power to drive these wages down.

We will discuss the effects of monopsony—which is when a single corporation dominates buying of a particular good or service—in greater detail in chapter seven. What I want to focus on here are the effects on America's farmers of having only one buyer for their crops and livestock. During Stage One of monopolization in America, from the beginning of the Reagan administration to the crash of 2008, no group of people was more harmed by the closing of markets than America's farmers. As badly as working Americans were shafted, the average farming family was treated, relatively, far worse.

Farmers and ranchers, we all know, are not like other workers. They are independent businesspeople—family businesspeople, typically—and their interests are supposed to be protected by a right to sell into open and competitive markets and to earn fair market prices for what they sell. That's why, in the 1920s and 1930s, when citizens were drawing up America's modern labor law regime, which placed a number of important limits on how employers can treat workers, both Republican and Democratic administrations did not extend these laws and regulations to farmers. Instead, as we will see in more detail in later chapters, they invested heavily in building up laws, agencies, and regulatory practices designed to ensure that the price of grains, livestock, milk, and produce would be governed not by any corporate boss but by supply and demand within carefully constructed marketplaces.

In such market systems, the most fundamental goal of political economic law is "non-discrimination." The aim of such law is simple—that everyone be given the same opportunity to succeed or fail. As we will see in more detail later, non-discrimination is key to equality of opportunity, hence to democracy and to the full liberty of the individual.

In farming, the traditional way to achieve non-discrimination is to ensure fair prices in an open market and to give farmers all the information they need to adjust their production to the realities of the moment. This is not always possible, however, when a corporation captures control over some key market gateway, such as a local slaughterhouse or grain silo. In such a case, to ensure equal opportunity requires forcing the gatekeeper corporation to treat everyone who sells into that market the same and never unfairly favor or disfavor any seller. Over the years Americans have developed many forms of common carrier law and practice to ensure equal access to all markets.

In the case of chickens, under the traditional system, farmers raised and fed their own birds, then carried them to markets where they sold them. For every pound of chicken, the farmer was paid a price that had been determined within a public market, based on supply and demand, perhaps adjusted slightly up or down based on the quality of their particular birds. Punishment was simple. A lesser or lazier farmer who brought a smaller flock to market had less to sell, hence walked off with less money. Even when the market price was low, such an open market system allowed smart farmers to adjust: they could, for instance, raise fewer chickens and devote their land and labor to other crops and animals.

Over the last generation, however, the rise of the Walmart model of control over America's retail markets has resulted in a top-down reorganization of every level of American agriculture. As the power of monopoly retailers has increased, many corporations under the sway of these retailers have also consolidated power. This is true, for instance, of slaughterhouse corporations like Tyson and grain handlers like Archer Daniels Midland. In many parts of the country, farmers now find only one potential buyer for their products. And, not surprisingly, these monopolists use their power to dictate prices for the animals and crops the farmers grow.

The result, since the Reagan administration, has been that the farmer has gone home from market with an ever-smaller share of what America's families spend each year on food. Earnings have been so bad, in fact, that over the last three decades millions of farm families have simply chosen to leave the land.

But Americans still need to eat, so corporations have come up with ways to keep some farmers working. In the case of chickens, Tyson and Pilgrim's Pride provided farmers with big loans—often guaranteed by the government—to build new and bigger sheds in which to house their chickens. They also introduced systems in which they provide the farmers with the chicks they are to grow and the feed and drugs they are to use in raising them. Under these systems, the corporations then pay the farmers for how efficiently they transform chicken feed into chicken flesh.[33]

As should be obvious, under this new system, the farmer has for all intents been transformed into a worker. The corporation makes all the decisions about what is to be raised and how, then provides all the inputs and tools, including capital. Then the corporation measures output. About the only thing the farmer actually owns is the debt and the waste. About the only thing the farmer actually controls is when exactly to declare bankruptcy.

This new system does not retain any of the traditional protections for the American farmer. These are not markets, by any definition of the word, and farmers are not paid market prices for their crops and livestock. Nor, thanks to the nature of the debt that they took on, can they easily shift to other products. Yet the growers are still not in any way covered by labor law, which places some basic limitations on the ability of corporations to discriminate in how they treat two people engaged in the same line of work.

As a result, corporations like Tyson and Pilgrim's Pride have been free to develop payment systems designed precisely to treat one farmer differently from the next, and to pay one farmer more or less than the next for the exact same amount of work. The corporations even have a name for this system of personalized and routinized discrimination. They call it the Tournament System.

According to the corporations, this Tournament System simply promotes efficiency and hard work. Farmers who do a better job, they say, will get paid more per pound. Those who do a lesser job get paid less. What is in fact taking place here, however, is that the corporations are taking advantage of the fact that there is no longer an open market where sellers and buyers discover the price through supply and demand. This means that every farmer must accept the price the corporation is willing to pay, and naturally the corporation chooses to pay every farmer less. But the corporations are now doing so in a way that makes it hard for all the farmers to join together and complain about the price, because when every farmer is paid a different price, no farmer has any idea what the fair market price should be.

And that's not all. Indeed, as any chicken farmer will eagerly explain to anyone who happens by, the system is worse even than that. At no point is there any auditing of the quality of the birds or the feed the corporation provides them. At no point is there any control on the weighing of the flock when the farmer delivers it to slaughter. The entire system, in short, gives to the corporation a power that is entirely arbitrary in nature. In place of rule of law, the farmer faces rule by whim of the master, the boss, the foreman.

As one farmer once told me, the result is "a kiss ass economy."[34] In the days of the open market, the farmers were a single community, all affected in the same way by the market price. Today, in place of community, farmers fearfully bicker with one another as they compete for the favor of the foreman.

This new system of serfdom was well developed long before the stock market crash of September 2008. Indeed, one of the few bright spots of the early years of the Obama administration was the new president's promise to do something to help America's farmers get something like a fair shake. It was a promise that the administration's agriculture secretary, Tom Vilsack, could have made good on simply by using the rule-making authority of his office to outlaw this corporate-controlled Tournament System.

Yet by 2010, under pressure from Republican defenders of the livestock corporations, the Obama administration suddenly quit the field, leaving America's chicken farmers—and indeed all of America's farmers and ranchers—to the mercies of JBS, Smithfield, Monsanto, Tyson, and a few other multinational corporations, most of which are now foreign owned.

The main message for the corporate lords of America and the world? You are at liberty to rule over your domains, and over your people. Both belong entirely to you. And every day, you can make your people dance to whatever tune you play, in whatever way you wish.

TWO

AUTOCRACY, AUTOMATIC

THE NEW JIG ECONOMY—TOURNAMENTS BY APP

Few Americans noticed the July 2012 launch of a new business called UberX. But over the next few years, millions would eagerly, even avidly embrace the service. For people who lived in cities where taking a taxi was a normal part of life, Uber offered lower prices, clean cars, and push-button dispatch. In suburbs and even rural areas where there were few if any cabs, Uber for the first time made it easy to hail a driver, improving the lives of millions.

As radical as this new service seemed, however, it was in key respects also a reincarnation of a form of monopolization Americans had seen many times before.

At bottom, Uber was a play to enclose a public service—the provision of reasonably priced taxi services, regulated by municipalities—within a framework of private control, aimed at private profit. As many have written, the same basic technologies at the heart of the Uber system could also be organized under a variety of alternative business models, including ones controlled by and for the public.[1] That Uber and its rival Lyft now largely control how we interact with these technologies is due mainly to the fact that these two corporations enjoyed the ability to swiftly attract enough investment capital to shape the public's perception of the nature of this technology and of the service the corporations themselves provided. They had enough money, in other words, to make their particular business models synonymous with the technology.[2]

Uber's expansion strategy was in fact little different from that of the monopolists of the plutocratic times or post-Reagan America. In 1901 it was the banker J. P. Morgan who engineered the creation of a near monopoly in steel production in the United States, and in 1986 it was Mitt Romney's Bain Capital that floated the radical expansion of Staples, Inc. In 2011, it was an initial investment by Benchmark Capital, followed by huge infusions of cash by groups including Japan's SoftBank and Saudi Arabia's sovereign wealth fund, that armed Uber with enough money to price its service below cost for years at a time. This allowed the corporation simultaneously to buy the goodwill of millions of customers, and to bankrupt or severely weaken almost all its rivals and potential rivals.[3]

But Uber also enjoyed three advantages compared to the corporate tools of the bankers of the 1890s and 1980s.

Uber's reach is much wider. The corporation's character as an online platform allowed it to scale at an unprecedented pace and to capture control over taxi services in a phenomenally wide range of locations, not only across America but around the world.

Uber knows much more. Every monopolist knows more about the business of the people who rely on it than those people know about the business of the monopolist. But compared to Standard Oil or the Pennsylvania Railroad, Uber enjoys much greater ability to store and use the information it collects on its drivers and its users.

Uber has a license to discriminate. One way Uber makes profitable use of all the data it collects on its riders and drivers is to set different prices or payments for the same service on a person-by-person basis. The corporation, in fact, has bragged to Wall Street investors that it is doing precisely that.[4]

A fundamental rule of the American political economy, as we saw in the last chapter, is that there be no favoritism in the provision of any essential service or good, that every seller and buyer be treated the same. For the first two centuries of our nation, Americans understood that laws against such discrimination were foundational to democracy, individual liberty, and equality of opportunity.

That's why Americans have traditionally required network monopolists such as railroads and telephone corporations to publicly post their prices and terms of service, and banned them from charging different prices or providing different services to different people and different businesses.[5] This is true of particular groups of people, as defined for instance by race or gender. It is also, importantly, true of the person or business as an individual.

Uber, however, like Google, Amazon, and today's other platform monopolists, has never been made subject to these traditional constraints on pricing and service.

Absent such rules, Uber's bosses have been free to treat every single driver differently. This means they can favor some drivers with more rides, and disfavor others, for whatever reason they choose. This means they can pay some drivers more per mile, and pay others less, for whatever reason they choose. This means they can make some drivers travel farther than others to pick up a ride, for whatever reason they choose. It means they can pay a particular driver at a certain rate one day, then pay him at a different rate the next. In short, Uber's bosses have been free to take the Tournament System model for pitting farmer against farmer, as perfected in recent times by slaughterhouse corporations like Tyson and Pilgrim's Pride, and update it for the twenty-first century by using their app to automate it.[6]

Absent traditional pricing rules, Uber's bosses are also free to build a similar sort of Tournament System for riders. In its statement to investors admitting that it engages in price discrimination, Uber implied that its goal was to charge richer people more than the rest of the population for the same level of service.[7] But the corporation's pricing system is actually designed simply to determine how much the people within a particular region are willing to pay for service, then charge that group accordingly. These relatively higher prices have nothing to do with demand; Uber charges them during rush hours and Uber charges them during off hours. And many factors other than having more money to spend can lead people to agree to pay more for a particular service. People who are more economically sophisticated often know how to pay less. People who are more economically desperate often have no choice but to pay more.

This is also true for how Uber treats you personally. Although what you see on your screen has been designed to look a lot like the free workings of a market system, in which the pricing of each particular ride you take is regulated by the most simple laws of supply and demand—with prices, for example, "surging" during rush hour—what is actually taking place is much different. Uber's system is designed to carefully study your travel habits and shopping habits, your spending habits on Monday versus your spending habits on Friday, all so it can figure out how to charge you the maximum amount for any particular ride, without driving you to decide to take the bus or walk instead.[8]

Uber's vast cache of data about where people go and when, we should not forget, not only provides an ever-more-perfect map of traffic to and from a community's bookshops and coffee shops and dance clubs and churches, but also to its backroom casinos and after-hours clubs, its pushers and dealers and sex clubs and bordellos.

All this information gives the corporation ever greater ability to understand just how badly you need a ride. Do you rush off every Thursday at 8 pm to see your boyfriend? Do you like to squeeze your Sunday visit to Mom between a morning round of golf and the afternoon NFL game? Every Tuesday and Thursday at 3 pm, do you have to get to your psychiatrist and back without your boss knowing?

Well, even if your boss doesn't know, Uber does. And Uber has the capacity to exploit its knowledge of your momentarily pressing needs to extract more money from you.

Uber has demonstrated its capacity and readiness to deliver different service to different people nowhere more perfectly than in its treatment of the public officials charged with ensuring the provision of safe and affordable taxi services. The corporation has repeatedly been charged with denying service to, and providing false information to, regulators around the world, including in Portland, Boston, Las Vegas, Australia, and France. Uber even developed a special term—"grayballing"—for such particularized targeting of individual law enforcers.[9]

The Organisation for Economic Co-operation and Development (OECD) recently described the general problem of such automated, highly targeted discrimination in dry language:

> The current evidence . . . shows that the technological means for online personalisation and price discrimination are extensive and developing rapidly, and difficult to detect in market monitoring research by authorities. It also shows that online marketplaces, platforms and social media use or can use data analytics and profiling techniques to . . . personalise the ranking of the offers in online marketplaces and platforms, and may be used to rank and target offers on the basis of estimated maximum willingness to pay of individuals, or to vary prices to reflect the cost of serving individual customers.[10]

Put more simply, Uber has developed a system that enables it to gain intimate knowledge about you and your habits and needs, then to jack up the price you pay for its service whenever and however it chooses. It is a system that allows the corporation to cut you off, for whatever reason, whenever it wishes. It is a system that combines the tools to engage in simple extortion with an almost unlimited license to do so.

Uber has mastered, in short, the tools and practices of the corporations that have already come to dominate Stage Two of the monopolization of America and that are fast supplanting the relatively simple exploitations of the lords of the last generation.

LIBERTY TO DISCRIMINATE

Popular histories tell us the Boston Tea Party was a rebellion against taxes. Yet as we see in the writings of Samuel Adams and others, America's revolutionaries viewed it mainly as a fight for liberty from the British East India Company's monopoly.[11] The revolutionaries objected to the idea of an all-powerful middleman corporation regulating their commerce. American colonists, they believed, were perfectly able to exchange goods and services with one another in markets of their own making with no outside regulator.

In the eighteenth century, there was no technological imperative whatsoever for any giant intermediary to exist. In the case of the East India Company, the corporation's power was the result of nothing more than a government charter that protected a particular group of traders from competition with other groups of traders. The artificial nature of the East India Company's power was made clear on February 22, 1784, six weeks after the Congress of the new United States signed a peace treaty with Britain. On that day the American ship *Empress of China* sailed from New York, bound for Canton with a cargo of ginseng. When the ship returned 14 months later, its traders sold its cargo of tea and porcelain on the open market. Without the active backing of the British state, the East India Company had no inherent power to stop the sale—let alone to determine anymore who sold what, or where or how they sold it, in America.

But over the next two centuries Americans would face many technologies that could not be broken into component pieces, the way a fleet of ships could be separated into individual vessels, or a company of investors could be separated into individual people. This was especially true of the railroad, telegraph, and other providers of essential intermediary services. These expensive and complex networks were built right into the physical world, and safe operation required great teams of people organized into intricate hierarchies. Time and again, however, Americans developed ways to ensure these essential intermediaries focused not on exploiting their gatekeeper position to manipulate and extort the public but on providing equal service to every seller and buyer.

In some cases, Americans chose direct public ownership of the intermediary or extremely close public regulation of private owners. We still see this today in commuter rail and bus networks and some local telephone, electricity, and water systems.[12]

In general, however, Americans have chosen to promote private control over vital intermediary monopolies. They have done so for a variety of reasons. These include practical considerations, such as that it can be far easier to convince people to contribute capital to a project by offering them a share in the profits than by dunning them for taxes. These also include political considerations, such as the desire to create a balance of power between strong private actors and strong public actors.

To ensure that these privately controlled systems served the public, Americans used various forms of common carrier law and other regulations that required these corporations to treat every customer the same. As we'll see in more detail later, some of these laws simply banned corporations from personalized discrimination in pricing or terms. Others aimed to prevent conflicts of interest over what they sold, by prohibiting intermediaries from integrating into the manufacture of goods that might compete with products being sold by their customers.

Americans often supplemented these simple restrictions with various types of open standards and codes to make it easy to connect one network to another and to make it easy for many companies to manufacture products to run on the same common networks. For instance, in the case of the electrical system, open standards means anyone can manufacture refrigerators or fans or lightbulbs or circular saws or wiring. It also means that one town's grid can connect to the next. In the case of the Internet, it means anyone can manufacture routers or write their own applications, and that one nation's network can connect to the next.

Such policies empowered Americans to take full advantage of all the important network technologies introduced since the railroad in the 1830s, without real worry that the heavily capitalized corporations that controlled these technologies would exploit their middleman position to steal other people's businesses or disrupt balances of political and economic power. Indeed, common carrier rules and policies have from the first served as a main pillar of American liberty and democracy and prosperity.

In the 1980s and 1990s, however, the neoliberal reactionaries of the Reagan and Clinton administrations, as they did with antitrust (and as we will discuss in greater depth in chapter seven), targeted many of the laws and policies designed to prevent such forms of discrimination.

Thus far, the effects of these radical changes have not reached to all corners of all networks. Non-discrimination rules still apply today to most traditional transportation and communications systems. Even airlines, widely derided for their wildly fluctuating pricing policies, enjoy little freedom to engage in true "first-degree" price discrimination, which is when the provider of a service charges each individual a specifically tailored price for the same service or delivers specifically tailored service for the same price.[13]

Similarly many antidiscrimination laws and policies have remained in effect in the digital economy in recent years, at least for periods of time. Non-discrimination principles, for instance, played a huge role in the big antitrust case against Microsoft in the late 1990s. That case aimed to prevent the corporation from favoring one Internet browser over another by reinforcing prohibitions against certain forms of vertical integration. Non-discrimination principles also underlay the "net neutrality" rules applied to telecommunications corporations and broadband providers in 2015.

Where we see the effects of the neoliberal revolution most dramatically is in the failure—by both Republicans and Democrats—ever to apply any sort of common carrier rules to online platforms, even after it became amply clear that Google, Amazon, and others had grown to a point where they provided essential services to other companies and to the public as a whole. This failure to apply common carrier to these giants is perhaps the single biggest factor behind the acceleration of the monopolization of the American economy we have witnessed in recent years. This de facto license to treat each seller and buyer differently, in combination with the ability of these platform monopolists to capture masses of data about other people's businesses, is what gives these corporations such unprecedented power to control and manipulate individual companies and people, and the economy as a whole.

Over the last decade or so, the platform monopolists have exploited this license to reorganize entire realms of human activity in ways that serve not the public but only the interests of the masters of these corporations. And the extent of the threat these corporations pose grows almost by the day, as Google, Facebook, Amazon, and a few other vital online platforms move to control and colonize more corners of human society. These corporations increasingly match individuals to specific shoes and clothes, specific restaurants and hotels, specific movies and music, specific games and gamers, and increasingly to particular books, sources of news, jobs, and potential spouses. Google and Amazon even increasingly aim to manage the flow and use of electricity through the wires of the grid and within our individual homes.[14]

As with America's chicken farmers and their relationship to corporations like Tyson and JBS, the result is the rise of systems of increasingly arbitrary governance and the destruction of the rule of law. The main difference between Walmart and the other dominant corporations and intermediaries of the last generation and Google, Amazon, and Uber, is that today's online giants are able to manipulate individual behavior and decision making not only on a day-to-day basis, but moment to moment.[15]

To give us some sense of how these manipulation systems work, let's look in detail at how Amazon, Google, and Facebook each shape some small portion of the human activities over which they have captured control. In the rest of this chapter, we will examine how Amazon regulates what consumers buy, how Google regulates where people go, and how Facebook (and Google) regulates what people read.

THE MASTER OF THE MARKET—AMAZON

In 2018, Walmart reported $514 billion in revenue, far more than any other corporation in the world. That a single retailer controls such a phenomenally large amount of America's consumer economy is proof, as we saw in the last chapter, of the revolutionary economic, political, and social effects of the overthrow of the American System of Liberty a generation ago. It also helps to illustrate another point we discussed in the last chapter, which is how much power Walmart can exercise over the individual suppliers who depend on it to get to market.

Yet when it comes to stock market valuation, we see a different picture. Although Amazon notched less than $178 billion in revenue in 2018, the corporation registered a total valuation of just below $1 trillion, putting it in competition with Apple and Microsoft for the crown as the world's most valuable corporation. Walmart by contrast ranked twentieth, with a valuation of only $250 billion.

The reason? Walmart's revenue in 2018 grew only about 3 percent over the year before, even in a boom economy. By contrast, Amazon's grew by more than 30 percent. To invest in a stock is to place a bet on a corporation's future profitability. Given that every day a greater percentage of total consumer purchases take place online, and given that Amazon already dominates online commerce, investors are simply concluding that Amazon will soon be doing more business than Walmart and will earn more—perhaps much more—from that business. They are betting, in short, that Amazon owns the future.

For hundreds of thousands of businesses, Amazon already owns today. The corporation wields more than sufficient power to make or break even large corporations swiftly, even suddenly. That's one reason why a growing number of politicians and enforcers around the world have begun to talk of the need to break up Amazon.

The most immediate concern of most of these enforcers is the conflict of interest between Amazon's role providing an essential platform on which other companies do business and its own fast-growing array of in-house products that it pits directly against the wares of its own customers.

Although no enforcer in the United States has yet moved to ban such unfair competition, in Europe federal officials in Brussels and the national government in Germany both appear to be targeting such behavior.[16] In India, the government has already forced Amazon to limit its sale of in-house brands.

This is an issue my team at the Open Markets Institute and I know well. We began to study Amazon's control over America's book market in late 2009, first wrote about the issue in early 2012, and first spoke to politicians and enforcers about the issue in 2013. Then in January 2017 Lina Khan of our team published what is now the standard analysis of the problem.[17]

What we also see today is that as fast as the enforcers and

politicians awaken to Amazon's monopoly power, Amazon is moving to shift its business model even faster.

A huge part of Amazon's business is still to take ownership over someone else's product and then resell it, the way other retailers do. Amazon calls this its "first-party" business. One measure of Amazon's power is that even the largest manufacturers of branded products now sell certain goods only on Amazon. They do so even though such deals—which Amazon calls "Exclusives"—serve mainly to concentrate more control in Amazon in ways that work against the interest of the manufacturers themselves.[18]

At the same time, Amazon has continued to grow its already-huge business by manufacturing its own "private label" brands to compete with those of these other companies. Amazon now designs and sells its own shoes, dresses, business suits, diapers, detergents, snack foods, electronics, books, movies, and videogames, as well as thousands of other products organized into some 150 in-house brands.[19] Amazon's ability to pit these products against even the biggest manufacturer is well understood. For instance, when an article reported that Amazon had begun to manufacture its own toys, the stock prices of Hasbro and Mattel plummeted.[20]

And Amazon wields this same basic power against many companies, including some of the best known in America. As a recent *Washington Post* article explained, "Amazon's latest tactic offers AmazonBasics batteries to shoppers searching for Energizer models, its Trek Support gel insoles to customers searching for Dr. Scholl's products, and its Basic Care nicotine gum to those searching for Nicorette's offering."[21]

Yet Amazon's real growth in recent years has taken place in lines of business that are leading the corporation in an entirely different direction than traditional retailers, including Walmart, toward a model that looks a lot like Uber's.

Under this new model, Amazon does little more than exploit its control over the marketplace to "match" sellers and buyers. Indeed, Amazon has succeeded in making itself the main place where other companies sell things. Rather than doing so on their own websites—in other words, on the open Internet—these companies now interact with buyers mainly across Amazon's vast, sprawling private platform.

Amazon CEO Jeff Bezos bragged about how rapidly this transition is taking place. In his annual letter to investors in April 2019, while noting that first-party sales had grown from $1.6 billion in 1999 to $117 billion in 2018, Bezos said that during that same period, third-party sales grew from $0.1 billion to $160 billion.

Bezos claimed the main reason for this success was that Amazon was doing such "a great job" helping these independent sellers "compete against" Amazon's own first-party business. Amazon, he wrote, adding his own italics, had provided other sellers with "*the very best selling tools we could imagine and build.*" The result, he said, was just terrible for Amazon. "To put it bluntly: *Third-party sellers are kicking our first party butt. Badly.*"[22]

From the point of view of the sellers themselves, who exactly is kicking whose butt looks somewhat different. These companies sell on Amazon because, online, increasingly there is no other place to find customers. As of early 2019, 66 percent of all individuals looking to buy online start their search for products on Amazon's website. If they are looking for a specific product, the figure is 74 percent. When it comes to commerce in consumer goods, Amazon has become the Internet. If you are not on Amazon, you are not really on the Internet, hence you are not really in the market.[23]

And Amazon is fast extending its control over online markets in four other key ways.

- *Delivery.* Amazon has invested tens of billions in warehousing and delivery, even buying up patented robotics technologies. Add to this its special deals with the post office and UPS, and the result is that, for a growing number of companies, Amazon now provides the only practical way to fulfill orders.
- *Procurement.* Amazon is signing contracts with local and state governments and federal agencies to manage their procurement contracts for them. Practically, this means Amazon has placed itself in between the seller and the taxpayer. Practically, this gives the corporation that much more direct power over

the companies that supply goods and services to the average buyer.[24]

- *Physical stores.* For most of its life, Amazon sold only online. It now sells groceries, snacks, books, and a growing array of general merchandise in physical stores. Every time Amazon executives open a batch of such stores, they drive down their rivals' stock market valuations, which ultimately makes sellers even more dependent on Amazon to get to market.
- *Hosting of data.* Amazon has invested tens of billions in server farms and software and now hosts the data of more than a million other companies.[25] Even when data is encrypted, Amazon can learn from and use this data to manipulate the flow of other people's businesses and of commerce generally on the Internet.

Each of these new capacities gives Amazon many additional ways to lure or lever other people's companies into dependence on its vast system of systems. And once these sellers do become dependent, they find that Amazon can manipulate their sales in an almost infinite number of ways, most importantly, through the corporation's control over how information—including the price of every good—is presented to the potential buyer. The ultimate result, almost always, is that Amazon gets to carve off a bigger and bigger share of each deal made on its website. In early 2019, Amazon's cut of the average deal struck on its platform topped 40 percent, roughly triple what it was a few years ago. The corporation, in short, has established itself as one of the biggest and most effective tax collectors in the world.[26]

And it's not as if these captive sellers have the ability to raise their prices, even if they spot an opportunity to do so. Amazon has long retained control over all pricing decisions on goods it buys and resells and has long manipulated the prices of other people's products for its own purposes. Until recently, third-party vendors on Amazon did retain full control over their own pricing. But as Amazon's power over the market has grown stronger, the corporation has increased its manipulation of other companies' prices. Just before Christmas 2017, for instance, Amazon arbitrarily decided to slash the prices charged by a number of third-party vendors up to 9 percent.[27]

There's a reason these vendors don't complain, even when Amazon breaks its own rules. If they do, there's a good chance Amazon will simply cut them off from the market. It's a tactic Amazon has used repeatedly in book publishing. The corporation stripped the buy buttons from Melville House in 2004, from Bloomsbury in 2008, from Macmillan in 2010, and from Hachette in 2014.

Another tactic Amazon routinely uses to get its way is simply not to police the sale of counterfeit items on its own website. Even when sellers harmed by such counterfeiting complain—as the shoemaker Birkenstock did repeatedly—Amazon has often continued to sell the bogus products even when it must know they are bogus.

So far, not one law enforcement official in the United States has raised a finger to protect the citizens who are being abused by Amazon. Which means that all other sellers now understand that Amazon's wishes, no matter how arbitrary, are the law of the land.[28] As one seller put it in a recent interview, "Amazon is the judge, the jury, and the executioner."[29]

One of the best measures of Amazon's power is its phenomenal surge in advertising profits, which went from a tiny line item in 2017 to $10 billion in 2018, and toward an estimated $38 billion in 2023.[30] In an open commercial system in which there are many sellers and many buyers, advertising is a way to attract attention. In a closed system, where a single corporation controls the access to market, advertising is a tool of extortion.[31] If you want Amazon to carry your goods, you have to pay whatever it demands to handle your goods. Increasingly, you also have to pay what it demands to advertise them to buyers.

Back in the day, Walmart's aim was simply to force manufacturers to give it lower prices so it could more swiftly undersell and bankrupt rival retailers. Now that Amazon has effectively killed off all real online rivals, its model is to capture control over the businesses of every seller and trader online, and then to pit everyone against everyone in a carefully orchestrated scramble to be placed first before the eyeballs of the busy buyer. At one and the same time, Amazon gets to sell both access to the market and various forms of protection from its own thuggish actions.[32]

And like Uber, Amazon is extending this automated mafia machine from seller to buyer. As the reporter Julia Angwin detailed recently, Amazon is fast developing the same abilities to manipulate buyers as well.[33] Or, more to the point, to manipulate you and your family. Into paying more. Into buying what they want to sell. Into sharing information you don't want to share. Into becoming one more cow for them to milk.

THE MASTER OF MAIN STREET—GOOGLE

By the time you read this book, Uber itself may be in real trouble. And the basic problem was evident long before Covid-19. Even before the corporation went public in May 2019, Uber had lost billions of dollars and had identified no clear path to profits. The corporation simply faced too much competition, from Lyft, from traditional taxis, from other forms of transportation.[34]

But no matter whether this particular ownership structure collapses or not, Uber's business model will live on, hence the various threats posed by that business model will live on. One way to get a sense of *who* might end up running Uber's business, or something very much like it, is to consider where Uber gets its mapping services.

In Uber's early days, one of its biggest investors was Google. Once Uber began to gain real traction, however, its executives moved to cut ties with Google, in order to ensure their corporation was less subject to paying rent to other monopolists and more fully in control of its own destiny. This meant kicking Google executive David Drummond off the Uber board.[35] More importantly, it meant developing its own mapping service. Between 2015 and 2017 Uber bought mapping technology and talent from Microsoft, purchased a startup named Otto that was run by one of the founders of Google's Waymo self-driving car division, and hired the former head of Google search to run Uber's own mapping operation.[36]

Then in April 2019, in advance of Uber's initial public offering of stock, executives admitted that the plan had failed. Uber, the executives reported, had paid Google $58 million over the previous three years to use the larger corporation's mapping services, and had agreed to pay some $245 million to settle a lawsuit for infringing on Google "trade secrets." Even more concerning, Uber had forked over some $631 million to Google for advertising and marketing.[37]

In fact, despite Uber's fight to liberate itself, Google and Google executives still owned large parts of the corporation at the time of the IPO.[38] More galling, Google had also invested in Uber's arch-rival Lyft and owned more than 5 percent of that corporation when it went public shortly before Uber's own IPO.[39]

In its pre-IPO filings Uber made clear to potential investors that this failure to win its independence from Google meant that the corporation's destiny was not in its own hands and certainly not in the hands of its customers. "We rely upon certain third parties to provide software for our products and offerings, including Google Maps for the mapping function that is critical to the functionality of our platform."

And the Uber executives made clear that this was not going to change any time soon. "We do not believe that an alternative mapping solution exists that can provide the global functionality that we require to offer our platform in all of the markets in which we operate. We do not control all mapping functions employed by our platform or Drivers using our platform, and it is possible that such mapping functions *may not be reliable*."[40]

In short, Uber depends on a landlord that can raise its rent and change its contract almost at will. In this sense, the corporation is really little different from one of the midsize manufacturers who depends on Amazon to get to market. Left unsaid by Uber was the fact that much of the extremely valuable data that the corporation gathers from its rides was also flowing straight into Google's data vaults.

The reason Uber found no real alternative to dependence on Google lies in two acquisitions Google made more than 15 years ago. First was the Android operating system for mobile phones, which Google purchased in 2005, then made available to almost any phone manufacturer in the world. Android was designed precisely, in the words of its original developer, to be "more aware of its owner's location and preferences" than other mobile phone systems.[41] After years of refinement by Google, Android is now one of the world's most powerful tools for tracking the movement of individuals, and it runs almost 90 percent of the world's mobile phones. The amount of detailed data Google is able to collect on anyone with an Android phone is phenomenal. Not only can an Android device tell exactly where you are, and the speed at which you are traveling, but it can sense whether you are riding a horse or bicycle, or jogging or climbing stairs. Google then combines all this information into the world's widest and deepest record of human movement across the face of the earth, a record of us both as individuals and as a species.

The second reason Uber found no real alternative to dependence on Google is that the corporation bought up control over most of the world's best mapping technologies. This included the fundamental technology behind Google Maps, which the corporation purchased from two Danish brothers in 2004. More recently, it includes at least 11 big acquisitions, the most important of which took place in 2013, the first full year of Uber's life, when Google purchased Waze, which at the time was the only large-scale independent mapping system left in the world.

Amazon has exploited its monopolization of the platform where sellers and buyers connect online to enclose many of America's most important markets for consumer goods, in ways that give the corporation ever greater capacity to micromanage commerce in America. Google, in similar fashion, has exploited its monopolization of mapping software to capture great and growing control over how human beings interact with our own streets and highways, both in America and around the world. As a result, Google now enjoys not only the ability to micromanage the movement of the individual through the world but increasingly enjoys the ability to determine the failure or success even of some of the most powerful and well-capitalized corporations in the world.

Uber and Lyft are not the only corporations threatened by Google's mastery of mapping. Until recently, manufacturers of cars and trucks were among the world's most powerful corporations. Today their future looks increasingly bleak, not because they lack the ability to make great vehicles, or to develop software for those vehicles, but because someone else owns the operating system for the roads and highways on which their vehicles must run.

The women and men who run these corporations are smart. They understand very clearly how Google and Apple exploited their control over mobile operating systems to almost seamlessly displace Motorola, Nokia, and other first-generation mobile phone manufacturers and to capture almost all the value in that industry.[42]

For the moment, most automakers have chosen to try to keep some control over mapping by forging alliances with one another. Given the century-long rivalry of these corporations, this is not always easy. The result thus far has been a patchwork of loose deals: between Ford and Volkswagen, between General Motors and Lyft, and among all the German carmakers together.[43] Toyota, meanwhile, has proposed an open-source self-driving system, on the model of Linux, to allow everyone to go their own way, but together.[44]

Yet here the carmakers face a second fundamental challenge to their traditional sovereignty: the institutional investors who control ever-bigger portions of these corporations may not give the executives all that much choice other than to join Chrysler and Nissan in turning the keys over to Google.

Consider for instance the role that the giant Tokyo based investment fund SoftBank plays within this system. With vast piles of cash—much of it from the Saudi government—SoftBank has become one of the most dogged engineers of technology monopolies in the world. This includes engineering the elimination of competition in ride hailing in much of the world.[45] In the case of self-driving cars, SoftBank now holds a stake in just about every play, including huge investments in the efforts by GM and Toyota to escape Google's control.[46]

As one reporter described SoftBank's new role in the automotive industry, "The overlapping investments and alliances have become so prevalent that they border on conflicts. And SoftBank sits at the center . . . From an investor standpoint, the interconnectedness makes the idea of picking a winner almost meaningless."[47]

In other words, SoftBank, the octopus that controls access to capital, will use its power and sway to force even the biggest of the carmakers into the grasp of the octopus that controls the streets, Google.

And don't count on any other corporation to come to the rescue. Even Apple, with its billions of dollars hoarded away, understands there is no way to match Google in mapping. For Apple, this is no theory but rather the lesson of hard competition. In 2016, after investing billions of dollars improving its own mapping software and databases, Apple realized that even a fast-growing share of iPhone users were switching to Google's map, with its wider and deeper—hence more useful—base of data.[48]

Rather than fight Google, Apple chose merely to collect huge fees from Google—an estimated $12 billion in 2019—for preloading their search on every iPhone. Apple chose, in other words, the quiet life of the landlord over the more bracing, but risky, life of the innovator.[49]

For automakers, the future looks bleak. Surrounded by systems controlled by Google, two second-tier automakers chose simply to strike deals directly with the corporation or its robot car division, Waymo. Fiat-Chrysler in mid-2018 agreed to manufacture nearly 70,000 Chrysler Pacificas for Waymo.[50] Then in February 2019 Renault-Nissan announced plans to work with Google on building self-driving cars.[51]

Absent a decision by a government agency to stand up to Google's dominance of mapping and related technologies, the day will soon come when Ford, GM, Toyota, and Mercedes will also all be forced to surrender to Google's control and accept a life of increasing senescence as benders of metal for the master of the map.

And as radical a concentration of wealth, power, and control as this would represent, we should keep in mind that Google's mastery of the world's streets barely touches on the full extent of Google's power to shape and direct online commerce and, indeed, human society itself. In the 20 years since its birth, Google has been left almost entirely free to monopolize whatever sections of online communications and commerce it has wished. And Google responded with at least 225 takeovers that helped the corporation corner control over much of the Internet itself. In addition to maps, Google now also plays a dominant role in searches, email, mobile, online video, operating systems, browsers, and online advertising technology, among many other monopoly positions. And it expands its reach every day. This includes the emerging "Internet of Things," which is designed to regulate the use of everything ranging from the appliances in your home to the electrical grid itself to the energy markets where hydrocarbons are traded. And this list of takeovers does not include the personal investments of top Google executives themselves.

Increasingly Google does not even need to buy other people's companies and technologies. As is true of Amazon, Google enjoys the ability to simply take their businesses at will. When Google speaks of the radical nature of the changes promised by artificial intelligence, it is really often just talking about all the data it has collected about other people's businesses and its ability to use that data to displace those businesses when it chooses.

And like Uber and Amazon, Google is also perfecting its ability to use these caches of information in an even more insidious way. It simply manipulates the sellers and buyers of various goods and services, as well as the various speakers and listeners, writers and readers in our society, in ways that allow the corporation to extort wealth, from everyone everywhere, just for doing what human beings do.

To understand the number and complexity of ways Google can discriminate in the information it delivers to you, let's turn back to the service of mapping. In this case we are talking not about how Google prices access to its maps for a corporation like Uber, but the quality of the mapping services it delivers to you and other individual people. Already today we live in a world in which it is absolutely possible for Google to steer some people along better routes, and to steer other people—perhaps you—onto slower and more costly side routes. There is almost an infinite number of reasons Google might want to manipulate your behavior in some direction or other. The corporation might wish to direct you, for instance, down a particular street to please some major advertiser. Or Google might wish to get you off the main road so some more important person can go faster.

We know that the tolls on the interstate highway system can be highly unfair to poor citizens. But at least those tolls are posted. And at least they apply to all people evenly. In the case of Google's mapping system, every decision made by that master mechanism is secret, hidden from everyone except Google itself. No government agency anywhere in the free world today is watching Google to prevent it from such blatant abuse of the absolute power that comes with providing each of its many essential services.

Our failure to apply common carrier rules to Google, to prevent the corporation from discriminating in the pricing and terms of the services it provides to different sellers and different buyers, has left that corporation free to build the most perfect system for micromanaging the movement of humans in the history of the world.

And every day the corporation invests vast new amounts of money and time in concentrating yet more power and control. In 2017, for instance, a division of Google named Sidewalk Labs announced plans to partner with the city of Toronto to build the world's most digitally connected neighborhood. The plan calls for the newly named "Quayside" section of the city to be outfitted with snow-melting sidewalks, robotic garbage collectors, self-driving taxis, even sensors to study how people use park benches.[52]

In April 2019 the Canadian Civil Liberties Association sued Toronto to force the city to cancel its contract with Google. "Canada is not Google's lab rat," the association's executive director said. "Our freedom from unlawful public surveillance is worth fighting for."[53] And to the surprise of many, Toronto's citizens won this fight; in May 2020, Google abandoned its plans.

Power to the people of Toronto. But—like New Yorkers' rejection of Amazon's "HQ2" investment in 2019—even this complete victory was largely symbolic. It left the core of Google's machine untouched. And that machine is already well on the way to controlling Toronto's streets and those of every other city in the world—and in much the same way, just about every other communications platform human beings use to interact with the world around them.

THE MASTERS OF TRUTH—FACEBOOK (AND GOOGLE)

Wired editor Nick Thompson is an old friend. I first met Nick in 2002, when we were both fellows at the Washington think tank New America. Over the years I have watched as Nick has perfected a particular way of using journalism to address concentrations of power by large corporations. Rather than write an economic analysis of the problem to help law enforcers act, Nick will frame the problem as a moral challenge for some leader inside the particular corporation in question. "Can so-and-so abandon his bad old ways?" Nick will ask. "Can so-and-so master his predatory behaviors?"

In early 2018 Nick wrote such an article about Facebook. The cover illustration—of a bruised Mark Zuckerberg—told the reader immediately that Nick did not intend to attack Zuckerberg—because others had already done that. Rather, it indicated that Nick planned to observe the Facebook CEO somewhat sympathetically. And this is precisely how the profile itself read. Yet at one point halfway through the article, Nick let down his guard. What slipped out was a sharp cry of horror, from this gifted journalist, about what Facebook was doing to his publication, his profession, and to American democracy.

"Every publisher knows that, at best, they are sharecroppers on Facebook's massive industrial farm," Nick wrote. "And journalists know that the man who owns the farm has the leverage. If Facebook wanted to, it could quietly turn any number of dials that would harm a publisher—by manipulating its traffic, its ad network, or its readers."[54]

Google and Facebook both look highly complex, and Google's structure certainly is complex. But ultimately the business models of these two corporations are very simple. Both corporations are designed to sell advertising—lots of it. That is why they collect so much information about us, why they so closely study our most intimate secrets. To make money, they combine their gatekeeper control over essential services with their license to discriminate in the services they deliver with the massive cache of data they collect on the people who sell and buy on their platforms. Google and Facebook then use their machines to steer the thoughts and actions of millions and millions of people, moment to moment. They then rent their manipulation machines, in the form of advertising, to anyone willing to pay for their use.

This model has proven phenomenally successful. In 2019 Google earned $120 billion just from advertising, while Facebook earned some $70 billion. Together the two captured roughly two-thirds of online ad revenue, and the total is growing fast.[55]

Unfortunately, from the point of view of the public, this model poses three huge problems.

First is that Google and Facebook have become the main spreaders of the lies and misinformation that have so disrupted our society in recent years. There is nothing new about propaganda; we can read about it in Thucydides's account of the Peloponnesian War. What is new is the scale, reach, and speed of today's manipulation machines.

When Google and Facebook built their manipulation machines, they did so in the expectation that corporations like Procter & Gamble would want to use them to steer buyers to, say, a more expensive version of Tide. Or that American Airlines might use them to steer buyers to a last-minute ticket to Cancun. But as we learned after the election of 2016, the manipulation machine is also of use to Vladimir Putin and others who want to steer the votes of citizens or stoke the rage of mobs. And Google and Facebook are more than glad to rent out their machines to them as well.

Second, a large portion of the advertising dollars that Google and Facebook pocket used to be spent somewhere else. Billions, for instance, used to go to newspapers and news magazines and local radio and television news teams.

In the early days of the Internet, companies like Craigslist also diverted money away from news outlets. But that was a long time ago, and by 2005 or so most publishers had learned how to adjust to the loss of classified advertising. Not this time; not against Google and Facebook. Between 2008 and 2017, as those two corporations diverted those billions of dollars in advertising revenue, newspaper newsroom employment fell by nearly half. Practically, this means 30,000 fewer reporters and editors walking beats in our towns and our state capitals. It means entire systems of specialized journalism have been wiped out entirely.[56]

The third thing Google and Facebook do is impose fear. I first came across this sort of fear in the book publishing industry in 2009. I discovered that many publishers, editors, and book authors would tell me horrifying stories about Amazon's abuse of its power over their businesses, but they would do so only behind closed doors. They feared that if they spoke in public Amazon would strip the buy buttons off their pages and cut them off from the market, just as the corporation later did to Macmillan and Hachette.

Today much the same is true of our newspaper journalists and publishers. Even as Google and Facebook bleed them dry, they dare not cry out for fear the giants will squeeze even harder. This is true across the United States. It is true across Europe. It is true around the world.

If there was ever any real doubt that Google and Facebook would intentionally exploit their power to promote their own political interests, consider what Nick wrote in May 2019, when in a second feature in *Wired* he revisited the subject of Facebook.

Once again Nick focused mainly on the drama and decisions within Facebook's executive suite. But once again he also snuck in a few words about his own fears, and indeed what Facebook had done to *Wired* after his previous article came out.

Shortly after *Wired* published Nick's first article on Zuckerberg in March 2018, "traffic from Facebook suddenly dropped by 90 percent, and for four weeks it stayed there," Nick wrote in May 2019. "After protestations, emails, and a *raised eyebrow or two about the coincidence*, Facebook finally got to the bottom of it. An ad run by a liquor advertiser . . . had been *mistakenly* categorized as engagement bait by the platform. In response, the algorithm had let all the air out of WIRED's tires. The publication could post whatever it wanted, but few would read it. Once the *error* was identified, traffic soared back."[57]

Nick then doubled down on what he'd written the previous year to make clear he knew exactly what Facebook had done. "It was a reminder that journalists are just sharecroppers on Facebook's giant farm."

Before we move on, let's make sure we all fully understand the lesson Nick wants us to learn. In response to the original March 2018 article, which overall provided a very flattering profile of Facebook, and which Nick structured to provide Facebook executives with ample room to prove their good intentions, the corporation's leadership responded by shutting off all traffic to *Wired* for a month.

The gravest threat to democracy in America today is not Donald Trump or Vladimir Putin or the Communist Party of China. The gravest threat is posed by Google and Facebook and Amazon. Not only do they spread other people's lies. Not only do they starve the journalists whose job it is to counter those lies. They actively punish the journalists who speak truth to them. And they have captured direct political control over all the corporations—and executives—who depend on them.

In his 1912 campaign for president, Woodrow Wilson spoke of the political dangers that come of concentrating economic power in only a few hands. "I cannot tell you how many men of business, how many important men of business, have communicated their real opinions about the situation in the United States to me privately and confidentially. They are afraid of somebody. They are afraid to make their real opinions known publicly; they tell them to me behind their hand. That means," Wilson concluded, "we are not masters of our own opinions."[58]

Today we see a similar pyramiding of power. The combination of monopoly control over access to markets, plus the monopolists' control of great masses of data on every seller and buyer, plus their license to discriminate in pricing and services, means even the most powerful corporations from Stage One of the monopolization in America—in other words, even the most powerful of the last generation of oligarchs—are fast being made subject to the wishes and whims of the new intermediaries.

Great masters of men who but five years ago ranked among the top tier of predators, who could alter the fates of hundreds of thousands or even millions of people with the flick of a forefinger, now themselves fawn and fuss and flatter, their lips carefully concealing their canines.

Who makes law in America today? Who chooses who wins and who loses? Increasingly it is the masters of Google and Amazon and Facebook and a few other corporations that control the gates into specific realms of human activity.

And when mere awesome economic power is not sufficient to achieve their ends, these masters resort to more direct forms of thuggery. Sometimes against journalists like Nick Thompson. Sometimes against politicians and regulators, as we saw with Uber's brass-knuckled multimillion-dollar campaign against New York City officials in 2015 and its generalized system of grayballing.[59] Sometimes against public critics like our team at Open Markets, as Google did in 2017 and as Facebook did in 2019.[60] Sometimes even, as we saw in the last chapter, against the grain farmer and pig farmer and warehouse worker and other folks just trying to get by.[61]

THE PUBLIC, ATOMIZED

In 1776, Adam Smith described how the market price of a good sends signals that enable people to change their actions. When a price is too low, suppliers turn to other lines of trade, other lines of business. When a price is too high, new suppliers will bring new production to market. In other words, basic supply and demand.

In 1946 the Austrian economist Friedrich Hayek used Smith's idea about how prices distribute information as part of an argument against centralized state control over an economy. A key assumption by both Smith and Hayek was that the price for any good or service would be clear to every member of the public. They assumed that how a particular good is priced naturally communicates to every citizen certain vital information, such as the existence of a shortage of tomatoes or chickens, or of a bumper crop of corn. This information, in turn, enables every buyer and seller to alter their economic behavior accordingly, such as by buying fewer tomatoes and more corn.

Market prices do something else as well. They also allow the public as a whole, and particular classes and groups of people, to take political action, if they think it necessary, to address the reason why a particular good is in short supply or oversupply. If the price of a particular good— say shoes—goes up and stays up, this may indicate that a monopolist has captured control of shoe manufacturing, and the time has come for the public to use the state to break this monopoly. If the price of wheat goes up and stays up, then maybe the time has come to investigate whether some trader has amassed a dangerous amount of power over the wheat supply or wheat handling capacity. And if that proves not to be the case, people can use the information to help them decide to build a new road to open new lands, or to open a new trade with a wheat-growing land across the sea.

In other words, it is the public price that plays a major role in making the public the public. It is one of the main factors that allows people, as a group, to stand together in the public square and town hall and to compare our personal experiences with one another in ways that allow us to identify patterns and structural problems, hence to act as a coherent community able to make wise decisions. Markets, in other words, are not only where we exchange goods and services with one another. Markets are not only institutions that provide the individual with liberty to conduct her own business, free from restraint. Well-structured markets are also one of the main institutions able to provide that most basic stuff of democracy, which is trustworthy information about potential problems within the workings of the political economy.

Compared to today, the harms that Smith and Hayek feared seem almost innocuous. Yes, mercantilism and monopolism, just as they feared, do lead to the warping of commercial activities toward wasteful and unnecessary ends. But when the prices of goods and services are still made public, and the public as a whole is able to understand how it is affected, then the public as a whole can take actions to fix the problem.

The problem with first-degree price discrimination, then, is not merely that it gives to a monopolist the ability to pick and choose winners and losers. It is not merely that it gives to a monopolist the ability to manipulate commercial interactions in ways that allow them to extort money and political favor from those who rely on them to get to market.

The problem with the license to engage in first-degree price discrimination is that even as it helps to concentrate all power and control in one or two private corporations, it simultaneously, by atomizing prices, atomizes the public. This is true when first-degree discrimination is imposed on sellers. It is true when it is imposed on buyers.

Consider the small corner of the political economy in which our chicken farmers make their living. Back in the days of competitive markets, farmers who didn't like the price offered by one processor could go to the next processor. If they did not like the prices offered by any processor, the fact that they were all presented with the same price enabled them to formulate common demands to these corporate buyers. And if that did not work, to formulate common demands—for reform—to their politicians.

Today, by contrast, when every farming family is given a different price, the farmers have no common information around which to organize. None of the farming families knows how exactly it is being exploited or to what degree. Every member of every farming family fears that if he or she complains, their family will be treated even worse or perhaps cut off entirely from the market.

And bad as this plucking of the chicken farmer's family may be, it takes place in a very real world of feathers and sweat and ammonia, at the gate of a processing plant where for a moment or two the farmer can look into the face of the foreman and beg. Or perhaps, if but for that most fleeting of human satisfactions, yell and spit.

In the world of Uber, Amazon, Google, and Facebook, all this manipulation, all this breaking of spirit and hope, this breaking of the public, is managed from afar, automatically, algorithmically.

The result is not merely that we live today in a kiss-ass economy, in which we must compete to please The Man. It is not merely that we live today, technically, subject entirely to another's will. Not merely that we are manipulated, moment by moment, by private masters who rule our commerce, our movement, even our thought.

It is that every one of us increasingly must now suffer alone, with ever less ability to commiserate with others about our common problems, because nowadays the power of the middleman is such as to make each of our problems unique, to make each of our problems solely a matter between us and the master.

The combination of monopoly plus massive caches of personalized data plus first-degree price discrimination means you have been set loose, to float entirely alone, like Pip in the midst of the vast sea, watching the little ship that carried our society sail into the maw of Leviathan.

THREE

THE AMERICAN
SYSTEM OF LIBERTY

FROM SUBJECT TO CITIZEN

IN 2009, SCIENTISTS AT THE LIBRARY OF CONGRESS REDISCOVERED
one of the most fundamental acts of the American Revolution.
Using a hyperspectral imaging camera to study an early draft of the
Declaration of Independence, they found that Thomas Jefferson at
one point had forcefully erased the word "subjects" then carefully
written in its place the word "citizens."

The most immediate effect of the Declaration was, of course, to
draw a new border between the people of the 13 colonies and
the people and government of Great Britain. The even more revolutionary effect of the Declaration was to reshape the political nature
and structure of the society inside the borders of the new nation. This
was the aim, as every schoolchild is taught, of the statements that
"all men are created equal," and that all possess "inalienable rights,"
including "Life, Liberty, and the pursuit of Happiness."

A scientist who took part in the discovery later said Jefferson's
erasure of the word "subjects" was so forceful that historians should
view the action itself as important. Jefferson crossed out many other
words in the draft, but he obliterated only this one. "It's almost
like . . . he didn't even want a record of it," she said. "Really, it sends
chills down the spine."[1]

I first read this story in the *Washington Post* in July 2010, soon after my book *Cornered* had been published. In my research I had come to understand that the people who had overthrown America's traditional antimonopoly regime had based much of their effort on the idea that competition policy should promote the "welfare" of the "consumer." This in turn was obviously based on the idea that within the political economy we should view the individual foremost as a "consumer." As a result, I already understood this conception of the individual as a "consumer" to be highly problematic. As we will see in chapter seven, it was consciously designed and wielded to promote forms of top-down, "command-and-control" socialism. What I had not yet fully thought through, however, was the role that the concept of "citizen" had played in constructing the American System of Liberty in the first place.

So, right at the moment I was first turning to the project that would become this book, the scientists in the Library of Congress provided me with an important clue. The American Revolution was obviously a fight *against* certain immediately perceived threats, such as the commercial power of the British East India Company and the taxing power of a parliament over which the Americans had no control. But it was also, necessarily, a fight *for* certain ideals, and *for* a certain vision of how society could be organized, and *for* a certain vision of what a human being could become. This story about Jefferson penning the word "citizen" is what helped me better to understand what the revolutionaries actually fought *for*.

Similarly, Jefferson's "citizens" also provided a clue to the principles the revolutionaries used in shaping the foundations of the American political economy. The American political economy is no mere pile of law inscribed in books, accreting like limestone on the bottom of the sea. It is a system based more or less perfectly on principles laid down at the time of the Revolution. And here too the concept of "citizen" helped me—and, I hope, will help us—to understand how the revolutionaries and later generations identified and refined these principles. And further, how they used these principles not only to

shape the law but to help guide them in how to use government itself as a tool to positively shape and construct American society and,
as we will see, the American citizen.

As we look at the American political economy today, it is ever
easier to understand what it is we are against. We see the threats. We
see which corporations and which business practices we must target
first. But as we rummage through our vast chest of antimonopoly
laws and policies, it is vital to understand also what we must stand
for, what we must fight for. As we glare at Google and Facebook
and Amazon, and sharpen our swords and broadaxes, we must also
look past these specific threats—as terrifying as they are—and plan
for the society we mean to have, and the people we mean to be, after
we win.

Not only will this vision inspire us to the fight, it will help us
practically by clarifying how exactly we must structure and harness
these corporations and technologies.

One of my main hopes in writing *Liberty from All Masters* is—as
we go about the task of structuring the political economy of our
twenty-first-century society—to provide us some guidance from the
past. The technologies we face today are in certain respects radically
different than any we have wrestled with before. But key aspects of
the problem remain the same as always, including the nature of human beings and the nature of commercial and political power within
human society. Indeed, even many of the basic facts of how corporate
organization shapes corporate behavior, and how corporations wield
any particular technology, remain the same.

The struggle for liberty did not begin in 1776. Nor, as we well
know, did it end there. In the pages to come, our story will range
back to the English Revolution in the seventeenth century, an event
that greatly shaped the thinking of America's revolutionaries. And
we will also look at periods in America's history when citizens fought
to achieve the full promise of the Declaration of Independence, such
as in the war to destroy slavery and, in the twentieth century, the
fight to destroy Jim Crow. In the pages to come we will also trace
the story through periods when citizens fought to adapt and update
the principles themselves to meet the challenges of new technologies

and new international threats, such as during the New Freedom and New Deal in the early decades of the twentieth century.

For our immediate next purposes what is most important about the revolutionary transformation of the individual from subject to citizen is that it allows us to begin the process of answering *how* the first generation of independent Americans set about securing liberty and democracy and building entirely new forms of community.

Americans made their Revolution at a time when only the most minimal and precarious forms of democracy and personal liberty existed—in the United Kingdom, in Holland—and when most European intellectuals believed that true liberty and democracy was for all intents impossible.

Jefferson himself, as he etched the word "citizens," could only hope that this act of political and spiritual imagination would ever have any real effect. Yet this conception of the individual as a citizen contained the seeds of the System of Liberty that Americans would construct over the next generation and would refine over the next two centuries of battles to protect and expand human liberty and democracy.

In painting over "subjects" and writing "citizens," Jefferson radically altered the relationship of the individual with the state and with other individuals. A subject exists below the state, or the king. A citizen is an equal part of the state. A subject petitions power. A citizen grants power.[2] A subject's allegiance is to the ruler. A citizen's allegiance is to fellow citizens.

This entire new web of relationships, in turn, is what sets our own story into motion. Because to perpetuate this new flat society of equal relationships between individual and individual, and to prevent the restoration of hierarchy and aristocracy, Americans had to establish new rules for how these individuals could *compete* with one another, not only in politics but in markets, in commerce, and in the accumulation of wealth and economic power. They had to construct a system that would promote and refine the vision of citizenship they had imagined. And they then had to protect and perpetuate that system over time.[3]

JEFFERSON AND/OR LIBERTY

My goal in focusing so closely on the movement of Jefferson's hands on the parchment, on the movement of his mind through the dreams and terrors and joys and horrors of human life, as he had read them in the pages of his histories and lived them in his public and private lives, is not to resurrect Thomas Jefferson the man. Long before Lin-Manuel Miranda wrote his musical celebrating Jefferson's archrival, Alexander Hamilton, Jefferson's personal reputation was in sharp decline. This reconsideration of the man Jefferson is of importance for understanding not just who he was but who we are and what we seek from him and other members of the founding generation.

Americans should feel honest horror at many of the actions of these men. This includes not only their failure to destroy slavery but also their policy of displacing Native Americans, a policy that led all but inevitably to extermination, even genocide. Even though our lives today are radically different, we should never dismiss such sentiments as anachronistic. Such horrified reactions help us to define who we are today. In the specific case of Jefferson, at the time he wrote the Declaration he personally held nearly 200 men, women, and children as slaves. As Edmund Morgan, the historian of colonial Virginia, put it, "To a large degree it may be said that Americans bought their independence with slave labor. The paradox is American, and it behooves Americans to understand it if they would understand themselves."[4]

In the specific case of Jefferson, his writings show his own profound disgust for the institution of slavery and its effects on the character of all the human beings involved. And yet in his personal life Jefferson failed to follow the example of contemporaries, such as George Washington, who freed their own enslaved people. Jefferson the man must own his own hypocrisies, his own failings, his own sins. And they are many.

In 1856, in his great oration on the Fourth of July, Frederick Douglass assailed the fundamental fraudulence of an America that chained and whipped and raped men, women, and children, and that destroyed families and even the ties between mother and child.

"You hurl your anathemas at the crowned headed tyrants of Russia and Austria, and pride yourselves on your Democratic Institutions, while you yourselves consent to be the mere tools and bodyguards of the tyrants of Virginia and Carolina," Douglass said. "Your shout of liberty and equality" is, he concluded, but "hollow mockery."[5]

The historian Henry Adams once called Jefferson the "Moses of democracy," and in the middle of the twentieth century Americans built a temple to Jefferson on the banks of the Potomac in Washington. In the coming years, perhaps we will choose to remove Jefferson's statue out from under the dome of that temple and replace it with a statue of some other Moses of democracy, perhaps Martin Luther King Jr. But, again, as we set about our task of reckoning with the specific threats posed to us and our society by twenty-first-century monopoly, how we reckon with Jefferson's personal failings need have no effect on how we wield his words and writings today.

Was Jefferson a seer? Or a mere scribe? A true believer in democracy? Or a wealthy demagogic poser? A tragic figure, a man who behind a benign smile loathed himself? Or a shameless hypocrite? Jefferson has been called all these things. But as we set about our task of reckoning with twenty-first-century monopoly, we need not answer any of these questions.

This story is not about the *man* Thomas Jefferson or any other individual. It is about the principles Jefferson and James Madison and other leaders of early America developed and put to practical use to shape and regulate competition among individuals within the American political economy. It is about the institutions and intellectual tools that they and their allies first framed and honed to achieve these ends.

Even more important, this book is about how these tools from the very first were also very much *our* tools, the people's tools. Yes, a few wealthy white men provided much of the original theoretical and institutional apparatus of American liberty and democracy. But let's not forget that the American people were able to make their demands felt right from the first. Let's not forget that thousands of common revolutionaries marched in the streets around the Declaration's drafters and often engaged in direct debate with them.[6]

And certainly, from the moment the Declaration was published, these basic tools of liberty were there for all to use. And use them the American people did. It was these tools and this language that landless whites would later use to secure more liberty for themselves. It was these tools and this language that Susan Anthony and John Bright and W. E. B. Du Bois used to fight, respectively, the suppression of women, and the disenfranchisement of British men, and the disenfranchisement of black Americans.

No one ever used these tools with more effect than Frederick Douglass. Before the Civil War, the abolitionist leader William Lloyd Garrison held that the U.S. Constitution was in essence a pro-slavery document. Douglass, who worked closely with Garrison for many years, ultimately rejected this argument and chose instead to make the Constitution his own. He voluntarily interpreted it as a liberty document and then wielded its emancipatory principles and structures to help enslaved people win their own liberty.

In a speech on July 6, 1863, during the Civil War, Douglass declared, "I hold that the federal government was never, in its essence, anything but an antislavery government. Abolish slavery tomorrow, and not a sentence or syllable of the Constitution need be altered. It was purposely so framed as to give no claim, no sanction to the claim of property in man. If in its origin slavery had any relation to the government, it was only as the scaffolding to the magnificent structure, to be removed as soon as the building was completed. There is in the Constitution no East, no West, no North, no South, no black, no white, no slave, no slaveholder, but all are citizens who are of American birth."[7]

Generation after generation, it was these tools and this language that have empowered different groups of Americans to make American liberty their own. It was this American System of Liberty that empowered the Americans of the nineteenth century to break the power of the planter and the financier who supported him. And that empowered the Americans of the twentieth century to defeat Nazi Germany and, later, Soviet Russia. It was this American System of Liberty that, in the years after the war, inspired millions in India and South Africa and Brazil and Mexico and Malaysia and Taiwan, and across all Europe, to establish their own systems for the mastering of private and public monopoly and the protection and expansion of democracy and individual liberty.

Our problem today is that long before we learned the full extent of Jefferson's personal weaknesses, the influence of pro-monopoly intellectuals had already led us to let go of his ideas. The result, as we saw in the previous two chapters, is the triumph of monopoly, and hence mass expropriation, the breakdown in rule of law, and the rise of autocratic and atomizing systems of control.

We should all feel at liberty to spit on the grave of any of the founders, should we wish. But we would be foolish to leave the tools they honed with such care out in the rain, rusting, unused. If we are to defeat Google and Amazon and Facebook and the other great private autocracies rising in our society, if we are once again to hold our destiny in our own hands as individuals and as a nation, if we are to understand how to rebuild the American System of Liberty so we can continue the work of Du Bois and King, we must now turn back to those first pages of America and read them afresh.

TO OWN ONE'S OWN SELF

The origins of the American System of Liberty actually lie outside America. The heart of Jefferson's Declaration was not a sudden striking inspiration out of nowhere. Rather it was more the culmination of a debate that had raged among English-speaking peoples for more than a century, back to the years of the English Revolution and Civil War in the mid-seventeenth century. Although that rebellion ultimately guttered into a vaguely liberal aristocratic system, with real power concentrated in a tiny class of landlords and bankers, the writings of the English radicals shaped much of the thinking of the Americans of a century later.[8]

We can trace regulation and prohibition of monopoly to the Old Testament and to ancient Babylonia.[9] And throughout medieval times in Europe the protection of competitive markets was a basic responsibility of local government. But antimonopolism in the modern political sense—in which the aim is to clearly limit certain powers so as to protect liberty of action and of speech, rule of law, democracy—took shape only in early seventeenth-century England. It was during the reign of Elizabeth I that we see the first political fights against monopoly, which was seen as corrupting of both government and commerce. It was in antimonopoly fights against King James that English reformers honed much of the thinking and rhetoric that would culminate in open rebellion against monarchy and ultimately the overthrow and beheading of King Charles I in 1649.[10]

The political writings of John Milton, the poet of *Paradise Lost*, provide one of the best guides to the fears and dreams of the intellectual leaders of the English Revolution. We see in Milton's essays and polemics highly sophisticated arguments in favor of freedom of worship, freedom of speech, freedom of the press, freedom from concentrated political power, as well as demands for a written constitution.

But, importantly, it's not only highly educated writers like Milton who made such demands. We also see that one of the more radical popular groups of the time, the Levelers, in 1647 called for popular suffrage, bans on monopolies, and a republican form of government.[11]

There is no doubt that America's revolutionaries were inspired both by the writings of Milton and other scholars and by the people's own antimonopolism of the English Revolution. This was true both of common Americans and the well-born. In the streets of Boston in the 1770s, the city's "lower classes" looked for inspiration to George Jones, the tailor who captured King Charles I in 1647 and later served as his executioner.[12] Madison's biographer Ralph Ketcham, meanwhile, describes how at Princeton Madison discovered that "enlightened men took for granted the pattern of thought which from Cromwell's day had opposed religious establishment, ecclesiastical hierarchy, courtly influence, and every other manifestation of privileged and therefore easily and inevitably corruptible power. The heroes of this tradition were Milton, Algernon Sidney, Locke." The ultimate result, among the young men who read these texts, was "a commitment to resist 'domination and tyranny.'"[13]

The bookshelves of America's revolutionaries were stocked not only with tracts from the English Revolution of the mid-seventeenth century but with the "dissenting writers" from the 100 years in between.[14] Alongside the preachers of rule of law such as Edward Coke, there were preachers of property rights like John Locke, preachers of democracy like William Penn, preachers of virtue like James Harrington, preachers of separations of powers such as Montesquieu. There were preachers of free speech like Thomas Paine, and preachers of liberal trade like Adam Smith, and preachers of freedom of conscience: not only Milton, but even more important for Americans, Milton's friend Roger Williams, the Puritan theologian who founded Rhode Island and who fought for separation of church and state and the abolition of slavery.

In recent decades, the people who fund the writings of libertarian essays and books have invested great amounts of money in efforts to claim that America was created foremost to protect certain specific forms of private property. But in fact no one of these ideas dominated. Instead, in the years leading up to the Revolution, we see an almost chaotic debate in which different ideas of liberty interacted with the actual experience of liberty in America and in Britain, not only among the learned but among all the people, in often unexpected ways. Thomas Paine's biographer, for instance, writes of how Paine's practice of Methodism contributed to his political education. "Within the chapel, commoners learned self-respect, self-government, self-reliance, and organizational skills. Often they learned to read and write and to speak 'in society.'"[15]

America's revolutionaries were practical men and women who faced a huge, almost impossible, challenge of engineering an entirely new political economy on the fly while threatened by powerful empires—Great Britain, France, Spain—not only across the seas but directly to the north, south, and west. With the quickening of revolution in the 1770s, they knew they had to bring some order to this chaotic debate about how to organize a system that would guard and promote all these many liberties together, and they had to do so swiftly and practically.

The revolutionaries needed to clarify a line of reasoning on the nature of the individual, the nature of property, the nature of competition, and the nature of community. The concept of "citizen" helped the revolutionaries identify three fundamental liberties on which to focus their political efforts. These were the liberty to think and believe as one wished; to participate fully in all political decisions; and to own one's own self in all economic life. Together, they formed a mutually reinforcing system. Either you have all three of these liberties or you have none. Each of the three is, at once, a means, a measure, and an end.

Over the years Americans have published innumerable histories of how earlier generations acted to ensure citizens' liberty to think and believe as they wished and to participate fully in all political decisions. Americans have also published many works on how earlier generations acted to secure their liberty from all forms of political bondage, including economic discrimination by race.

Few recent histories, however, have focused on how earlier generations set about practically achieving the liberty to own one's own self in *all* economic life, other than in the case of bondage slavery. My goal in the rest of this chapter and the next three is to identify how exactly earlier generations defined this particular liberty, how they structured institutions to achieve these aims, and how they responded to a variety of political and technological challenges to these institutional structures over the course of two centuries together as a national community.

A CITIZEN MUST HAVE PROPERTY

One of the hottest debates in American society today is *Who qualifies as a citizen?* Who gets to stand inside the border and who must remain outside? If allowed inside, how long must a person wait to have full access to the law, and how long must they wait to be able to vote? The debate is so controversial that many progressives today want to all but abandon the word "citizen." To many it seems but code for nativism, tribalism.

There is absolutely nothing new about this debate. The founding generation faced much the same set of questions on July 5, 1776.

Who was to share in this new common sovereignty they had declared? And who was now subject to it? In much of the new country, the initial answer was that citizenship must be reserved for men who held real property, mainly in the form of land.

In the years since, this initial focus on ownership of land has led many to conclude that the American Revolution, and especially the framing of the Constitution, were both fundamentally antidemocratic actions. According to this view, the aim from the first was to concentrate control in the hands of an aristocracy, an oligarchy. And certainly there were many among the founders who held that the prime goal of society should indeed be to protect the right of the individual not only to acquire property, but to use it as that individual alone saw fit. And further that this included a right to hold human beings as property.

But another of Jefferson's edits in the Declaration belies this simple story.

Less than a month before the Declaration, the Fifth Virginia Convention had unanimously adopted a "Declaration of Rights" written by the planter George Mason. This included the statement that the "inherent rights" of the individual include "the enjoyment of life and liberty, with the means of acquiring and possessing property, and pursuing and obtaining happiness and safety."

In simplifying this phrase to "Life, Liberty, and the pursuit of Happiness," Jefferson and the other signers of the Declaration tell us they saw property not as an end in itself, but as a means to other things. Indeed, much the same would prove true in the Constitution itself. There, the word "property" appears only once, in an Article IV clause that refers to government property.[16] As the constitutional scholar Akhil Reed Amar has written, what we in fact see here is "a plain commitment to people over property."[17]

The somewhat paradoxical answer as to why so many of the founders initially believed that citizenship should be tied to ownership of land is that they believed property was the only way to truly secure the liberty of an individual to think and believe as one wished and to participate fully in all political decisions. To be a full citizen, they held, a person must be economically *independent*. In the first days of the Republic, most assumed this meant owning enough land to feed and clothe one's family.

The reasoning here is simple. If citizens do not depend on any other person for sustenance, then they will be able to think critically and speak freely in public. Only someone who never need beg anything of anyone—someone fully immune to all threats and manipulations—can be counted on to represent his own personal interests, and the interest of the public, at all times.

One of the clearest defenders of this idea was John Adams, a founder who did not own enslaved people and didn't have all that much land.

Like the other founders, Adams had been steeped in such thinking through his studies of the English Revolution. One guiding essay was a 1660 polemic by Milton, in which he condemned a political world characterized by "the perpetual bowings and cringings of an abject people."[18] A few decades later the English politician Algernon Sidney provided a more positive vision of who would make a good citizen. "Liberty," he wrote, "solely consists of an independency on the will of another; and by the name of slave we understand a man who can neither dispose of his person or goods, but enjoys all at the will of his master."[19]

For Adams and other founders, this distrust of any man who was subject to some master was not mere theory, not mere book learning. Having grown up in the colonial period, they had all witnessed individual cravenness and servility, up close, in their neighbors and perhaps in themselves. And they wanted to protect their new democracy from all such sycophancy and toadyism, and from all such distortions of democratic debate.

For Adams and many other founders, the question was not a matter of race, and they did not limit their effort to exclude only enslaved people from the voting rolls. They also sought to exclude all bonded servants.[20] Adams also made clear that his distrust carried over to renters and tenants, even those without debt.

In a letter to John Taylor, the Virginia politician and constitutional scholar, Adams imagined the political relationship between a rich landowner and those who live on his land. "If he is a humane, easy, generous landlord, will not his tenants feel an attachment to him? Will he not have influence among them? Will they not naturally think and vote as he votes? If, on the contrary, he is an austere, griping, racking, rack-renting tyrant, will not his tenants be afraid to offend him? Will not some, if not all of them, pretend to think with him, and vote as he would have them?"[21]

For Adams, the problem was not only a matter of the wealthy manipulating the simple people. If anything, what Adams most feared was a similar corruption of the educated and well-born, not least those who held political power. The very wealthy have ample tools with which to "govern the state underhand," Adams wrote. "The persons elected into office will be their tools, and in constant fear of them, will behave like mere puppets danced upon their wires."[22]

The Declaration of Independence, then, can perhaps best be understood as a declaration of independence of man from man. And in these first moments of the nation, many founders believed the only way to measure such independence was through secure ownership of land.

PROPERTY MUST BE DISTRIBUTED

A truism of American history is that formal party politics began only in 1792, when Jefferson and Madison formed their "Democratic-Republican" party to oppose what they viewed as the monopolizing and concentrating tendencies of Treasury Secretary Alexander Hamilton and his allies. From the first, the goal of their new party was to extend the border of citizenship outward, to bring more people into the common sovereignty. The goal, in other words, was to make republican citizenship more democratic.

The result of such thinking was the second fundamental decision of the founding period: property should be divided to as great a degree as possible. If independence required property, and if the nation was to be not an aristocracy but a democracy, then all free men should have property. The only problem with this commonly told history of America's early democracy is the timing. In fact, we can trace demands to distribute property to the propertyless, mainly in the form of land, to the earliest days of the Republic.

There were many reasons why early Americans feared concentration of power over property. One was simple class resentment. Adams himself, who ended up for a time leading the Federalist Party created by Hamilton, personally expressed this basic anger against wealth and privilege in 1776. "That exuberance of pride, which has produced an insolent domination in a few, a very few, opulent, monopolizing families [must] be brought down nearer to the confines of reason and moderation."[23]

A second was the belief that such monopolization of land was immoral. While serving as ambassador to France, Jefferson was shocked to find indigent peasants living next to the uncultivated hunting estates of the rich. It is this "unequal division of property which occasions the numberless instances of wretchedness which I had observed," he wrote. "The consequence of this enormous inequality" is to produce "misery" for "the bulk of mankind." Jefferson's conclusion? Legislatures cannot "invent too many devices for subdividing property."[24]

A third was fear of counterrevolution. After the English Revolution, control over land and political power had been swiftly concentrated in the hands of the very largest landlords, along with a rising class of bankers. Most Americans were appalled by the idea that their Revolution might do little more than transfer power from a parliament of landlords and bankers in London to a parliament of landlords and bankers in America. And at the time, this did not seem like an abstract danger. The ranks of men calling themselves "patriots" included Lord Baltimore, master of 23 vast estates in Maryland totaling 190,000 acres. (Baltimore's land was worked not by enslaved people but by tenants.)[25] They also included Robert Livingston, who controlled 160,000 acres in the Hudson Valley. Indeed, when Livingston joined the American rebellion in 1775, many of his tenants opted to remain loyal to Britain. In their eyes, any government supported by Livingston was not a government that would support them, hence it was better to "stand by the king."[26]

A fourth was fear of the mob. As Daniel Webster, the Massachusetts senator and orator, wrote in 1820, "Those who have not property, and see their neighbors possess much more than they think them to need, cannot be favorable to laws made for the protection of property. When this class becomes numerous, it grows clamorous. It looks on property as its prey and plunder, and is naturally ready, at all times, for violence and revolution."[27]

Jefferson, even before putting his final touches on the Declaration, had already taken steps to ensure a much wider distribution of land, at least in his native Virginia. In his draft constitution for the state, published in June 1776, Jefferson attempted to ensure that every white adult male would own at least 50 acres through a direct distribution of lands held directly by the state.

Although this proposal failed, Jefferson and his allies did succeed in passing two other laws, in 1776 and in 1785, that together resulted in a system for limiting the concentration of land ownership in Virginia. Traditionally, upon the death of a landowner, his holdings would pass to his firstborn son. After these changes—to the laws of entail and primogeniture—such lands were divided equally among all the children.[28] Jefferson later proudly held that in Virginia, these laws "laid the ax to the foot of pseudoaristocracy."[29] And certainly some aristocrats agreed. One planter, Landon Carter, horrified by the new laws, called Jefferson a "midday drunkard" who had betrayed his class.[30]

In these early years many founders also embraced the idea of a progressive taxation of property that would hit large landholders hardest. In a 1785 letter to Madison, Jefferson wrote that "Another means of silently lessening the inequality of property is to exempt all from taxation below a certain point, and to tax the higher portions of property in geometrical progression as they rise."[31] In the years before the Civil War, citizens in at least seven states enacted progressive taxation of land.[32]

Noah Webster, who would later author America's first dictionary, in 1787 imagined that the laws and taxes designed to distribute land and reduce the power of great landowners would function as a sort of antimonopoly *system*. "Wherever we cast our eyes, we see this truth, that property is the basis of power." Therefore, he wrote, "an equality of property, with a *necessity of alienation constantly operating to destroy combinations of powerful families*, is the very soul of a republic."[33]

ALL THE PROPERTIES OF THE INDIVIDUAL

This fight between those who meant to restrict the status of "citizen" to a landed few and those who meant to extend citizenship to the many was the first great political fight within the new nation. And it was a fight that evolved swiftly, as the democratic republicans soon moved beyond their call merely to distribute land to every white adult citizen. They also developed a set of sophisticated arguments designed to seat the independence of the individual in many other forms of property besides land.

One of the most common criticisms of Jefferson and the democratic republicans is that they were radical agrarians who imagined a society of independent farmers living in an idyllic world of buzzing bees and tinkling cowbells while giving no thought to the sorts of industry necessary for material growth and national defense. To be sure, a somewhat pastoral vision infused a short book Jefferson wrote while the Revolutionary War still raged, *Notes on the State of Virginia*. Yet once America had won its independence, Jefferson and his allies focused at least as closely on the development of manufacturing as did the Federalists. It was Jefferson himself, in fact, who imported the production techniques that laid the foundation for mass manufacturing in America.[34] As Annette Gordon-Reed and Peter Onuf put it in their smart recent book on Jefferson's ways of perceiving and thinking, the idea that he believed that "Americans should remain forever in the agricultural state of development" is a "gross mischaracterization of his actual beliefs . . . He could not have been the progressive he was and think that way."[35]

Where we most clearly see the practical nature of the democratic republican approach to power and politics is in the efforts to expand the ranks of citizenship.

Most basic was support for the right of the poor and middling soldiers who had fought in the Revolution, including those who were entirely landless, to participate in politics. The goal was not to reward their skill at arms with land at some point in the future and thereby establish them as "yeoman" citizens in the tradition of the republican periods of English and Roman history. It was to ensure that even if these soldiers never owned half an acre, they could take part as full citizens in all the immediate debates and decisions of the day.[36]

Democratic republicans also strongly supported the same rights for artisans and mechanics. Even before the end of the Revolutionary War, Ben Franklin was inviting individuals with such skills to settle as full citizens in the new republic. The work of such people, Franklin said, was just as "necessary and useful" as the work of the farmer and indeed was necessary to supply the "Cultivators of the Earth with Houses, and with Furniture and Utensils."[37]

The Constitution recognized ideas could be property too and indeed helped to create that property by establishing systems of patent and copyright to protect the individual thinker and writer.[38] But soon after the framing, Madison and others had begun to speak of property as any of a wide variety of skills and attributes that a person may develop and possess.

In the political competition of the early days of the nation, between those who sought to limit citizenship and those who sought to expand it, Madison put this thinking to practical use. In doing so he looked back more to Edward Coke's fights against King James's monopolies than to Locke's famous definition of property as whatsoever a man might make or grow with "his labour."[39] In a 1792 essay called "Property," Madison wrote: "That is not a just government, nor is property secure under it, where arbitrary restrictions, exemptions, and monopolies deny to part of its citizens that free use of their faculties, and free choice of their occupations, which not only constitute their property in the general sense of the word; but are the means of acquiring property strictly so called."[40]

In this same essay, Madison pushed even further away from the idea that citizenship must be seated in ownership of land or, for that matter, even some other particular faculty or skill. "In a word," Madison said, "as a man is said to have a right to his property, he may be equally said to have a property in his rights." Madison then went on to clarify that such rights include his freedom of expression, his religious opinions, and his own personal safety.

"Government is instituted to protect property of every sort; as well that which lies in the various rights of individuals, as that which the term particularly expresses," Madison concluded. "This being the end of government, that alone is a just government, which impartially secures to every man, whatever is his own."[41]

Under pressure, Madison was willing even to entirely abandon any pretense that citizenship need be connected with any form of personal property whatsoever. When the wealthy New York landowner Gouverneur Morris, during the constitutional debates, proposed to restrict the vote to freeholders, Madison made clear he believed all men had an absolute right to consent in their own government and to participate fully.

Madison made clear he agreed with Morris that owning property was important. "Viewing the subject in its merits alone, the freeholders of the Country would be the safest depositories of Republican liberty," he said in direct response to Morris.[42]

"But this does not satisfy the fundamental principle that men cannot be justly bound by laws in making of which they have no part."[43]

Madison, in the words of Ketcham, believed that "If a conflict arose, it was more just to weaken property rights than personal rights." Indeed, Madison "consistently regarded the doctrine of consent as more vital than mere protection of property."[44]

Yet in his debates with Morris, Madison had also set a challenge for himself. "In future times a great majority of the people will not only be without landed, but any other sort of, property," he said. "These will either combine under the influence of their common situation; in which case, the rights of property & the public liberty, will not be secure in their hands: or which is more probable, they will become the tools of opulence & ambition."

That's why, only four years later, Madison would turn back to the task of figuring out how to make each individual citizen as economically independent as possible. For our history of America's System of Liberty, it is not Madison's absolute support of the right of all citizens to vote that is most important. It is his effort—carried forward by later generations—to redefine property in ways that would promote the true economic independence of as great a proportion of these citizens as possible.

RULE OF LAW

In 1780, John Adams drafted a Constitution for the state of Massachusetts. In the preamble, he wrote: "It is the duty of the people . . . in framing a constitution of government, to provide for an equitable mode of making laws, as well as for an impartial interpretation, and a faithful execution of them." Later in the document he expressed the goal even more concisely. "The end," Adams wrote, is "a government of laws and not of men."[45]

The argument that independence required property had carried Adams and the other founders straight—indeed ineluctably—to a focus on rule of law. The line of reasoning was simple. If someone can take what you own, at will, you are as much under that person's sway as if you did not own any property at all.

Here again, Adams and the other founders were able to study the lessons of English history. A century before, under the centralized monopoly rule of a strong king, no property was safe. Under such rule, the sovereign was able to give and take, to create and destroy, property for whatever reason he or she might choose. From the point of view of the king, this was no flaw. Rather it was key to creating a perfect pyramid of power in which the sovereign could force even the most powerful to bend to his will.

Perhaps the most honest defense of such a system was made by King James. In words that would have gladdened Donald Trump, he said, in 1610, "Kings make and unmake their subjects; they have power of raising and casting down; of life and of death." Kings, James went on, "make of their subjects like men at the chess; a pawn to take a Bishop or a Knight, and to cry up or down any of their subjects as they do their money."[46]

One way the sovereign manipulated the powerful was to grant

and revoke the license to live on one particular estate or another. Another way, directly pertinent to our discussion here, was to grant and revoke lucrative patents and other monopolies. Queen Elizabeth, for instance, awarded her favorite, Walter Raleigh, with monopolies in cloth, tin, wine, even playing cards.[47]

The immediate goal of such arbitrary bestowals of power—a goal very much intended by the sovereign—was to atomize both the aristocracy and the people and to keep them hustling for place and pennies, in concentric circles, around the court.

The inevitable result of such arbitrary bestowals was to deprive—sometimes suddenly—many ordinary people of their ability to pursue their work, such as the manufacture of cloth or tin or playing cards, or the importing of wine. As Edward Coke put it in Parliament in 1614, "The monopolizer engrosseth to himself what should be free to all men."

That's why the fight to bring the monarch under the control of the common law centered, for most of the early years of the seventeenth century, on a fight against monopoly. Indeed, it was Parliament's vote in 1624 to declare all "royal patents" forever illegal, and to leave all decisions over monopoly to the common law, that counts as the first great victory over arbitrary power of the modern era.[48]

At the time of the American Revolution, the prerogatives of the king remained highly restricted. But even if the king enjoyed far less arbitrary power than before, the British political economy was still a very hierarchical world, with many forms of unrestrained power. The Scottish philosopher David Hume in 1742 described this "civilized monarchy" as a world characterized by "a long train of dependence from the prince to the peasant, which is . . . sufficient to beget in every one an inclination to please his superiors and to form himself upon those models, which are most acceptable to people of condition and education."[49]

As Adams and the other founders were well aware, this train of dependence continued straight into America, and the fear that someone powerful could take the property of someone less powerful remained very real. This indeed was one of the main lessons of the fight with the British East India Company, which was held by many merchants to be a threat to their properties.[50]

Educated Americans of the time were well versed in the fights between Parliament and the king in the seventeenth century. And the writings of Edward Coke were especially favored by Adams, who described him as "the oracle of the law," and by Jefferson, who credited Coke with "the profounder learning" in the "doctrines of British liberties."[51]

Adams's immediate goal in writing the Massachusetts Constitution was to establish a clear separation of powers among the legislature, the executive branch, and the courts. But it is also very clear that when he speaks of "a government of laws and not of men," he and his allies fully intend that these basic rules apply not only to public officials but also to anyone wielding the power of a great estate or corporation and indeed to all monopolies and any other forms of private government.

As we today move toward dealing with Amazon and Google, the most important lesson we must keep in mind is that the arbitrary nature of their power—as we saw in the last chapter—directly undermines rule of law and in its place establishes a rule of man, of Mark Zuckerberg, of Jeff Bezos. Hence our most important goal is to restore a "government of laws and not of men." To do so requires constructing a system in which every individual—and their property—enjoys equal protection from arbitrary power and equal access to the market, with no favoritism and no discrimination whatsoever.

A COMMUNITY OF THINKERS

In the years after the Revolution, Americans who lived through this radical breaking of one society and making of another often spoke of how they had come to understand themselves and the world in entirely new ways.

"We see with other eyes, we hear with other ears; and think with other thoughts, than those we formerly used," Thomas Paine wrote in a 1782 letter. "We are now really another people, and cannot again go back to ignorance and prejudice. The mind once enlightened cannot again become dark."[52]

John Adams, looking back on the founding from the age of 83, said the Revolution had little to do with the actual war for political independence from Britain. The "real American Revolution" was a "radical change" in "Principles, Opinions, Sentiments, and Affections," he wrote. "The Revolution was in the minds and hearts of the people."[53]

In recent decades Americans have been much more comfortable analyzing big changes in society through political and economic, rather than spiritual, lenses. Even in the case of Paine and Adams, it can be tempting to view their statements as but the byproduct of political revolution, or perhaps even a stepping-stone toward political revolution.

Yet these testaments of radical change in one's own intellect, one's own soul, were very much an intended result of the Revolution. Many of the founders, and many of those whose writings inspired them, fully understood that in creating a new architecture of power in society, they were also creating a new architecture of mind and thought and spirit.

We see this in a remarkable document from 1654 by Roger Williams, the theologian who founded Rhode Island and whose thinking influenced Adams and other founders. In a pamphlet published while he was living in London, Williams directly connected religious and political freedom. The aim must be, Williams wrote, "A true and absolute Soul-freedom to all the people of the Land impartially; so that no person be forced to pray nor pay, otherwise then as his Soul believeth and consenteth."[54]

Among the founders, we see this most famously in James Madison's editing of the text of the Virginia Declaration of Rights, which was adopted on June 12, 1776. Madison felt that the original language promising the "fullest Toleration" of religion implied that one religion—Anglicanism—was the right religion, while others should at best be abided. Madison succeeded in getting the wording changed to "all men are entitled to the free exercise of religion, according to the dictates of conscience."[55]

"Conscience," Madison wrote later, "is the most sacred of all property."[56]

Many over the years have faulted America's founders for creating an atomistic society, with every individual a discrete and lonely island. This is a critique I understand well, having lived and worked for many years in South America, often among people who believe that the way to establish individual liberty is by first strengthening community. Yet what we see in the early United States is almost the exact opposite of atomism. It is an entirely new vision of how to achieve community, with ties between citizen and citizen, and between citizen and God, forged through direct interaction with one another, on terms of absolute equality in the market, in the town hall, and in spiritual debate. We see a vision of a community of free thinkers able to use both reason and a sense of morality— as exercised day to day through open and democratic debate—to govern themselves and their world.[57]

Many have similarly faulted America's founders for unleashing a liberty of appetite, in the form of an economic system that depends on every individual acting foremost to serve one's own selfish interest. And certainly, in the debates over how to structure checks and balances, it is evident that the founders believed selfishness lies in every person. Yet at the same time we see here also an effort to free the individual, at least some of the time, from the dictates of gross appetite so as to liberate the citizen to truly deliberate.

Americans today are often not comfortable speaking of issues of faith. But it is vital to remember that the founding generation measured liberty not only in the number of town halls where citizens could debate, and not only in the amount of wealth that was created by citizens free to run their farms and businesses without interference by powerful private actors. They also measured liberty in the number and variety of churches and faiths available to the citizen.[58]

Over the course of just a few years before and after the Declaration, white male Americans made their society a bastion of not merely political and commercial liberty but also intellectual and spiritual liberty, with these citizens free to believe what they wanted, how they wanted, when they wanted. Similar liberty existed elsewhere, in Britain especially, but it was a liberty mainly for the aristocrat, and even then it was highly circumscribed. In America, citizens democratized this liberty. They dragged it outside academy, club, and class and began to make it a liberty for every white male everywhere.

In the eyes of the founders, the full liberty of both citizen and society depended on the creation of open competition and debate in all human activities and hence on the destruction of all economic, political, and spiritual monopoly.

Of the many distillations of what Americans wrought in these years, perhaps the most concise and eloquent summation was written by W. E. B. Du Bois. America's great contribution to the world, he wrote in 1935, is "a vision of democratic self-government: the domination of political life by the intelligent decision of free and self-sustaining men."

Americans first dreamed of liberty. Then they used that liberty to build a system to allow themselves—even those still in chains—to keep dreaming.

FOUR

CITIZENS BY DESIGN

THE RULE OF 160

NEXT TIME YOU'RE IN A WINDOW SEAT IN A FLIGHT OVER THE center of America, take a look at the landscape below. You'll see long lines, made by roads and fences and the edges of fields, stretching to the horizon, north and south, east and west, cutting the farmland into little squares. Fly over Europe or Asia, or for that matter most of the eastern United States, and the lines that divide farm from farm curve and meander, tracing the contour of hills and the banks of rivers and streams. This gridding of America has nothing to do with the relative flatness of the Heartland. Rather it is the product of a scientific system for structuring society, developed in the earliest days of the United States.

At the end of the Revolutionary War, America's citizens found themselves with clear new borders, not only around the 13 states along the Atlantic but extending also around the lands that would later form Ohio, Indiana, Illinois, Michigan, Wisconsin, and northeast Minnesota. These lands, long claimed by France, then for a time by Britain, had been transferred—at least according to European law—to U.S. control by the Treaty of Paris. One of the first acts of the new Continental Congress was to draw a plan to bring these territories into the Union as new states.

Here again we see the hand and mind of Jefferson at work, as he was the person Congress charged with sketching the plan. This made sense in two respects. Jefferson himself had been trained in surveying and cartography by his father, and the citizens of his state of Virginia had recently ceded to the federal government their claim to much of the land that made up these territories. The result, known as the Northwest Ordinance, was revolutionary in many ways, starting with the very surveys themselves. To our ears today the instructions in the act sound like plain common sense. "The plats of the townships . . . shall be marked by subdivisions into lots of one mile square, or 640 acres . . . and numbered from 1 to 36 . . . The lines shall be measured with a chain; shall be plainly marked by chaps on the trees, and exactly described on a plat."[1] But in the mid-1780s this rational process for the transformation of meadows, forests, and hills into largely exchangeable squares of "property" was largely new. And the system of public surveys that Jefferson and his colleagues devised would be emulated around the world.[2]

The Ordinance was, more importantly, also revolutionary in the ends it sought. The document was the first great positive attempt by the citizens of the new nation to achieve the promise of rough equality made in the Declaration, and to do so according to the revolutionaries' carefully conceived idea of the citizen. The immediate aim of the authors of the Ordinance was to provide tens of thousands of American families with enough land to raise crops and livestock sufficient to feed themselves, and to trade in nearby markets for the tools, clothing, housewares, and books they required. The result was a decision to provide each family, for a reasonable price, with 160 acres of land, or a "quarter-section" of each of the newly marked-off squares. Thus the revolutionaries would also achieve a yet-more-primary aim—of transforming the men in these families into fully "independent" citizens.

American democracy is full of contradictions, and often they are tragic. Even as men in the cities of the East carefully traced lines across their parchment maps, other men and women and children lived in towns and villages and settlements, farming and hunting these lands that for centuries or more had been their home. Although some of the men in the East felt a vague sense of stewardship over the people already on the land, the system of settlement American leaders put into place also opened the way to the exploitation, displacement, confinement, and murder of many of these people. And the political leaders fully understood this at the time. As Secretary of War Henry Knox wrote in 1794, "our modes of population have been more destructive to the Indian natives than the conduct of the conquerors of Mexico and Peru."[3]

This was no mere accident of history. It was not an inevitable collision of peoples with different views of how to organize society and live in the world, and the outcome was not preordained. On the contrary, as the historian Jerry Ostler has compellingly argued, the text of the Ordinance essentially "legalized wars of 'extirpation' or 'extermination,' terms synonymous with genocide by most definitions." Although the Ordinance theoretically compels the U.S. government to observe the "utmost good faith ... towards the Indians" and promises never to disturb "their property, rights, and liberty," Ostler notes that the Ordinance also "legalized genocidal war against" the Indians should they "reject" the "gift of civilization."[4] At its very best, American policy, as Richard White writes in *The Middle Ground*, never aimed at anything more than "amalgamation and imperial benevolence" and at enabling Americans to believe they were acting for the "greatest good" of the Indians even as they "demanded more and more land." In Aziz Rana's useful framing, it was a "settler empire" in which the "liberty" of some people depended on the "subordination" of others.[5]

But the lesson here is not simply that American democracy stands on these graves. The Northwest Ordinance was in fact many projects rolled into one. It was a document of empire—claiming absolute sovereignty over lands, in perpetuity, where other people lived, based on claims the founders knew full well were based ultimately only on might. It was a statement of national defense against the European empires—Britain, France, Spain—then playing for control of these same lands. And it was a desperate fiscal measure to provide a bankrupt government with a pittance of revenue from the sale of these "public" lands.

What we also see in the Ordinance is one of the foundational statements in the establishment of the American System of Liberty. The particular approach America's first citizens took to distributing these lands amounts to nothing less than a conscious effort to mass manufacture more citizens, through the chopping up of vast stretches of landscape into citizen-sized properties and the subsidization of their sale. The approach pioneered here provided a pattern for how Americans would make and protect liberty and democracy for many generations to come. Indeed, for the next two centuries, in some ways straight to today, this figure, of 160 acres, would prove one of the most important definitions of what it meant to be an independent citizen in America. As the Missouri senator Thomas Hart Benton summarized the goal in 1854, "The freeholder . . . is the natural supporter of a free government, and it should be the policy of republics to multiply their freeholders as it is the policy of monarchies to multiply tenants."[6]

In the specific case of farmland, we see the number 160 return time and again over well more than a century in various plans to "develop" America's lands. We see it in the Preemption Acts of 1830 and 1841, which aimed to regulate the distribution of land to squatters.[7] We see it in the Homestead Act of 1862, which extended the practices of the Northwest Ordinance to as-yet-undeveloped lands west of the Mississippi River. We see it in the Southern Homestead Act of 1866, which aimed to distribute public lands in Florida, Louisiana, Alabama, Mississippi, and Arkansas to formerly enslaved black citizens, and to landless whites who had remained loyal to the Union (this project largely failed during the southern war against Reconstruction).[8] We see it in the Timber Culture Act of 1872, the Desert Land Act of 1877, and the Reclamation Act of 1902, all of which tailored these rules to lands not fit for traditional cultivation of grains.[9] In all these programs, Congress, in distributing the land—or the water that made the land economically valuable—limited any one family to 160 acres.[10]

The mid-nineteenth century was also a time when the federal government gave hundreds of thousands of acres to large corporations, especially railroads, to subsidize construction of this vital new infrastructure. Here too the patterns put into place in the Northwest Ordinance helped shape and control these monopoly powers. The Pacific Railroad Act of 1862, for instance, promised to give the corporations that built a railroad to California land the equivalent of 40 farmsteads of 160 acres each for every mile constructed, then structured the deal to encourage the selling of these plots to settlers.[11]

As recently as 1950 we see this 160-acre limit holding strong. The same year Sam Walton drove through the checkerboard landscape of Arkansas into Bentonville, Congress tried to raise the amount of public irrigation water available to any one farmer in Colorado's San Luis Valley to enough to work 480 acres. President Harry Truman, who for years had ploughed the soil on small farms in Missouri and who proved to be one of the most democratic-minded presidents in American history, vetoed the bill.[12]

And the model worked, at least measured by the original aim of keeping America's farmlands largely in the hands of families. In 1850, America's farms averaged 203 acres each; in 1860, 199 acres; in 1870, 153 acres.[13] During the New Deal of the 1930s, the size of the average farm covered by the Farm Tenant Act was 133 acres.[14] Further, this dividing of land into citizen-sized farmsteads would prove a basic model for how to divvy up many other forms of property in America. This included the store that Sam Walton bought in the early 1950s; the idea here being that the business of retail should also be broken into citizen-sized plots much like the business of farming. And this model included most manufacturing or service businesses that were not made radically more efficient by enclosure within the walls of vast, centralized, highly capitalized factories.

In the last chapter we saw how the concept of the individual as a citizen and the identification of a core set of interlocking liberties clarified a line of reasoning about the relationship between the individual and various forms of property. In this chapter, we will look at the institutions America's new citizens established to create, protect, and develop these various forms of property, in ways that promoted individual liberty. In other words, we will look at how these new citizens set about structuring their new society to achieve their ultimate political, moral, and spiritual ends.

On August 7, 1789, the first Congress elected under the new Constitution enacted the Ordinance as one of the first laws of the new nation. America's first president, George Washington, soon signed the law into effect.[15] Although Americans today have largely forgotten the Northwest Ordinance, for much of our history many citizens celebrated the act as nothing less than "a charter for freedom."[16] Or as the Massachusetts senator George Frisbie Hoar put it at the time of its centennial, "The Ordinance . . . is one of the three title deeds of American constitutional liberty."[17]

THE STATE AS A TOOL OF LIBERTY

In the years before the Revolution, when all power traced back ultimately to the sovereign, many writers in the colonies and Britain defined liberty mainly as an absence of government. The "traditional dogma," as one historian has put it, held "that freedom meant *release* from the authority of government."[18]

This dogma remains as strong, if not stronger, today. As we'll discuss in chapter seven, supporters of modern libertarianism have spent a great deal of money promoting the idea that the state should do nothing more than serve as a "night watchman" and, at most, guard against crimes like murder and rape.[19]

To be sure, at the time of the Revolution many Americans did want mainly to be left alone, to retreat to their homestead, hang a "no trespassing" sign, and rest a long rifle across their knees. Yet the majority of America's revolutionaries also clearly aimed at something far grander than what the political theorist Philip Pettit calls "the absence of interference" with the individual "by arbitrary powers."[20]

As we saw in the previous chapter, the Declaration of Independence created a radical new understanding of *who* is the state, by establishing that "we" are the state, each citizen holding an equal share of sovereignty. The Declaration also created a radical new understanding of the *purpose* of the state. In America, the purpose is, ultimately, to protect against all dangerous concentrations of power at home and abroad—be it the great landlord or the British East India Company.

What we see in the Ordinance is a guide to *how* the founders expected America's new citizens to use their state. The result is a vision of the state as not merely a sharpened broadax to bring down every so often upon the extraordinarily powerful. Rather, Americans from the first saw their state as a tool they could use to actively structure the character both of their society and of the individuals within it. Indeed, the Ordinance—one of the first expressions of America's new national Congress—shows in great detail how America's first citizens consciously and intentionally aimed to use the American System of Liberty to design a particular type of nation and a particular type of citizen.

In addition to the Ordinance's division of farmland into citizen-sized farms and its distribution of these 160-acre plots to the citizens themselves, this design includes:

- The prohibition of slavery in all lands north and west of the Ohio River.
- The extension of the right to vote to all "free male inhabitants of full age," no matter their race or religion, or whether they had previously been enslaved.[21]
- The collecting of citizens into townships, based on the belief that "republican institutions would only take root where orderly and industrious settlers were organized in compact settlements."[22]
- Support for public education through the reservation of one lot in every township "for the maintenance of public schools."[23]
- Government regulation of the market, in this case through direct federal control over the supply of land available for purchase at any one moment.[24]
- The liberal use of subsidies and incentives, both in the form of setting low prices for the land and the direct provision of credit to buyers, to lure citizens to the land.
- A prohibition on primogeniture to help prevent the future concentration of ownership over the lands.[25]

Almost simultaneously, citizens used the Constitution also to establish the post office system as a central function of the new state. The most important public infrastructure in U.S. history, the U.S. Postal Service was designed to ensure the rapid and non-discriminatory transmission of information—political, commercial, personal—between citizen and citizen, and community and community, across the vast reaches of the new nation.[26]

Of vital importance, there are real differences between the American vision of the state and other visions, such as the French system put in place after the revolution of 1789, and these differences are maintained to some extent to this day. Most Americans did not envision a small cadre of trained professionals managing the state for the good of the people but rather a system in which all citizens shared in direct control. And the goal in America was not to determine how a citizen should think through various forms of public indoctrination.

Rather than impose any national curriculum, citizens instead aimed to use the state to distribute and protect the ability of citizens to learn for themselves, to debate among themselves, to make decisions among themselves, and to establish schools within their own communities. The expectation was that future generations of independent citizens would also use the state to develop and protect the systems necessary to birth subsequent generations of independent, well-informed, free-thinking citizens fully able to learn, debate, deliberate, and decide. As one promoter of the Ordinance said at the time, the aim was to distribute property and power in a way that would ensure the United States would be ruled by "an enlightened people."[27]

What we see here is a vision of public progress that stands atop a vision of personal progress, both made possible by public action.

Madison today is often held up by libertarians as one of the main believers in a minimal state. In truth, Madison strongly rejected the idea of liberty from government. As one biographer writes, Madison believed that "under a government of consent, properly constructed to prevent domination by faction, freedom could mean the use of power in the public interest."[28] In a 1792 essay Madison belittled the idea that "because the people *may* betray themselves, they ought to give themselves up, blindfold, to those who have an interest in betraying them." The American way, he wrote, is to "conclude that the people ought to be enlightened, to be awakened, to be united, that after establishing a government they should watch over it, *as well as obey it*."[29]

In another essay from that same year Madison explained how basing independence on property ownership, as promoted by the Northwest Ordinance, helped citizens to watch over their government. "The class of citizens who provide at once their own food and their own raiment," he wrote, "may be viewed as the most truly independent and happy. They are more: they are the best basis of public liberty, and the strongest bulwark of public safety. It follows, that the greater the proportion of this class to the whole society, the more free, the more independent, and the more happy must be the society itself."[30]

In the eighteenth century and ever since, many Americans have honestly struggled to make sense of what seems like a paradox—that the power of the state is absolute in relation to any one person or group of people, and that the only purpose of this power must be to liberate the individual to rule one's own self and to take part in ruling one's own community.

But for many Americans, this paradox was not hard to master, even many generations after the Revolution. Abraham Lincoln, perhaps the most famous child of the Ordinance, at the beginning of the Civil War put it thus: "It is a struggle for maintaining in the world, that form and substance of government, whose leading object is, to elevate the condition of men—to lift artificial weights from all shoulders—to clear the path of laudable pursuit for all—to afford all, an unfettered start, and a fair chance, in the race of life."[31]

And a full century after the Ordinance, that most quintessential of American spirits, Walt Whitman, in his book *Democratic Vistas*, distilled this prime goal of state power into the simplest of statements.

The ultimate job of the American system? To "train communities through all their grades, beginning with individuals and ending there again, to rule themselves." The reason? To make of each citizen "a separate and complete subject for freedom, worldly thrift and happiness, and for a fair chance for growth."[32]

Then repeat.

MARKETS AS SYSTEMS OF LIBERTY

In March 1776, less than four months before the Declaration, Adam Smith published *The Wealth of Nations*. The timing was no mere coincidence. Smith's thinking was deeply shaped by debates in America on how to structure markets and the fight against the East India Company. As one of Smith's biographers put it, "The American Colonies constitute the experimental evidence of the essential truth of the book, without which many of its leading positions had been little more than theory."[33] Indeed, *The Wealth of Nations* contains dozens of examples taken from America.

The Wealth of Nations would in turn shape thinking in America to this day. As early as 1790, Thomas Jefferson called it "the best book extant" on economic questions.[34]

Yet even had Smith never lived, America's new citizens would have been more than able to make the markets of the new nation work. Contrary to the modern libertarian myth that early America was a paradise of laissez-faire, the writings and actions of the founding generation make amply clear they had learned through close study and direct experience that the market is simply another form of human institution one could use to achieve specific ends.

The basic "economic" purposes of the market were well understood in America long before the Revolution. These were: to organize the efficient exchange of goods, to rely on simple rules of supply and demand to discover a coherent price for these goods, and to make that price public. Americans had also long understood how to achieve these ends. In Britain, protecting the market against monopolizers and other cheats had since the early Middle Ages been one of the main services provided by local authorities and the king.[35] In colonial America, in addition to targeting high prices, officials had also long worked to ensure the healthfulness of foods and the cleanliness of the market itself. And they were just as diligent about protecting local sellers against middlemen and other gatekeepers. The American market "could hardly be called 'free,'" historian William Novak has written. "The urban marketplace was probably the most visible, potent expression of public control over buying and selling."[36]

These regulations worked. Indeed, a main complaint of the revolutionaries was that local market systems had broken down due to the war. Abigail Adams, in a letter to husband John, in early 1777 wrote of "a general cry against the merchants, against monopolizers etc. who tis said have created a partial scarcity . . . not only of luxury, but even the necessaries of life."[37] In Philadelphia a year later, a newspaper published an anonymous warning: "To all FORESTALLERS and RAISERS of the prices of GOODS and PROVISIONS. Take notice that a storm is brewing again[st] you."[38]

By the Revolution Americans had also developed a remarkably sophisticated understanding of markets as tools to achieve not merely economic ends but social and political—even moral—ends. In other words, the founders fully understood they could use markets to structure relationships among individuals in ways that would help them build and reinforce the new republican citizen and the new republican nation.

Three ideas especially would come to shape thinking in America about how to structure and use markets:

Markets Can Promote Equality. The Northwest Ordinance contains two key lessons about equality. First and most obvious is the general effort to limit ownership by any one citizen to 160 acres of land. It is almost impossible to imagine a better expression of "equality" than this effort to ensure not only that every citizen is independent but, at least at the starting gate, roughly equally independent. From the point of view of structuring the market itself, also important is the sharp dismissal by the authors of the Ordinance of the idea that any private corporation should govern—or be a powerful player within—the market for the sale of lands. Unlike in the development of such proprietary colonies as Virginia and Pennsylvania, or the Cooperstown region of New York, the citizens who wrote the Ordinance intended there to be no hierarchy between smaller freeholders and a dominant class of corporate masters.

Markets Can Protect the Liberty of Individuals. The most important lesson of the American rebellion against the East India Company is that the individual must have complete liberty to bring one's properties to market and to exchange them directly with one's neighbors. This vision of liberty traces, as we saw in the last chapter, straight to the English Parliament's fights against the monopolies of Queen Elizabeth and King James.[39] A key result of such thinking is to view the citizen foremost not as a buyer but as a producer—of crops, products, work, ideas. As a producer, the citizen's most important interest is the liberty to sell. Over the coming generations, Americans shaped their antimonopoly laws to protect themselves as makers and sellers of things and work in ways that also helped protect themselves as buyers of things and work.

Markets Can Forge Community. This is true most obviously in that markets bring people physically together—to exchange goods. One byproduct is that people also get to talk to one another. Another is that their awareness of their mutual interdependence, one with another, is reinforced. The best depiction of such interdependence is at the beginning of *The Wealth of Nations*, where Smith uses a description of specialization of labor in a pin factory to illustrate how cooperation within a market system can result in vastly higher levels of production.[40]

Smith's immediate political message in this passage is that when people break down barriers to trade, everyone ends up with more material wealth. But Smith also intended to communicate something more, an idea that carried over from his first book, *The Theory of Moral Sentiments*.[41] This is a vision of society as a complex community of highly unique souls, in which markets, even while fostering the independence of the individual, also foster a hive-like interdependence that makes everyone not only more productive and wealthy but more sociable and happy.

THE PEOPLE RULE—NOT THE CORPORATION

From today's perspective, it's almost impossible to imagine the depth of the hatred—even terror—many citizens felt toward the business corporation around the time of the Revolution. These fears were due in part to the old stories of Queen Elizabeth and King James using corporate monopolies to reinforce systems of arbitrary rule. They were also due to the very fresh experience of having an intermediary—the East India Company—insert itself between the seller and buyer in America in ways that empowered its executives to regulate the lives of individuals and commerce as a whole.

Far more viscerally terrifying, however, were the reports of what the East India Company had actually done in India, to the Indian people. By the early years of the American Republic, the fantastically destructive effects of the corporation's complete monopoly control over India's economy, combined with its mission to extract as much wealth as possible for executives and investors, had been amply detailed.

One of the most damning of all descriptions of the East India Company came in a speech by Edmund Burke, the British parliamentarian and author often credited with framing the basic principles of modern conservatism. A strong believer in constitutional restrictions on power, Burke closely studied the East India Company's actions in America and in India. In 1783, Burke described what the corporation had done to the regions of India under its direct control.

When the company arrived in India, Burke said, Indian society was prosperous and in good order. "In all the cities were multitudes of merchants and bankers, for all occasions of monied assistance; and on the other hand, the native princes were in condition to obtain credit from them. The manufacturer was paid by the return of commodities . . . [T]he country was full of . . . inns and hospitals, where the traveller and the poor were relieved. All ranks of people had their place in the public concern, and their share in the common stock and the common prosperity."

But, Burke continued, the East India Company introduced a new system. "It was their policy to consider hoards of money as crimes; to regard moderate rents as frauds on the [corporation]; and to view, in the lesser princes, any claim of exemption from more than settled tribute, as an act of rebellion. Accordingly, all the castles were, one after the other, plundered and destroyed. The native princes were expelled; the hospitals fell to ruin; the reservoirs of water went to decay; the merchants, bankers, and manufacturers disappeared; and sterility, indigence, and depopulation, overspread the face of these once flourishing provinces."[42]

Adam Smith, in less dramatic language, agreed. From his point of view, the problem was that the corporate structure of the East India Company destroyed all sense of ownership and responsibility, not only in the investors in England but also in the executives working and living in India. The result was absolute power tied to absolute appetite, with no one at any point in this chain of command having any real interest in using the corporation's power for anything but "plunder." As Smith described the investors specifically: "No other sovereigns ever were, or, from the nature of things, ever could be, so perfectly indifferent about the happiness or misery of their subjects, the improvement or waste of their dominions, the glory or disgrace of their administration; as, from irresistible moral causes, the greater part of the proprietors of such a mercantile company are, and necessarily must be."[43]

Partly in reaction to such stories, Americans in the first years of the new nation created very few corporations—only 33 from 1781 to 1790.[44] But they soon realized there was a problem with this approach. The nearly four million people who, by 1790, lived in the 13 new states greatly needed new roads and bridges and factories to connect and build the new nation. Few individuals had sufficient funds to float big projects on their own. And most towns and states had yet to develop any real ability to tax their citizens. As a result, by the first year of Washington's presidency, Americans had begun to explore new ways to structure corporations, ways that would provide investors with a sufficient sense of protection to convince them to put money into a venture while also providing citizens with assurances that the new corporation would not turn predatory like the East India Company.

What resulted were two different approaches to regulating corporations, only the second of which is remotely like how we manage the task today.

The first approach was simply to require that the state legislature vote to grant a charter before any corporation could begin operations. Citizens used these charters to require that corporations always serve the public interest, through close restrictions on the powers and licenses of the corporations. These included putting limits on the life of each corporation to ensure it would expire once it had served its purpose, be it the building of a bridge or the establishment of a new public service.[45]

The second approach was to foster competition. By early in the nineteenth century, Americans had begun to give out multiple charters for the same line of business. As the businessman and economist Samuel Blodget Jr., writing in 1806, explained the thinking, "if two baking companies are thereby permitted, bread may be cheaper in consequence; or if there are two banks thus instituted . . . more of the people will be favored by loans . . . and a further increase will reduce even the rate of interest."[46]

As Americans came to perfect these twin restrictions on the corporation, citizens began to feel comfortable licensing many more corporations to do business. Between 1800 and 1817, citizens approved almost 1,800 new enterprises, with Massachusetts citizens alone creating more than in all of Europe at the time.[47]

By early in the nineteenth century, however, many Americans had begun to fear that the process of chartering corporations, rather than democratizing the corporation, was instead resulting in the corruption of state legislators.[48] As a result, New Yorkers began to experiment with a radical new approach to corporations, one that would ultimately birth the system we know today. The idea was to let entrepreneurs simply launch a new business without any specific legislative approval at all. Investors still had to file for a corporate charter, and their enterprise was still expected to serve the public interest. But in a very American twist, the expectation was that these new corporations would be regulated more by the need to compete against other corporations within a market than by rules built into the charter.

New Yorkers first tried this "freedom to incorporate" model for manufacturing enterprises in 1811. But citizens in other states moved much more slowly. It was not until 1837 that Connecticut adopted a similar model, with New Jersey following in 1846 and Ohio in 1856.[49]

Indeed, Americans kept sharp restrictions on the corporation in place in almost every state until a full century after the founding. Not until after the Civil War were bankers and executives able finally to almost entirely escape America's traditional system of strictures on the corporation. They did so by combining the new "rights" theoretically granted by the Fourteenth Amendment to the Constitution with the powers concentrated by new technologies like the railroad and new corporate structures called trusts.

But it's important not to get too far ahead of ourselves; we will cover the late nineteenth century in the next chapter. What's important now is to keep in mind that right into the 1870s, the American approach to regulating corporations largely succeeded not only in preventing monopoly but in keeping corporations ultimately under the people's control.

THE PEOPLE RULE—NOT THE FINANCIER

Ever since the often intense political rivalry between Thomas Jefferson and Alexander Hamilton in the 1790s, many historians have tried to fit these two men into a simple framework, with Hamilton as the brilliant financier who set the United States on firm financial footing and Jefferson as the naïve preacher of a moneyless agrarian idyll. As one recent biographer wrote, Hamilton's prowess at "monetiz[ing]" the economy made American "society fluid and open to merit, [and made] industry both rewarding and necessary."[50] Jefferson, by contrast, was an "oppositionist" who "codified" a "knee-jerk pattern of response to government policies."[51]

It's certainly true that Jefferson and Madison and other democratic republicans viewed Hamilton and his allies as a threat to all efforts to establish a democracy of rough equality in America. They believed Hamilton intended to use control over America's banking system not only to concentrate the capital necessary to develop the nation but to concentrate political power and control in his own hands and those of his banker friends and allies.[52]

There was ample reason for this fear. Fresh in their minds was the "reign of the financier" Robert Morris, the Philadelphia merchant and banker who in the early 1780s dominated federal politics and who was once charged by the Pennsylvania government with being a "pecuniary dictator."[53] Then there were Hamilton's own schemes while he served in government. This included his complex plan to encourage speculators to buy up debts the government owed to Revolutionary War soldiers, at pennies on the dollar, then arrange for the government to redeem the debts in full. Not only did Hamilton's plan aim to vastly enrich these few financiers at the direct expense of true patriots, and the public at large, it also aimed to turn these financiers into appendages of government, eager to do favors for those in power so as to protect their properties. To many Americans, Hamilton's financial system looked much like the corrupt system of patronage and use of banking power perfected in Britain by Robert Walpole in the early eighteenth century.[54]

As Madison described Hamilton's plan to Jefferson in 1791, "the stock-jobbers will become the praetorian band of the Government, at once its tool and its tyrant; bribed by its largesses, and overawing it by clamors and combinations."[55] Writing years later, Jefferson adopted a tone only slightly less outraged. "Hamilton's financial system," he wrote, "had two objects, 1st, as a puzzle, to exclude popular understanding and inquiry; 2nd, as a machine for the corruption of the legislature."[56]

In the event, the democratic republicans responded not by seeking to tamp down or restrain the business of banking but by working with allies in individual states to promote a radical democratization and decentralization of the business of banking. Their basic idea was that the more banks and bankers there were, and the more widely they and their capital were spread across the states, the harder it would be for any one banker or group of bankers in New York or Philadelphia to concentrate real power. Further, the democratic republicans believed that more banks would mean more money available to more people to build new farms and businesses. In all, Americans established at least 25 private banks between 1790 and 1800, 62 between 1801 and 1811, and a total of more than 300 banks by 1820.[57]

The one type of bank America's democratic republicans did not want to see was a federally chartered bank. Many believed the federal government lacked the capacity to guard against the use of such a bank to corrupt members of Congress and state legislators in ways that would concentrate dangerous amounts of power.

In the early 1830s this thinking resulted in a decision by President Andrew Jackson to oppose renewal of the federal charter for the Second Bank of the United States, run by the Philadelphia financier Nicholas Biddle. In theory, Biddle's bank was supposed to serve as a sort of privately run "central bank" able to regulate money supply and interest rates across the United States. But Jackson and others believed Biddle had figured out how to distribute credit in ways that corrupted policymakers and centralized power much in the tradition of Hamilton a generation earlier.

The Jackson administration ultimately prevailed in what came to be known as the Bank War. But victory came at a huge cost. During the fight the administration found itself opposed by a wide variety of powerful men who feared Biddle's power or sought to curry his favor. Then Biddle responded to his loss by pulling back credit from across the country, helping trigger a devastating economic crash in 1834, which in turn contributed to the great Panic of 1837, perhaps the worst depression in American history until the 1930s.[58] One victim of this depression was the highly progressive administration of President Martin Van Buren, who had served one term as Jackson's vice president and who moved into the White House just as the panic took hold.

Even years later, in a history of American political parties he published in 1867, Van Buren's rage at the bankers was palpable. Hamilton "established the money power on precisely the same foundations upon which it had been raised in England," Van Buren wrote. "A party adhering inflexibly to the leading principle of that school . . . survived his own overthrow, is still in existence, and will continue to exist as long as ours remains a free Government, and as long as the characters and dispositions of men remain what they are. To combat the democratic spirit of the country was the object of its original establishment, an object which it has pursued with unflagging diligence."[59]

It was not until early in the twentieth century, during the administration of Woodrow Wilson, that the American people would again attempt to create a central bank, and then only when they believed they had designed a framework of federal regulation able to prevent any sort of favoritism or concentration of personal power and had built an executive branch strong enough and smart enough to do so.

THE AMERICAN THEORY OF COMPETITION—
CHECKS AND BALANCES

America's revolutionaries may have aimed to create a new society, even a new type of individual. Yet these utopians were also extreme cynics with a very dark view of the rivalry and selfishness that governed human behavior even at moments of deadly threat. This cynicism was the product of their own experiences in America's Revolutionary War, when the new government had to fight avarice and sloth and cowardice to feed, clothe, and arm soldiers even as they froze in the field.

As Madison put it in *The Federalist Papers*, "the nature of man" has "rendered them much more disposed to vex and oppress each other than to co-operate for their common good." Madison's views did not mellow with age. Near the end of his life he wrote, "Man is known to be a selfish, as well as a social being. Respect for character, though often a salutary restraint, is but too often overruled by other motives ... We all know that conscience is not a sufficient safeguard; and besides, that conscience itself may be deluded."[60]

In the words of one of Thomas Paine's biographers, the revolutionaries "worked from the idea that the driving force behind every political development, the key determinant of every political controversy, is power. Power was understood as the exercise of dominion by some men over the lives of others, and it was seen as a permanent temptation in human affairs."[61]

Hence, what we see in the new citizens' careful thinking about how to use markets, corporations, banks, and the state is an effort to structure these human institutions in ways that would allow them to better direct and deflect economic and political power, or in other words the competition that is inevitable in all human society, in ways that would enable them actually to achieve their utopian vision.

The first step was to greatly strengthen the federal government.

The last key piece of the system America's new citizens put into place to build and protect their new society was a full-blown institutional structure to engineer competition at all levels of society, between individual and individual, and group and group, to ensure that power in the new nation would always be subject to rule of law and never to that of man. This was of course the Constitution, with its careful system of checks and balances.[62]

The immediate goal of the Constitution was to concentrate more power in the federal government. Despite the Ordinance's great positive statement of democratic purpose, fully realized, the first national government of the United States lacked the strength to enforce the vision Congress had sketched on the parchment map, and also lacked the strength to protect the nation from foreign threats. But concentrating more power in the federal government immediately raised another equally pressing question, which was how to protect the individual and the public as a whole from the power vested in this new state.

Americans did not invent the idea of checks and balances. Nearly a half century before the Constitutional Convention, the Scottish Enlightenment philosopher David Hume wrote that political thinkers had long since "established it as a maxim" that in "fixing the several checks and controls of the constitution, every man ought to be supposed a knave, and to have no other end, in all his actions, than private interest."[63] What Americans did introduce was the idea that the Constitution could be, in its entirety, structured as an antimonopoly document.

As every American schoolchild is supposed to be taught, this first generation of citizens carefully divided the power of the state into different branches of government and different houses of legislature. As we sometimes forget, the citizens also carefully engineered rivalry between their state governments and the federal government by intentionally overlapping the responsibilities of these two sovereigns. Doing so provided yet another check, in the form of the ability to—at any moment, for any reason—use the state governments to address dangerous concentrations of power within the federal government or vice versa.

What is most important for our purposes, and yet what is all-too-seldom remembered in America today, is that these first citizens viewed the Constitution itself as their most complete statement of intent to break all dangerous concentrations of power everywhere.

Over the years, many have focused on the fact that the framers did not write an express prohibition of monopoly. The intent of such an argument is to be able to declare that since the framers never put real federal limits on the power of the banker and trader, Americans today should also refrain from doing so. This theory is often based on a 1787 letter Jefferson sent to Madison, in which he famously proposed a "restriction against monopolies" in the Bill of Rights. As recently as June 2019, the head of the Antitrust Division in the Justice Department, Makan Delrahim, made exactly this argument.[64]

Yet it is clear that America's first citizens believed the Constitution applied not merely to the political system but applied to the political economy as well. We see this in Madison's statement in "Federalist 10" that the "first object of government" must be "the protection of different and unequal faculties of acquiring property."[65] It is also clear these citizens thought very much about monopoly, not least in their conscious—and at the time, somewhat contentious— establishment of two distinct types of monopoly. One was a system of patents and copyrights to protect the individual innovator from the power of the banker and trader. The other, as noted above, was the post office network, to ensure the inexpensive and neutral transmission of information—especially news—to all corners of the new nation.

A far better guide to what these citizens actually expected their new Constitution to accomplish lies in Madison's reply to Jefferson's interest in writing an antimonopoly clause into the Bill of Rights. Madison agreed that monopolies are "among the greatest nuisances." But he also made clear he believed the Constitution already provided ample protections against private concentrations of power. "Monopolies are sacrifices of the many to the few . . . Where the power, as with us, is in the many," the "danger cannot be very great that the few will be thus favored."[66] Jefferson soon agreed that no antimonopoly provision was necessary. Perhaps just as important is the fact that the participants in the Constitutional Convention repeatedly rejected—"by a great majority"—proposals to endow the U.S. government with the power to grant corporate charters.[67]

In short, these first citizens believed the Constitution—with its intricate systems for the breaking of political power—provided ample protection against economic monopoly. Further, they believed the Constitution was more than supple enough to allow citizens to adapt it to meet any conceivable economic threat or opportunity that might arise.[68]

In the end, America's first citizens did more than simply engineer the most sophisticated mechanism in human history for distributing political and economic power. They also birthed a mature, and revolutionary, *theory of competition* within society, based on the belief that rivalry among individuals could be directed in ways that would ensure that such competition was constructive and not destructive in nature. And they established a set of principles to guide the engineering of this competition not only within government but in every place within society, at every moment.

As Madison explained in *The Federalist Papers*, the goal must be to trace the "policy of supplying, by opposite and rival interests, the defect of better motives . . . through the *whole system* of human affairs, *private as well as public*."[69]

And so Americans entered the nineteenth century armed with a System of Liberty designed not only to protect the individual against all concentrations of power but to empower individuals to think and act and make and build a new world.

THE BROADAX AND THE COTTON GIN

And so they did. All the energy of self-interest in the individual, boxed like coal fire under a boiler by these carefully wrought institutions, now powered a period of phenomenal innovation and building by America's new citizens. In recent decades, the world has witnessed many instances of extreme material growth, in Europe after the Second World War, in Asia more recently. Yet never has the world seen anything quite like the explosion of energy in America in the first half of the nineteenth century.

We see this not only in the invention of new technologies and products, which included the steamboat, fire hydrant, wire cable suspension bridge, sewing machine, combine harvester, steam shovel, vulcanized rubber, circular saw, rotary printing press, Columbiad cannon, escalator, repeating rifle, safety elevator, electrical telegraph, and lightbulb. As profoundly important were the new methods of manufacturing that Americans developed. Jefferson in a 1785 letter introduced the concept of "interchangeable parts," which means that the gears designed for one particular watch on an assembly line will fit every other watch on that line. This concept, after being perfected by the Springfield Armory for the process of manufacturing rifles, came to provide the technological basis for American mass manufacturing and for much of America's material prosperity. Whereas European systems of production aimed largely to serve aristocrats, this new American system of production generally aimed to serve all individuals in the nation.[70]

By the 1830s European travelers had begun to depict American enterprise in tones approaching awe. The French writer Alexis de Tocqueville, the most famous of these observers, wrote, "In the United States the greatest undertakings and speculations are executed without difficulty, because the whole population is engaged in productive industry . . . The consequence is that a stranger is constantly amazed by the immense public works executed by a nation which contains, so to speak, no rich men." Americans, he went on, "have joined the Hudson to the Mississippi, and made the Atlantic Ocean communicate with the Gulf of Mexico, across a continent of more than five hundred leagues in extent . . . But what most astonishes me in the United States is not so much the marvelous grandeur of some undertakings, as the innumerable multitude of small ones."[71]

Americans themselves increasingly celebrated the competitive nature of their new society and even fostered it. Elkanah Watson, the inventor of the country fair, in 1820 wrote that he had introduced prizes for livestock and crops in order to spur "envy" and "competition." The way to a good society, he opined, was through "a general strife."[72]

But the America of these years was not only or even mainly a world defined by individual rapacity and selfishness. Americans also created a fantastic array of entirely new communities that tied individuals together in new ways and toward new ends. As the historian Gordon Wood writes: "Newly independent American men and women came together to form hundreds and thousands of new voluntary associations expressive of a wide array of benevolent goals— mechanics' societies, humane societies, societies for the prevention of pauperism, orphans asylums, missionary societies, marine societies, tract societies, Bible societies, temperance associations, Sabbatarian groups, peace societies, societies for the suppression of vice and immorality, societies for the relief of poor widows, societies for the promotion of industry, indeed societies for just about anything and everything that was good and humanitarian."[73]

The result, Wood concludes, was "the most liberal, the most democratic, the most commercially minded, and the most modern people in the world."[74]

But America was of course also a nation of slavery. And these innovative energies were also applied to many of the economic systems of the South. This includes Eli Whitney's cotton gin, patented in 1794. By making it much easier to separate cotton seeds from cotton fiber, the gin cleared the way to growing and exporting vastly greater crops of cotton. The result, by the 1830s, was an international system of manufacturing and trade, centered in Britain and largely controlled by British bankers and merchants, that rested ultimately on the backs of the enslaved people and tenants in America who grew and picked that cotton.[75] Although the democratic republicans in Washington may have been able to break the power of Nicholas Biddle's Philadelphia bank, they had no hope of mastering an international system of finance that was based on the other side of the Atlantic, in London.

Then there were the social and economic effects of the Panic of 1837. Much like the Great Depression of the 1930s and the financial crisis of 2007–2008, this collapse hit poor and middle-class Americans much harder than the rich, and in many cases helped the already well-off to further concentrate control, as planters and other land monopolists drove bankrupt citizens off their farms, especially in the South.[76]

By the 1830s, the planters who controlled politics in the South had also begun to perfect an entirely new governing philosophy. This philosophy, centered on the use of racist theories to justify the grotesque subjugation and enslavement of human being by human being, was openly and absolutely opposed not only to the institutions of the founders but to their most fundamental principles.

We will look at the intersection of power and race in more depth in later chapters. For our purposes here, an infamous speech by Alexander H. Stephens, the vice president of the new Confederacy, in Savannah, on March 21, 1861, serves to capture just how far the lords of the South had strayed from the goals of America's founders.

"The prevailing ideas entertained by [Jefferson] and most of the leading statesmen at the time of the formation of the old Constitution, were that the enslavement of the African was in violation of the laws of nature; that it was wrong in principle, socially, morally and politically," Stephens said. "It was an evil they knew not well how to deal with, but the general opinion of the men of that day was that, somehow or other, in the order of Providence, the institution would be evanescent and pass away . . . Those ideas, however, were fundamentally wrong. They rested upon the assumption of the equality of the races . . . Our new government is founded upon exactly the opposite idea, its foundations are laid, its corner-stone rests upon the great truth that the Negro is not equal to the white man. That slavery—subordination to the superior race—is his natural and normal condition. This, our new government, is the first in the history of the world based upon this great physical and moral truth."[77]

The structure of private monopoly power—in the nation, around the world—was made clear in January 1861, before Confederate soldiers fired the first cannon at Fort Sumter. Abraham Lincoln had been elected president, and South Carolina had announced its plans to secede from the Union. New York City mayor Fernando Wood proposed that Manhattan, Long Island, and Staten Island also secede to protect the ties between Wall Street's bankers and the slave system. "The profits, luxuries, the necessities—nay, even the physical existence of" New York, Wood said, "depend upon continuance of slave labor and the prosperity of the slave master."

Wood asked New York's Common Council to declare the city "independent" so it could "make common cause with the south." The Council approved the plan and—for a time—prohibited the passage of federal troops through the city.[78]

America's democratic republican citizens understood fully the power they had to break. As the abolitionist senator from Massachusetts Charles Sumner put it, the "Money Power has joined hands with the Slave Power. Selfish, grasping, subtle, tyrannical, like its ally, it will not brook opposition. It claims the Commonwealth as its own and too successfully enlists in its support that needy talent and easy virtue which are needed to maintain its sway."[79]

America's democratic republican citizens also understood exactly the idea they had to reestablish. It was that son of free-soil Illinois, Abraham Lincoln, who expressed this challenge most simply. "We all declare for liberty; but in using the same *word* we do not all mean the same *thing*. With some the word liberty may mean for each man to do as he pleases with himself, and the product of his labor; while with others the same word may mean for some men to do as they please with other men, and the product of other men's labor."[80]

The fight, in 1861 as in 1776, was to establish liberty from all masters, everywhere.

"TRUTH UTTERED IN ACTION"

When the fight was finally joined, the principles and institutions of the founders had created exactly the sort of citizen necessary for the moment, exactly the sort of citizen originally intended. Opposition to slavery in America traces almost to the first days of the first colonies. But it was the Declaration, with its simple statement of equality, that created a gnawing pressure that worked on the souls and minds of early citizens. As Americans struggled to create all sorts of new "properties," the hypocrisy of defending property in man grew only more odious.

Nowhere did this spirit play a bigger role than in states established under the Northwest Ordinance. In addition to providing a model for dividing properties into citizen-sized plots, the act did something equally revolutionary in fencing slavery out.[81] As the constitutional scholar Akhil Reed Amar has written, the Ordinance "structured a footrace between free-soilers hoping to move into the Northwest and slave owners aiming to carry their property and culture into the southwest."[82] Many, including Lincoln's own family, came from the South in search of a land without slavery.[83]

By the 1840s these new states had become the center of the anti-slavery movement, the home of the Liberty Party, and of Van Buren's Free Soil Party, and of the new Republican Party. To some degree, the opposition to slavery was simple self-interest. When white men came to understand slavery was not dying, and indeed that the planters had captured control of the Democratic Party, in the words of W. E. B. Du Bois they "came to oppose slavery not so much from moral as from the economic fear of being reduced by competition to the level of slaves."[84]

Yet we also see in these years a reawakening to the full nature of American citizenship. In 1837, on the fiftieth anniversary of the Northwest Ordinance, Ohio citizens had celebrated "Those truly excellent laws of Congress, [which] furnished a perfect mould for well proportioned republicans."[85]

And indeed, what we see here is a largely conscious fight against racism by people who fully understood that the planters were wielding race as a tool to break democracy. In his 1855 version of his autobiography, Frederick Douglass sought to unify all Americans in rebellion against both planter and banker. "The difference between the white slave, and the black slave, is this: the latter belongs to *one* slaveholder, and the former belongs to *all* the slaveholders, collectively," Douglass wrote. "The white slave has taken from him, by indirection, what the black slave has taken from him, directly, and without ceremony. Both are plundered, and by the same plunderers."[86]

Pennsylvania congressman Thaddeus Stevens, a leading abolitionist, made sure to clarify that the Civil War was a fight for equal rights for all. "This is not a white man's Government," Stevens said in a speech. "To say so is political blasphemy, for it violates the fundamental principles of our gospel of liberty. This is Man's Government, the Government of all men alike; not that all men will have equal power and sway within it. Accidental circumstances, natural and acquired endowment and ability, will vary their fortunes. But equal rights to all the privileges of the Government is innate in every immortal being, no matter what the shape or color of the tabernacle which it inhabits."[87]

When the southern states seceded, America's citizens, four generations after the founding, faced their greatest test. The result, over the course of the Civil War, was that nearly a million free men would march south from the citizen-sized farms of the old Northwest.[88] During these same years, the promise of equality and liberty in a land without slavery sapped the South of vast reserves of men and money, as entire regions of many southern states seceded from the Confederacy. In some instances these regions remained loyal to the Union. In other cases, soldiers simply went home, as tens of thousands of men refused to fight for the liberty of the planter.[89]

One of our best witnesses to how the idea of liberty worked on the minds of Americans during this struggle is again Whitman, who served both as journalist and nurse during the war. "Probably no future age can know, but I well know, how the gist of this fiercest and most resolute of the world's warlike contentions resided exclusively in the unnamed, unknown rank and file; and how the brunt of its labor of death was, to all essential purposes, volunteer'd. The People, of their own choice, fighting, dying for their own idea, insolently attack'd by the secession-slave-power, and its very existence imperil'd."[90]

But the Civil War was, of course, not merely or even mainly a white man's fight. It was also a fight in which black men and black women set themselves free and made themselves into full American citizens.

Before the war, no one did more than Douglass to foster the idea that slaves must become full citizens, no different than any other citizen. As we saw in the last chapter, Douglass rejected the argument that the Constitution was a pro-slavery document. Douglass also made clear that the goal of black citizens must be full economic independence in the form of land, education, and rule of law; that black citizens must have the same power of the vote as white, and that the original "great principles" of America were his principles.[91]

But Douglass made clear he did not believe reason alone, prayer alone, simple willingness to live peacefully as a citizen on a farm or with a store alone were sufficient to break the power of the planters. He also understood that both the freeman and slave had to fight.

Just before his friend John Brown's raid on Harpers Ferry, Douglass wrote an editorial titled "The Ballot and the Bullet." The idea that the international system of slavery could be overthrown without war was "nonsense," he said. The winning of "hearts and consciences" was a necessary first step. But "truth to be efficient must be uttered in action as well as in speech."[92]

In the coming few years no one proved more energetic or creative than Douglass in shaping and defining the purposes of the war, in filling the ranks of the army with freemen and enslaved people who had escaped, in demanding equal pay for these men, in asserting their citizenship.

Once a black man could "get upon his person the brass letters U.S. . . . , an eagle on his button, and a musket on his shoulder, and bullets in his pocket, there is no power on earth . . . which can deny that he has earned the right of citizenship in the United States," Douglass said in an 1863 speech.[93]

The result? As this most masterful maker of new citizens would put it years later, "When the recruiting officers . . . were going up and down the street begging for men to enlist, when the cause of the Union hung in the balance, when foreign powers were ready to recognize the South, the negro with arms of iron and fingers of steel, grasped the Union cause and held it together!"[94]

Thus citizens of all races and backgrounds combined to break the last relic of feudal monopoly outlaw power in America. Thus they joined to complete the full promise of 1776.

And yet, within but a few years, the greatest battles of the war began to tarnish beneath the failure of the American people to deliver to the black man precisely what it had promised to the white man in year one of the new nation: land. Although Congress moved swiftly to pass a special Homestead Act to distribute public lands in five southern states to the freed people of the South, neither the Johnson nor the Grant administrations enforced the law. Nor did Congress or the executive branch ever move to effectively break apart and redistribute the lands engrossed by the slaveholders in Virginia, the Carolinas, or Georgia.

A century later, Martin Luther King Jr. spoke of what resulted. "In 1863 the Negro was given abstract freedom expressed in luminous rhetoric. But in an agrarian economy he was given no land to make liberation concrete. After the war the government granted white settlers, without cost, millions of acres of land in the West, thus providing America's new white peasants from Europe with an economic floor. But at the same time its oldest peasantry, the Negro, was denied everything but a legal status he could not use, could not consolidate, could not even defend."[95]

Du Bois, in *Black Reconstruction*, cut even more swiftly to what it meant to be liberated and then left without any real property. "The slave went free, stood a brief moment in the sun, then moved back again towards slavery."[96]

FIVE

TO DEMOCRATIZE THE MACHINE

CITIZENS MASTER THE MASTERS—AGAIN

IN AUGUST 1910, THEODORE ROOSEVELT ORDERED HIS TRAIN TO stop in Osawatomie, Kansas, so he could speak to the farmers and shopkeepers of the town about his plan to tame America's monopolies. "Combinations in industry are the result of an imperative economic law which cannot be repealed by political legislation," he bellowed from the rear platform. "The effort at prohibiting all combination has substantially failed. The way out lies, not in attempting to prevent such combinations, but in completely controlling them in the interest of the public welfare."[1]

It was less than two years since Roosevelt had turned both the White House and leadership of the Republican Party over to his vice president, William Howard Taft. Now he wanted the presidency back. Recently returned from safari across West Africa, where he had shot elephants, lions, rhinos, and hippos, Roosevelt's promise was simple. He would bring the great corporate and banking beasts that threatened America to heel. And he would do so with the flaming spirit of John Brown, who in 1856 had led 40 abolitionists in battle against more than 200 pro-slavery "border ruffians" right there in Osawatomie. The apocalypse had come. And Roosevelt was ready to loose the fateful .405 cartridges of his terrible swift Winchester.

To this day, most American historians continue to fall for the myth that Teddy Roosevelt was a "trustbuster." As his Osawatomie speech shows, along with his larger New Nationalism program, what he actually promised was to blend state and private power into a top-down command-and-control system of governance that would have made even Alexander Hamilton queasy.

Born to wealthy parents in Manhattan, Roosevelt had in fact long made clear his disdain for antimonopoly law. In 1907, as president, he had even called on Congress to overturn the Sherman Antitrust Act. "It is profoundly immoral to put or keep on the statute books a law, nominally in the interest of public morality, that really puts a premium on public immorality, by undertaking to forbid honest men from doing what must be done under modern business conditions, so that the law itself provides that its own infraction must be the condition precedent upon business success."[2]

In the run-up to the 1912 election, Roosevelt collected some of the bright minds of the day. These young men believed that President Taft had been captured by the masters of industry. But unlike the populists in the Democratic Party, who demanded strong enforcement of antimonopoly law, the intellectuals in Roosevelt's camp advocated instead a complete overthrow of many of the checks and balances put in place in the early years of the United States. Let the capitalists complete their concentration of power, they said. They would then use the state to direct those great combinations toward good.

Walter Lippmann, in the first years of his long career as a journalist and essayist, still under the sway of the socialist teachings popular at this time, in his book *Drift and Mastery* provided a concise statement of Roosevelt's new philosophy. "We don't imagine the trusts are going to drift naturally into the service of human life. We think they can be made to serve it if the American people compel them."[3] In place of checks and balances, Lippmann imagined a political economy governed by "the scientific spirit" and ruled by phalanxes of experts. The protection of democracy, Lippmann wrote, depended now on "the new science of administration. The development of that science is the only answer."[4]

Even more influential was Herbert Croly, a son of New York

writers. After marrying into wealth, Croly dabbled in architectural criticism until bursting to prominence with the 1909 book *The Promise of American Life*, in which he celebrated, much to Roosevelt's delight, Hamiltonian nationalism, the concentration of control in a few outstanding leaders of men, and the use of state power to reward these "friends" of the administration with power and pelf.[5] In a passage that essentially defended a return to the autocratic practices of Queen Elizabeth and King James (and that also well presaged President Trump's more recent efforts to use the Justice Department and State Department to promote his personal interests), Croly wrote, "in economic warfare, the fighting can never be fair for long, and it is the business of the state to see that its own friends are victorious . . . It must help those men to win who are most capable of using their winnings for the benefit of society." Croly called this vision "constructive discrimination."[6]

Roosevelt himself appeared less concerned about philosophy than about simply getting his own hands on the levers of control.[7] In the first big antitrust case of his presidency, in 1902 against the banker J. P. Morgan's Northern Securities holding company, his goal seemed less to protect rule of law than to chastise a man Roosevelt once termed a "rival operator" with whom he must either "come to an agreement" or "ruin."[8] In recent years, some have feared President Trump might misuse antitrust laws to concentrate personal power. To the extent Roosevelt used antitrust, it was with the intention of making himself boss, king, kaiser.

With the Republican Party still backing Taft, Roosevelt turned for support to the then-powerful Progressive Party, a sprawling confabulation of reformers pursuing many theories of change. His main competitor for the nomination was the Wisconsin senator Robert La Follette. In his *Autobiography* a year later, La Follette delivered one of the most scathing indictments any American politician ever published about a rival, and he focused specifically on Roosevelt's embrace of monopoly power.

"Since Lincoln's time no man had been offered such an opportunity to strike an effective blow for his country as was presented to Roosevelt," La Follette wrote.[9] "Instead, in his messages and public addresses, one finds the new President setting himself up as superior to the law."[10]

Most damaging, La Follette wrote, was Roosevelt's "denunciation" of the Sherman Antitrust Act. This served as "an executive sanction to violate the law. It opened the floodgates for trust organization, and upon Theodore Roosevelt, more than any other man, must rest the responsibility for the gravest problem ever to menace the industrial freedom of the American people."[11]

The presidential election of 1912 was one of the most important in the history of the United States. Citizens believed themselves threatened by the greatest concentration of private power since the days of the slave masters, only this time the threat was posed by Wall Street financiers exercising their power through the industrial corporation and bank. During the campaign, the main candidates presented America's voters with a bluntly honest debate that focused on different ways to structure and organize economic and political power.

Both major parties vehemently opposed—sometimes in the language of Armageddon—Roosevelt's call to concentrate and centralize economic power in the state. Making the case for the Republicans, President Taft offered a vision largely British in nature, in which the government would use antimonopoly law to ensure that the lords of industry would not combine their powers into an oligarchic dictatorship over the state itself. But Taft also intended to leave these powerful men largely free to operate as autocratically as they wished *within* the walls of their industrial and banking estates. The Democrats, meanwhile, put forth a man named Woodrow Wilson, a constitutional scholar from Virginia with brilliant oratorical skills and a mystical turn. Wilson presented himself as the reincarnation of Jefferson and Madison and Lincoln, and promised to restore the democratic republic of the founding and of Gettysburg.[12] Americans, Wilson preached, could easily avoid the traps of both statism and estatism. The key was not to use the state to direct the entire political economy but rather to use its antimonopoly powers to prevent any private actor from capturing such an ability. To the extent there would be any direction of the overall political economy, it would come from the American people themselves, their will expressed through democratic deliberation.

Human beings tend to view politics through the lens of the great leader, the great man. And Wilson's powerful intellect, masterful use of language and imagery, and great political dexterity certainly played a huge role in his election and in the later success of his policies, which he called the New Freedom in direct contradistinction to Roosevelt's New Nationalism. Yet in many respects Wilson was more a spokesperson for a citizen-led movement against the monopolists, and against the concentration of wealth and power, that had been building for two decades.

To understand the politics of the New Freedom, and later of the New Deal, it is vital to recognize the role played by these antimonopoly citizens, who at the time generally referred to themselves as "populists."

This populist movement in America traced to groups of farmers, skilled working people, and shopkeepers—both white and black—who began organizing outside any party with the aim of using the ideology and language and tools of the founders to break the power of the monopolists and financers who increasingly threatened individual liberty and democracy. It was a movement that had long since captured real power, building up sufficient sway within the national Democratic Party to take the presidential nomination three times. In 1896, 1900, and 1908, the populists had sent their candidate—the small-town lawyer and orator William Jennings Bryan—to battle against the corporate and banking lords gathered under the Republican banner.[13]

By the time the Democrats nominated Wilson, the populist movement had both greatly expanded and to some extent gone mainstream, as the fears and goals of the farmer, skilled worker, and small shopkeeper in the South and Midwest had become the fears and goals of moderate and even conservative citizens in every town, and almost every line of business across the nation. The basic tenets of populism had also been embraced by a growing legion of progressive intellectuals—such as the lawyer Louis Brandeis—who believed that the American System of Liberty could be used even to make heavy industry, network technologies, and banking safe for democracy.

Woodrow Wilson was a deeply flawed man. Like Roosevelt, he was racist, and once in power he completed the segregation of the federal government, a process Roosevelt had set in motion in 1906.[14] But during the campaign, Wilson was able to ride this wave of popular rage and hope in ways that helped to fully reconnect citizens to the original principles and language of the American System of Liberty.

Wilson spoke more bravely than Roosevelt of the threats posed by the monopolists and more practically of the nature of their power. "The masters of the government of the United States are the combined capitalists and manufacturers of the United States," he said.[15] "By tyranny, as we fight it now, we mean control of the law, of legislation and adjudication, by organizations which do not represent the people, by means which are private and selfish. We mean, specifically, the conduct of our affairs and the shaping of our legislation in the interest of special bodies of capital and those who organize their use. We mean the exploitation of the people by legal and political means."[16]

Wilson also efficiently belittled Roosevelt's command-and-control, "Iron Heel" approach to regulating monopoly.[17] Roosevelt, Wilson said, "proposes to use monopoly in order to make us happy. [T]he project is one of those projects which all history cries out against as impossible . . . These gentlemen are not proposing the methods of liberty but are proposing the methods of control. A control among a free people is intolerable."

After winning the White House, Wilson, as we will discuss in more detail shortly, helped to clear the way for the single most important reestablishment of citizen control over the American political economy since the founding. In doing so, he was simply delivering to the citizens of America what they had demanded for more than a generation; indeed Wilson's presidency was the culmination of

America's second citizens' rebellion. But whereas in 1861 America's farmer citizens and shopkeeper citizens had stood against the planters, this time they marched against both the monopolist and the financier who stood behind him.

In doing so, America's citizens established the basic ideas, principles, rhetoric, and institutional structures that would guide Franklin Roosevelt's New Deal twenty years later and that ensured that twentieth-century industrial America was organized not according to any new science of power, or any blind faith in strongman leaders, but rather the democratic republican thinking of America's first citizens more than a century earlier.

RAILROADING THEIR WAY TO MONOPOLY

To understand the revolutionary nature of Wilson's New Freedom, and its importance in establishing the intellectual framework of the New Deal policies of the 1930s, we must first address the extreme concentration of economic power in the United States in the period between the end of the Civil War and the election of 1912. This period, sometimes referred to as the plutocratic era, has long baffled historians. How was it that power and wealth became so fantastically concentrated immediately after 750,000 Americans died in a war that redeemed for all men—at least for a moment—the liberty promised in the Declaration?[18] How was it that the whole American System of Liberty, built with such care over so many decades, suddenly failed?[19]

The confusion derives in part from the fact that many historians have embraced the same deterministic arguments used by Teddy Roosevelt and his team of young men. Looking through that frame, later writers often concluded that the rise of monopoly and other forms of concentrated power was inevitable, due perhaps to some inherent characteristic within capitalism. Many therefore missed the obvious story: the American System of Liberty was assiduously subverted by men who consciously intended to concentrate autocratic control over America's citizens.

Immediately after the Civil War, a very different future had seemed possible. The power of the last great outlaw monopolists—the slave masters—had been broken, along with the rule of the lash. Citizens were using the Homestead Act and the Southern Homestead Act to manufacture new independent citizens through the distribution of 160-acre farms, much the same as in the days of the Northwest Ordinance. Most important, the American people had passed three great amendments to the Constitution—to ban slavery, to guarantee citizenship and equal protection of law to individuals of all races, and to protect the right of all men to vote, no matter their race, no matter whether they had ever been enslaved.

Yet during the presidency of Ulysses S. Grant, a citizen farmer who by the end of the Civil War had risen to command all U.S. armies, it became more and more evident that the money power had somehow broken fully loose from all government constraint.

During these years Americans were treated to a series of chaotic business conflicts and speculations, sometimes followed by devastating economic panics and collapses. One of the most audacious occurred only six months after Grant took office in 1869. The stock manipulator and railroad mogul Jay Gould, along with his partner in financial buccaneering, Jim Fisk, engineered a corner on the market for gold on Wall Street. Gould later claimed his effort was part of a complicated plan to raise the price of wheat and shift money to western farmers so they could afford to ship their grains east on his railroad. But few believed this story. And within days, Grant ordered the government to sell bullion in order to break the corner. This shattered not only the price of gold but also the price of grains and other commodities—and of the stock market itself—in the first of four "Black Friday" crashes in American history.[20]

To many Americans, such speculations were a sign of simple moral corruption. This was the message of Mark Twain in the 1873 novel *The Gilded Age*, which told a story of Washington influence peddling, and which provided us with the name some historians have used to describe the era as a whole. More bluntly, in an 1871 essay titled "The Revised Catechism," the sometimes nihilistic Twain wrote, "What is the chief end of man?—to get rich. In what way?—

dishonestly if we can; honestly if we must." Decades later, after the rise of Theodore Roosevelt and the concentration of power on Wall Street, Twain would write, "Jay Gould taught the entire nation to make a god of the money and the man, no matter how the money might have been acquired."[21]

Yet the real story was more one of financiers—then often called "robber barons"—breaking free from the structures and strictures that had held them in check for America's first century. At a time when citizens had not yet armed the federal government with strong and fully modern regulatory agencies to counter the power of concentrated capital, America's financiers enjoyed almost unlimited license to engage in experiments in corporate and bank structure and market speculation and manipulation.[22]

Three fundamental changes from antebellum America helped power their efforts.

One was that the biggest financiers had far deeper pots of cash with which to play. During the emergency of the war, as the Lincoln administration had experimented with a variety of instruments to pay for soldiers and materiel, J. P. Morgan, Jay Gould, Jay Cooke, and other New York bankers had concentrated much of that capital in their own hands. Although the National Bank Act of 1863 established strong, modern regulations on banking activities, including a ban on bankers owning non-banking businesses, the United States still lacked any central regulator to keep watch over Wall Street, and the newly crowned czars of finance were left largely free to entrench their power.

A second change was the introduction of new legal forms for the business corporation. In 1882, John D. Rockefeller's Standard Oil Company created the first interlocking system of ownership to tie many corporations into one, which they called a "trust." Tycoons in the whiskey, lead, and sugar industries soon followed. Then in 1888, New Jersey created the nation's most liberal general incorporation law, making it much easier to create holding companies able to operate easily across state borders. This new law in turn triggered a second burst of concentration.[23]

The single biggest change was the maturation of revolutionary

new technologies—especially the railroad and telegraph. These technologies did more than simply link people and towns more closely
together. They also provided corporate masters with an extremely effective means of projecting power over distance in radically faster ways,
and positioned them as essential middlemen able to exert extreme
leverage in their battles for absolute supremacy in particular markets.

The railroad was, in fact, the most important source of the power
of both Standard Oil and Carnegie Steel, two of the biggest and
most politically potent corporations in U.S. history, relative to the
overall economy in which they operated. Normally it was the railroad that held sway over the shipper, thanks to the power that came
from being able to favor one company's shipments over another's.
But both Standard and Carnegie controlled inputs—including lu-
bricating oils and steel—that the railroads themselves needed. This
enabled them to force the railroads to help them in their efforts to
bankrupt or otherwise displace their rivals.

As a New York State investigative commission put it in 1880,
"The parties whom [Standard Oil] have driven to the wall have had
ample capital, and equal ability in the persecution of their business
in all things save their ability to acquire facilities for transportation."
Or as Hans Thorelli, perhaps the most sophisticated historian of
antimonopoly law, would put it many years later, "Standard's monopolization of transportation facilities held the key to its success."[24]

Unlike today's historians, the Americans of the late nineteenth
century, steeped as they were in the language and practice of democratic republicanism, fully understood not only the nature of the threat
posed by these monopolists but the direction from which it came.

Indeed, by the early 1870s, many Americans began to fear that
America's capitalists had finally and fully escaped the box that the
founders had put them into. One of the strongest early warnings
came from Charles Francis Adams Jr., great-grandson of John Adams. The new monopolists, Adams wrote in an essay on Gould, Fisk,
and the railroad boss Cornelius Vanderbilt, embody "the autocratic
power of Caesarism introduced into corporate life."

Forty years before the full implications of Theodore Roosevelt's vision became clear, Adams predicted it "only remains for

the coming man to . . . put Caesarism at once in control of the corporation and of the proletariat."

LINCOLN'S LAST VICTORY

By the 1880s it was clear that the Republican Party had fallen into the grip of the monopolist and financier almost as completely as the Democratic Party of the 1850s had become the tool of the slave master and the "money power." But the remnants of the party of Lincoln, Douglass, Van Buren, Sumner, and Stevens—with its close ideological ties to the Democratic-Republican Party of Madison and Jefferson—did wage one last campaign to preserve the American System of Liberty.

In the late 1880s this democratic republican wing of the Republican Party passed two bills that aimed to break and harness the new monopolists. One worked. One failed. The one that worked was an effort to use common carrier principles and law to neutralize the power of the new technologies, especially the railroad.

Americans of the nineteenth century fully understood that providers of essential services, such as railroad and telegraph corporations, and even banks, could pose especially dangerous economic and political threats to the public. In response, citizens passed a wide range of laws at the state and local level to carefully limit the powers of these corporations. They also began to use the powers of the federal government. Even before the Civil War, for instance, citizens had inserted strong non-discrimination rules into the Pacific Telegraph Act of 1860, in the form of a requirement that all messages receive equal treatment.[25] The National Bank Act of 1863, which modernized the U.S. monetary system to allow the federal government to pay for the war, decreed a complete separation between banking and commerce so as to protect the business of lending from conflicts of interest. Then immediately after the war, Senator John Sherman authored the National Telegraph Act of 1866 to extend the rule of common carriage across the nation as a whole.[26]

For a period it seemed that the judiciary fully shared this belief. The idea that the public has an absolute right to regulate certain types of business had in fact recently been expressed in resounding terms by the chief justice of the Supreme Court, Morrison Waite, in his opinion in *Munn v. Illinois* in 1876. In that case, 9 of 14 grain elevators in Chicago had been charged with fixing prices for handling and storing grain, and the state of Illinois had responded by regulating the prices and terms on which these companies could do business. The grain monopolists then sued the state, arguing that the elevators were fully private in nature, and that public officials had no right to take such action against private properties.

Waite's first conclusion was that the grain elevators constituted "a 'virtual' monopoly," based on the fact that the "vast productions" of grain from the "great States of the West" must pass through these elevators to get to "the States on the seashore."

Waite then explained why all monopolists of vital goods and services must answer to the public. "Property does become clothed with a public interest when used in a manner to make it of public consequence, and affect the community at large," he wrote. "When, therefore, one devotes his property to a use in which the public has an interest, he, in effect, grants to the public an interest in that use, and must submit to be controlled by the public for the common good, to the extent of the interest he has thus created. He may withdraw his grant by discontinuing the use; but, so long as he maintains the use, he must submit to the control."

Then, quoting seventeenth-century legal scholar Matthew Hale, Waite concluded that the public can therefore reasonably require that the owner of such a monopoly attend the public "at due times," keep their properties "in due order," and "take but reasonable toll."

The *Munn* decision was not unanimous, and the dissent in the case—with Supreme Court justice Stephen Johnson Field calling the decision "subversive of the rights of private property"—served as a warning of the new fashion afoot: applying the philosophy of the slave masters to the monopoly corporation and bank. And sure enough, in 1886, the Supreme Court in *Wabash, St. Louis and Pacific Railway Co. v. Illinois* all but entirely took away from the states the regulatory powers that had been so strongly defended by the *Munn* decision, with the majority basing its argument on the idea that such regulatory actions by state officials violated the Commerce Clause of the Constitution.

The prospect that America's railroad barons, along with any corporation and bank already strong enough to demand special treatment from the railroads, would now be entirely untethered from all public authority raised a tight knot of fears across the nation. The most immediate fear was simply that these powers would now gouge individual members of the public or fail to provide reasonable service. More fundamental was the fear that the railroad masters would now engage in discriminations that allowed them to extort not only cash from those subject to their power but political favors as well, in ways subversive of democracy itself.

As members of Congress set out to fix the damage done by the *Wabash* decision, one of their most important guides to the fundamental dangers posed by the license to discriminate was a new book by a Yale professor named Arthur Hadley.

"[D]iscriminations made between individuals," Hadley wrote in *Railroad Transportation*, in 1885, "is the most serious evil connected with our present methods of railroad management. Trade adjusts itself to almost any system of classification, and sometimes even to local discriminations. But where two individuals, under like circumstances, receive different treatment, no such adjustment is possible."[27]

One result of such personalized discrimination, Hadley warned, is that "Differences are made which are sufficient to cripple all smaller competitors, and sooner or later drive them to the wall, and concentrate industry in a few hands."[28] "[T]he great majority of local and personal discriminations are in favor of the strong," he wrote. "As such they do great harm to the community by increasing inequalities of power."[29]

More dangerous yet was the direct collapse of rule of law, hence of the security of private property. "Where the system of granting special privileges becomes deeply rooted," Hadley wrote, "a great many are granted without any principle at all, through the caprice or favoritism of the railroad companies and their agents."[30]

In 1886 Republican senator Shelby Cullom responded to these fears by drawing up a bill designed to prohibit railroads from engaging in most forms of price discrimination, and that established a five-person commission to make sure the laws were enforced.[31] Backed strongly by Republicans and Democrats from the Midwest and South, but opposed by most Republicans from the banker-controlled states of the Northeast, the Interstate Commerce Act was passed and signed into law in 1887 by Grover Cleveland, a Democrat from New York state.[32]

The Interstate Commerce Act would prove to be a highly incomplete law. In the years to come it would require many adjustments to ensure that railroads charged reasonable prices and provided reasonably efficient and effective service, and that the financiers were not able to manipulate capital structures in ways that allowed them to overcharge the public.[33] But the law also got one really big thing right in outlawing discrimination. The era of the railroad lord was over, and though the families of Cornelius Vanderbilt, E. H. Harriman, Leland Stanford, and Jay Gould would retain great wealth to this day, never again would one man or group of men be able to leverage the railroad monopolies to the apex of power. The same, obviously, was also true for any powerful industrialist who aimed to follow the path of John D. Rockefeller and Andrew Carnegie.

In the years to come, America's citizens extended the principles of common carriage to the telegraph, telephone, pipeline, trucking, air travel, broadcast, and Internet industries. Each time, they aimed specifically to prevent these corporations from discriminating in the delivery of their services. The basic goal was always to ensure that these public systems would serve the public, and not be transformed into tools for the extortion of money and political power in the name of a few private masters. In other words, the Interstate Commerce Act would prove to be one of the most important foundations of American democracy in our nation's history.

THE BANKERS BREAK LOOSE

Three years later, in 1890, the old Lincoln wing of the Republican Party made its final attack on the money power. This time their tool was a law designed to outlaw the trust ownership structure that

Standard Oil had first mastered in 1882, and also—in very general terms—all other monopolies and artificial restraints on trade.

The main backer of the act was Ohio senator John Sherman, whose brother, General William Tecumseh Sherman, helped break the power of the Confederacy by marching his army across Georgia to the sea. The text of the Sherman Antitrust Act itself was short, as its original authors wanted it to have the simplicity of a constitutional statement. Yet Senator Sherman himself delivered a long speech on March 21, 1890, in defense of his bill, in which he made clear that he and his allies intended for the law to fully restore the original structures of the American System of Liberty.

"The popular mind is agitated with problems that may disturb social order," Sherman said. "Among them all none is more threatening than the inequality of condition, of wealth, and opportunity that has grown within a single generation out of the concentration of capital into vast combinations to control production and trade and to break down competition."[34]

In one of the most oft-cited statements from the speech, Sherman said what was at stake was American democracy itself. "If we will not endure a king as a political power, we should not endure a king over the production, transportation, and sale of any of the necessities of life. If we would not submit to an emperor, we should not submit to an autocrat of trade, with power to prevent competition and to fix the price of any commodity."[35]

To ensure a proper understanding of the immediate purpose of the law, Sherman made clear that it was the "liberty" of the individual, as a producer, that the law must protect foremost. In words that blended the lessons of Madison, Smith, and Locke, Sherman said, "It is the right of every man to work, labor, and produce in any lawful vocation and to transport his production on equal terms and conditions and under like circumstances. This is industrial liberty, and lies at the foundation of the equality of all rights and privileges."[36]

Sherman's speech is a glorious document, one of the most important expressions of democratic republican thinking in our nation's history, a resounding updating for the railroad age of the original

American vision of propertied independence for the farmer, working person, shopkeeper, artist, and manufacturer. There was no speech quite like it in the fight for the Interstate Commerce Act. There would be few speeches like it—not even from Bryan—until the days of Wilson and Brandeis a generation later. It should therefore serve as the true touchstone for all enforcement of modern antimonopoly law and policy in the United States and indeed in the democracies of the world.

Yet Senator Sherman's antitrust law itself, when put to the test, did not merely fail, it did so in spectacular fashion, serving mainly to accelerate the very consolidation of economic and political power that it sought to arrest and reverse.

At the time and in the years since, there has been much speculation about how the lawyers in the conference committee may have deliberately altered the original text of the law in ways designed not only to limit its effect, but to provide loopholes wide enough for the most elephantine of monopolists to amble through.[37] Similarly, there has been much debate about the Senate's decision not to establish a commission similar to that of the Interstate Commerce Act but instead to trust enforcement to the judiciary. But for the sake of our story, it does not matter whether the Sherman Act was intentionally sabotaged or whether the drafters simply lacked the ability to imagine the future cunning of the financiers and corporate executives with whom they were doing battle.

The fact is that even before the courts had really begun to make sense of their new responsibilities, America's bankers responded with a series of mergers that created monopolies or near monopolies in dozens of businesses, ranging from the manufacture of locomotives, writing paper, cans, steam pumps, window glass, and pneumatic tools to the mining of salt and the distillation of sugar. Many of the monopolies that would dominate American and indeed world business for decades—including the chemical giant DuPont and Otis Elevator—were created or took their modern form during this time. In the case of electricity, one of the most durable cartels in history was created when J. P. Morgan in 1892 engineered the capture of control over the patents of both General Electric and Westinghouse and used that control to govern development of the entire electric power industry for decades.[38]

The "consolidation craze" that followed passage of the Sherman Antitrust Act, Hans Thorelli later wrote, "wrought an almost revolutionary change in the legal and financial structure of major segments of American industry."[39] From an "economic, social, and political point of view the industrial consolidation movement was doubtless of more momentous significance than any other development in American society around the turn of the century." Not even the Spanish-American War and America's emergence as a power in Asia, following the decision to colonize the Philippines, "affected American civilization . . . as much as the emergence of the giant concern as the dominant element in scores of the nation's industries."[40]

By 1901 Morgan had consolidated sufficient mastery of the capital market to break even the power of the steel magnate Andrew Carnegie. With Elbert Gary's Federal Steel Company as his corporate tool, Morgan backed Carnegie into a position where he had no real choice but to sell out. The resulting deal made Carnegie the richest man in the world. And it made the monopoly that resulted—U.S. Steel—the largest corporation in the world, the first ever valued over $1 billion, with 532,000 workers and a 67 percent share of America's booming market for steel.[41]

By 1903, according to figures compiled by the Wall Street publisher John Moody, the lords of Wall Street had rolled 8,664 companies into 445 corporations, most of which dominated entirely one market or another. And with Roosevelt in the White House, more was to come, including Morgan's participation in the "rationalization" of America's telephone industry, under the banner of AT&T, beginning in 1907.[42]

Less than two generations had passed since the American people had broken the power of the slave masters and the money masters who financed them. Barely more than 15 years had passed since Congress had taken from the money lords their ability to leverage the railroad monopolies to extort their way to wealth and autocratic control. Now the money power was back and more awesome than ever. It was able to leverage the monopoly industrial corporation, the monopoly trading corporation, and the monopoly of the technological patent to gain more or less autocratic control over vast swaths of the U.S. political economy.

More dangerous yet, Roosevelt's embrace of monopolization had effectively licensed a tiny group of financiers, led by J. P. Morgan, to concentrate de facto control over the money power itself, through the weaving of an intricate web of cross ownership and control that extended from bank to bank and corporation to corporation. As La Follette explained in 1913, "The trusts and combinations at the beginning of Theodore Roosevelt's term were but a handful. Limited in number, they stood unsupported, each by itself. They had not yet been fused and welded together with the Morgan system of interlocking directorates."[43]

Indeed, as Moody detailed, J. P. Morgan's group had even brokered a peace with the Rockefeller family and their own immensely powerful Wall Street operation, centered on the National City Bank, which today we know as Citigroup. "They are not only friendly, but they are allied to each other by many close ties," Moody wrote. "It is felt and recognized on every hand in Wall Street to-day, that they are harmonious in nearly all particulars."[44]

The full extent of the power that had been concentrated by Wall Street would not be made clear until Congress in 1912 approved a special subcommittee to investigate whether a banking trust did indeed exist on Wall Street. The committee report, published in early 1913, just before Wilson took office, found that Morgan and a few other Wall Street bankers had indeed captured control over America's credit system.

"The acts of this inner group [have] been more destructive of competition than anything accomplished by the trusts," the report explained, "for they strike at the very vitals of potential competition in every industry that is under their protection, a condition which if permitted to continue, will render impossible all attempts to restore normal competitive conditions in the industrial world." At present, the report concluded, America's business leaders had been reduced to "being subject to the tribute and good will of this handful of self-constituted trustees of the national prosperity."[45]

It was at this time that Louis Brandeis finally turned his full attention to the threat posed by corporate and banking monopoly, first in the role of freelance agitator and then increasingly as Wilson's intellectual partner in his antimonopoly thinking and writing. Raised in Louisville, Kentucky, Brandeis had practiced corporate law in Boston, where he earned the nickname "The People's Lawyer" by leading fights against abusive employers and railroad monopolies—including Morgan's use of the New Haven railroad to monopolize urban railway service in the Northeast. Like Wilson, Brandeis held that citizens must use the original principles of the American System of Liberty to guide the breaking and neutralization of the power of twentieth-century monopolists.

These few bankers, Brandeis warned, had captured control over the gate to the credit system itself. "Though properly but middlemen," he wrote, "these bankers bestride as masters America's business world, so that practically no large enterprise can be undertaken successfully without their participation or approval." The "most potent factor in their control of business is not the possession of extraordinary ability or huge wealth. The key to their power is Combination—concentration intensive and comprehensive."[46]

More galling yet, the bankers had captured their position using the funds deposited in their banks by the same hardworking and honest citizens whom they were now pillaging. "The goose that lays golden eggs has been considered a most valuable possession," Brandeis wrote. "But even more profitable is the privilege of taking the golden eggs laid by somebody else's goose. The investment bankers and their associates now enjoy that privilege. They control the people through the people's own money."[47]

The good news? The solution was simple and easy to understand. "We must break the Money Trust," Brandeis concluded. "Or the Money Trust will break us."[48]

THE AMERICAN SYSTEM OF LIBERTY MADE ANEW

Woodrow Wilson was in office only 16 months before Germany invaded Belgium on August 4, 1914, to start what we now call the

First World War. Yet in that time his administration oversaw the most extensive reconstruction of the whole U.S. political economy since the Constitution and the Northwest Ordinance. This included the introduction or preparation of:

- The Federal Reserve Act, to establish a publicly controlled central bank to regulate Wall Street bankers and America's money supply.
- The Clayton Antitrust Act, to clarify and strengthen the Sherman Antitrust Act and to distribute the same antimonopoly enforcement powers to every U.S. state.
- The Federal Trade Commission (FTC) Act, to create a regulatory agency—headed by a five-person commission—to promote "constructive" rather than "destructive" competition.[49]
- A progressive income tax, to ensure a more equal distribution of wealth in the nation.
- The breaking of the system of tariffs that had long protected America's monopolists from foreign competition.
- The first breakup of AT&T, in which the government forced the telephone corporation to spin off the Western Union telegraph network, to stop all acquisitions unless approved by the Justice Department, to connect its network to smaller telephone companies, and to charge reasonable prices.[50]

Under Roosevelt and Taft, antitrust enforcement had been ad hoc, sporadic, hypocritical, discriminatory, dangerous. The Wilson administration now carefully updated America's whole antimonopoly system to promote rule of law, and distribution of power and opportunity, for a twentieth-century industrial era that looked fantastically different from the world of the founders. In place of the plow, stagecoach, and sailing ship, the new economy was a place of vast factories filled with immense machines, nation-spanning communications and transportation networks, electric power, chain stores, automobiles, and even airplanes.

Exactly as at the founding, and in close echo of Senator Sherman's speech, Wilson, Brandeis, and their allies in Congress organized their thinking around a vision of the citizen as an individual seeking liberty to bring properties to market. Further, as Brandeis himself made clear, they were fully aware they were not simply making a smart new political economy but were also shaping the nature of American democracy itself and designing citizens capable of protecting that democracy.

"Democracy," Brandeis wrote in a 1922 letter, "substitutes self restraint for external restraint . . . It demands continuous sacrifice by the individual and more exigent obedience to moral laws than any other form of government. Success in any democratic undertaking must proceed from the individual. It is possible only where the process of perfecting the individual is pursued." In words that could have come from Madison, Brandeis said, "always and everywhere, the intellectual, moral, and spiritual development of . . . the individual is both a necessary means and the end sought."[51]

The new administration's approach was also highly pragmatic. Indeed, despite their repeated emphasis on the danger of size, and despite being often derided as backward looking and naïve, from the first Wilson, Brandeis, and their allies set out to ensure that the American people could benefit from nation-spanning transportation and communications networks, mass manufacture, and automation. To strike the right balance between their fear of bigness and their understanding that some industrial activities must be big, they carefully divided the political economy into three distinct realms, then adapted their competition philosophy to each particular set of human activities.

First, in the case of networked industries like railroads, telephones, and electricity, the democratic republicans of the early twentieth century aimed to treat these services as essential to the public. The goal was not to make them smaller but rather to make them neutral, in the sense that these intermediaries, with great potential power over the lives and businesses of others, had to provide the same pricing and terms of service to all comers. The intellectual and political challenge here was in fact relatively easy, given the lessons from the success of the Interstate Commerce Act and the fact that many of that act's original problems had been fixed by the Mann-Elkins Act of 1910.[52] (Numerous American communities took a far more direct approach to ensuring the widespread, affordable, and non-discriminatory provision of such services, which was—along the model of the original U.S. Postal Service—to own them directly.)

Second, and more challenging, these reformers of the industrial age needed to develop a formula for enterprises engaged in the art of applying science to mass production, for instance, making chemicals and metals or automobiles and tractors. In such instances, enforcers took a much more liberal approach to vertical integration, not wanting to get in the way of the engineers—in enterprises such as Ford and General Electric—who were experimenting constantly with different methods of construction and assembly.

In the industrial realm, the debate over bigness was far more engaged and complex. By this time, J. P. Morgan had largely rolled up the American steel industry into the vast and sprawling U.S. steel, based on the idea that such rationalization was more efficient. By contrast, in 1912, Brandeis had become fascinated with a study comparing the German steel industry, which was organized into a partial cartel, to the American industry. The study detailed how, even though the German government allowed companies to coordinate pricing and output levels in primary steel, the resulting competition in "specialty production" delivered far higher quality, lower prices, and more innovation than the American model.[53]

One result of such thinking, over the years to come, was a policy that aimed simply to ensure that at least four firms engaged in every industrial activity. Another result, beginning in the late 1930s, was a policy of forcing large industrial firms to license their patents for free to any comer.[54]

Third, in sectors of the economy that did not require high degrees of scientific expertise—such as farming, retail, and banking—the aim was to promote as wide a distribution of power and opportunity as possible, hence as wide a distribution of property, not only in the form of land but in the form of citizen-sized independent businesses. The new administration therefore adopted policies that promoted local control over retail, over livestock and grain markets, and over banking, essentially in the spirit of the Northwest Ordinance with its citizen-sized properties. In almost all such lines of business, the aim was to prohibit vertical integration and predatory pricing.[55]

In each of these three approaches, the Wilson administration aimed to set simple, easy-to-understand, bright-line rules to ensure citizens, businesses, enforcers, and the courts understood what was legal and what not. And in industries undergoing rapid technological change, it had empowered the FTC to carefully track industrial structures, conduct detailed research, and, when necessary, propose new rules.

One way to understand just how fully Wilson and Brandeis aimed to update the principles of the founding for the twentieth century is to look at their attitude toward the nature of the business corporation itself. Hearkening directly to the earliest days of the Republic, they held that the large industrial corporation was essentially public in nature and must be made ultimately to serve the public. In a statement published during his first year in office, Wilson wrote, "A modern . . . corporation cannot in any proper sense be said to base its rights and powers upon the principles of private property. Its powers are wholly derived from legislation. It possesses them for the convenience of business at the sufferance of the public."[56]

If there was a single, paramount aim of their entire system, it was to once and for all break the power of Hamilton's system, the power of concentrated capital, the power of Wall Street, the power of money, over the lives of individual citizens and businesses and over the nation as a whole. Wilson and Brandeis understood that it was the corporation that allowed the financier to reach into the world to extract, exploit, divert, and suppress. Stopping this required not only regulation of Wall Street but the use of antimonopoly law to disrupt the ability of the capitalist to engineer corporate monopolies powerful enough to manipulate main street.

In *The Promise of American Life*, Herbert Croly belittled Madison and Jefferson and their followers for failing to develop the tools necessary to protect their original vision of America. The founders' system of liberty, Croly wrote, "has failed because it did not bring with it any machinery adequate even to its own insipid and barren purposes."[57] Wilson and Brandeis now answered Croly's challenge by building both federal and state-level institutions strong enough and sophisticated enough to do just that. Theirs was also a system flexible enough—thanks to the mission and structure of the FTC—to adjust to suddenly changing circumstance and technology.[58]

In 1916, Wilson appointed Brandeis to the Supreme Court, ensuring that one of the authors of their revolution would be able to help protect it in the years to come. He did so over a set of vicious objections based mainly on the fact that Brandeis was Jewish.

When Franklin Roosevelt and the New Dealers began their work in the 1930s, they built upon the intellectual and institutional base established during the New Freedom. Indeed, over the course of the twentieth century, it was upon this intellectual and institutional base—this second System of Liberty—that the American people would complete the rebuilding of something like real democracy.

A COMMUNITY OF UNIONS, COOPERATIVES, AND ASSOCIATIONS

President Wilson signed the Clayton Antitrust Act into law on October 5, 1914. The following day, he sent the pen he had used to Samuel Gompers, head of the American Federation of Labor, the largest alliance of unions in the nation. Twelve days later, Wilson wrote that "justice has been done to the laborer." He then connected this directly to the antimonopoly provisions of the Act, saying the outcome was but "the natural and inevitable corollary of a law whose object is individual freedom and initiative as against any kind of private domination."[59]

It may seem strange that an antitrust law would be of such immediate concern to a labor leader and to working people. Yet going back to the founding, American common law had viewed the union of the worker in pretty much the same light as the business corporation. In much the way the corporation joined the money capital of many investors, this thinking went, the union joined the labor capital of many workers. This thinking, in short, was based on a vision of work itself as a type of property.

The idea that monopoly was a threat to working people was, in fact, very much on Senator Sherman's mind as he drafted and defended his bill in 1890. Monopoly, he said, "commands the price of labor without fear of strikes, for in its field it allows no competition."[60] Yet part of the tragedy of the original Sherman Antitrust Act is that, in addition to failing to rein in corporate monopolists, for more than a decade it ended up providing those same corporate monopolists with a perfect tool to break strikes by workers and efforts by farmers to form cooperatives. The monopolists used the language in the act prohibiting "restraints of trade" to claim that unions and cooperatives—in essence—were illegal cartels.[61]

To stop this gross abuse of the law, the Wilson administration and Congress inserted language into Section 6 of the Clayton Antitrust Act. Nothing "in the antitrust laws," this section read, "shall be construed to forbid the existence of labor, agricultural, and horticultural organizations, instituted for the purposes of mutual help." Nor "shall such organizations, or the members thereof, be held or construed to be illegal combinations or conspiracies in restraint of trade."

In Section 20 of the Clayton Antitrust Act, they added, "no such restraining order or injunction shall prohibit any person or persons whether single or in concert, from terminating any relation of employment, or from ceasing to perform any work or labor, or from recommending, advising, or persuading others by peaceful means to do so."

In other words, the Clayton Antitrust Act—in addition to greatly strengthening U.S. federal law against monopoly—also made it unequivocally clear that citizens have a right to form labor unions and farmer cooperatives, to strike, and to encourage others to strike. In his autobiography, Gompers would later write that "Sections 6 and 20 [of the Clayton Act] constitute the charter of industrial freedom or, as I called it, 'Labor's Magna Charta.'"[62]

Once again, Wilson and Brandeis were simply aiming to restore a principle that traced to the early days of the Republic. In this case, it was the liberty to join unions and similar groups. Much like America's farmers, America's workers had established precedents for peaceful democratic organizing that served to inspire people around the world and indeed deeply influenced the thinking even of Karl Marx and Friedrich Engels.[63]

These precedents included the General Trades Union, which launched the first nationwide labor organization in 1834. It included, that same year, the first election of a labor leader—New York's Ely Moore—to Congress. It included President Van Buren's March 1840 executive order declaring that no person should work more than ten hours on a federal project.[64] It included a March 1842 ruling by the Massachusetts Supreme Court that labor unions could not be charged with criminal conspiracy for forming closed shops or strikes. "We cannot perceive," Chief Justice Lemuel Shaw wrote then, "that it is criminal for men to agree together to exercise their own acknowledged rights."[65] It included President Grant's 1869 proclamation establishing an eight-hour day for all laborers, workmen, and mechanics employed by the government.

Throughout these years, America's working people—like America's farmers and shopkeepers—were staunch enemies of monopoly, which they saw as a threat to their skills and their properties. As the labor leader Terence Powderly said in 1886, "He is a true Knight of Labor who with one hand clutches anarchy by the throat, and with the other strangles monopoly."[66]

The Wilson administration during these years also took more positive actions to make it easier for farmers to create cooperatives. This included the 1916 Federal Farm Loan Act. This act promoted the creation of locally organized and owned "land banks" to provide credit to farmers who otherwise found it hard to secure loans. In the words of Wilson, this put farmers "upon an equality with all others who have genuine assets."[67] It also included taking the first steps to frame and pass what is now known as the Capper-Volstead Act, which formalized farmers' rights to form cooperatives for both the sale of their products and the purchase of supplies. And it included the first federal efforts to regulate markets for wheat and other grains, cotton, and commodity market futures in ways designed to stabilize the income of farmers.[68]

From today's perspective, perhaps most surprising was the third area in which Wilson and Brandeis promoted liberty to associate. In addition to advancing that liberty for working people and farmers, they worked with Congress to extend this liberty also to the independent business owner and the trained professional. The idea here was that these individuals should be allowed to join together in trade associations, professional associations, and other organizations that would enable them to identify common problems and threats, as long as they did not engage in any outright cartelization.

Brandeis was especially fascinated with the promise of such associations of independent entrepreneurs. As the historians Gerald Berk and Laura Phillips Sawyer have detailed, Brandeis believed that independent businesspeople should be free to discuss the nature of their work with one another and to set standards, just like doctors and lawyers. Such an approach, he believed, would enable these businesses to focus more on improving products and processes rather than simply on trying to cut prices and wages.[69]

The vision of American capitalism the Wilson administration and Congress put into place just before the First World War could not be more clear. On one hand, limit absolutely the ability of bankers, financiers, and the superwealthy to combine their own capital and power. On the other, make it as easy as possible for working people, farmers, independent business owners, and professionals to cooperate with one another, not only to protect their rights and interests but to improve their products and services.

Here again we see, as in the earliest days of the Republic, a vision of competition as a form of cooperation, a way to forge a community of citizens based not on some utopian vision of human nature but on an honest appraisal of human character. It was a vision that understood that humans would always seek foremost their own personal advantage, leavened by the belief that such rivalry could be shaped to promote a better society for everyone.

A "PSYCHOLOGICAL BIRD" IN EVERY POT

In the 1912 presidential campaign, W. E. B. Du Bois endorsed Woodrow Wilson and praised the New Freedom. Since the Civil War and Reconstruction, this marked the first time that an important

African American leader had broken with the Republican Party come election time. And Du Bois was someone important. A historian and civil rights activist born in Massachusetts just after the Civil War, in 1909 Du Bois had helped to found the National Association for the Advancement of Colored People (NAACP), where he would write and edit the journal *The Crisis* for the next 20 years. Though often today remembered for his late-career support for democratic Marxism, Du Bois in the early decades of the twentieth century was perhaps the single greatest prophet of American liberty, playing a role in many respects as important as that of Brandeis.

Du Bois's endorsement was not based on any particular love for Wilson or trust in the man or his administration. As Du Bois was fully aware, Wilson's home state of Virginia was still segregated, and the college over which Wilson had presided, Princeton, was the only Ivy League school that did not admit blacks.[70] Yet Du Bois's endorsement played a major role in some 100,000 African Americans deciding to vote for the nominee put forth by a party that had once been led by John C. Calhoun and Jefferson Davis.[71]

It was a hard decision made in hard times. Over the previous few years Teddy Roosevelt and the plutocrats had smashed the last remnants of the Republican Party of Lincoln and Stevens to chase the votes of white southern men. True, Roosevelt had shocked the nation by inviting the famous educator Booker T. Washington to dinner in 1901. But as soon as Roosevelt secured a second term in 1904, he shut and bolted the door. By the end of his time in office, Roosevelt had appointed fewer blacks than any of his predecessors, including the Democrat Grover Cleveland.[72] And Roosevelt's successor, Taft, had largely followed the same course.[73]

The African American rebellion against Roosevelt and the Republicans was not based merely on broken promises. Roosevelt had taken to outright disparagement of blacks as a "backward race" that was "altogether inferior to the whites."[74] Perhaps most outrageously, Roosevelt had used a February 1905 speech in honor of Abraham Lincoln to appeal for "white racial purity."[75]

If any African Americans had any doubt about Roosevelt's true character, he disabused them through his treatment of the all-black First Battalion of the 25th Infantry Regiment of the U.S. Army, after citizens in Brownsville, Texas, in 1906 charged that men in the unit had shot a bartender to death. The battalion was one of the most decorated in the U.S. military, with a total of six Medal of Honor winners in battles ranging from Cuba to the Philippines. This unit had even reinforced Roosevelt's own Rough Riders at a "desperate moment" in his charge up San Juan Hill.

Although the white citizens of Brownsville could offer no proof of their charges, Roosevelt discharged 167 of the 170 men in the battalion without honor, cutting off pensions even to men with 25 years of service.

It didn't take long, however, for Du Bois and other black leaders to discover that Wilson was in certain respects even worse than Roosevelt. Not only did Wilson refuse to appoint black ambassadors to Santo Domingo and Haiti, positions long reserved for African Americans, but he allowed Treasury Secretary William McAdoo and Postmaster General Albert Burleson to segregate their departments of government. In Georgia, the collector of internal revenue simply fired all black employees, saying, "There are no government positions for Negroes in the South. A Negro's place is in the corn field."[76]

The disillusionment came to a head in a meeting between Wilson and African Americans in the White House in 1914. William Monroe Trotter, a black newspaper publisher and activist who like Du Bois had endorsed Wilson in 1912, at one point asked, "Have you a 'New Freedom' for white Americans and a new slavery for your Afro-American fellow citizens? God forbid!"[77]

Yet that was exactly what was happening. The New Freedom, this new American democracy, was in fact designed mainly for white Americans. To be sure, to some extent the New Freedom did provide some new opportunities for African Americans; after all, the same antimonopoly policies that protected white businesses and farms helped to protect African American businesses and farms.[78] But this was a mere byproduct of laws designed for others, what we might call trickle-down liberty.

Jim Crow has often been described as mainly a political tool of the powerful to prevent working people of different races and cultures from locking arms with one another. And to be sure, race has been used many times to tear white from black, and to suppress the votes of both African Americans and poor whites.

Martin Luther King Jr., just after the Selma march in 1965, retold the well-known story of one such time, in the early days of the populist movement, when in many parts of the South whites and blacks had marched side by side to, in King's words, "drive the Bourbon interests from the command posts of political power."

The Bourbon interests answered this challenge, King said, by preaching race hatred. "To meet this threat, the southern aristocracy began immediately to engineer this development of a segregated society," he explained. "If it may be said of the slavery era that the white man took the world and gave the Negro Jesus, then it may be said of the Reconstruction era that the southern aristocracy took the world and gave the poor white man Jim Crow. He gave him Jim Crow. And when his wrinkled stomach cried out for the food that his empty pockets could not provide, he ate Jim Crow, a psychological bird that told him that no matter how bad off he was, at least he was a white man, better than the black man."[79]

King's story of how the white aristocracy used Jim Crow to divide white from black is not wrong in most fundamentals. But in a history of a democracy, and with citizens as well educated in the nature of power as those of the United States, it is important not to discount the conscious efforts by many white men to actively repress the black man and exclude him from citizenship without any help from the masters themselves.

Yes, time and again, the masters have used race to divide. And yes, time and again, great numbers of poor and middle-class whites embraced promises of favored treatment in exchange for beating their quondam allies. Yet we also see the active and intentional creation and enforcement, by middle- and working-class white men especially, of race-based unions and race-based business cartels, designed simultaneously to take wealth and power from those above them and to carefully prevent citizens from other races and cultures, especially African Americans, from sharing in any bounty that might result.

We can trace such race-based organizing to long before the Civil War itself, not least to a series of riots in the 1830s in Philadelphia, Washington, Baltimore, New York, and elsewhere that aimed to keep free African Americans out of certain skilled jobs. One of the most infamous examples of this attitude is Andrew Johnson, the Tennessee haberdasher who rose to the presidency upon the assassination of Lincoln. From the earliest days of Reconstruction Johnson worked hard to ensure that any land, jobs, or schooling that the federal government might distribute or subsidize would go only to poor white men, and never to any freed black man.[80]

To the extent the 1912 election confirmed anything about American racism, it was that both national parties had fully embraced Jim Crow. Which in turn made it that much easier for organizations like Samuel Gompers's AFL to formally allow any of their member unions to exclude African Americans for any reason whatsoever.[81] (The American racism of these years, as Daniel Okrent details in *The Guarded Gate*, also helped to shape attitudes in Europe, and especially Germany, in the period leading up to the Nazi takeover.[82])

Du Bois himself, in 1917, as President Wilson prepared to take America to war in Europe, made one last demand to extend the promise of the New Freedom to the African American man and woman. In an essay in his magazine *The Crisis*, in emulation of Frederick Douglass's similar demand of Lincoln more than 50 years earlier, he wrote:

> Let us enter this war for Liberty with clean hands. May no blood-smeared garments bind our feet when we rise to make the world safe for Democracy . . . We cannot lynch 2,867 untried black men and women in thirty-one years and pose successfully as leaders of

civilization. Rather let us bow our shamed heads and in sack cloth and ashes declare that when in awful war we raise our weapons against the enemies of mankind, so, too, and in that same hour here at home we raise our hands to Heaven and pledge our sacred honor to make our own America a real land of the free:

To stop lynching and mob violence.

To stop disfranchisement for race and sex.

To abolish Jim Crow cars.

To resist the attempt to establish an American ghetto.

To stop race discrimination in Trade Unions, in Civil Service, in places of public accommodation, and in the Public School.

To secure Justice for all men in the courts.

To insist that individual desert and ability shall be the test of real American manhood and not adventitious differences of race or color or descent.

Awake! Put on thy strength, America—put on thy beautiful robes. Become not a bye word and jest among the nations by the hypocrisy of your word and contradiction of your deeds.[83]

Yet the pleas of Du Bois and the rest of America's black-skinned half citizens failed. America's race crisis, if anything, became even worse after the war, as the nation witnessed some of the most deadly race riots in history, including in downtown Washington, as white citizens sought to shove America's new black soldier citizens back to the end of the line and down into the boiler rooms and muck rooms of the capital. The federal government itself, as Richard Rothstein, Ira Katznelson, and others have detailed, became an active enforcer of Jim Crow in farming, services, and housing, from the New Deal well into the 1960s. Even as American soldiers fought to shatter the religious ghettos of Europe, progressive social "engineers" like Rex Tugwell were engineering racial ghettos in every city in America and driving black farmers off their land.[84] If anything, "redlining" of black neighborhoods by the federal government amounted to a form of institutionalized monopolization of housing for the exclusive use of whites.[85]

The New Freedom broke the back of the autocracy of the financier and corporate master and cleared the way for the restoration of the American System of Liberty. But Wilson left America with a democracy with hard borders or, rather, with a hard caste system based mainly on the color of one's skin. In short, he left it not yet truly a democracy at all.[86]

THE FIRST PAGE— REDEEMED AT LAST?

NO OVERHEAD CONTROL

In May 1935, Louis Brandeis spoke some of his most famous words, not in testimony to Congress or in a Court opinion, but rather in a personal message to Franklin Roosevelt. A unanimous Supreme Court had just declared a key program of the early New Deal unconstitutional.[1] Meeting afterward with one of the president's aides, Brandeis wanted to make sure Roosevelt fully understood the decision.

"This is the end of this business of centralization," Brandeis said. "I want you to go back and tell the President that we're not going to let this government centralize everything. It's come to an end. As for your young men, you call them together and tell them to get out of Washington—tell them to go home, back to the states. That is where they must do their work."[2]

What so enraged Brandeis was the National Industrial Recovery Act (NIRA). Entering the White House at the worst period of the Great Depression, Roosevelt had carried into office an unwieldy alliance. This included many officials who viewed the world through the lens of Wilson and Brandeis and who believed the main challenge was to break any concentration of private or public power that threatened liberty and democracy. It also included a number of officials who, in the tradition of Theodore Roosevelt and Herbert Croly, promoted what at the time was often called "overhead control" of the economy.[3] This second group was led by a Columbia University economist named Rexford Tugwell, a strong advocate of using the state to radically restructure social and economic relations. Indeed, Tugwell had traveled to the Soviet Union in 1927 in large part to study the Communist regime's political economy.

As one leading historian of the New Deal, Arthur Schlesinger Jr., later wrote, the result was a "struggle between the social planners, who thought in terms of an organic economy and a managed society; and the neo-Brandeisians, who thought in terms of the decentralization of decision and the revitalization of choice."[4]

What the planners had come up with in the NIRA was a scheme for direct government control over pricing, wages, and production levels for almost every industry in America. When Brandeis promoted trade associations in the 1910s and 1920s, his vision was that they be governed by their members. The NIRA planners' version, by contrast, called for top-down direction of these businesses through government-run cartels, whose diktats would be enforced by fines and other punishments. Their immediate goal, the planners said, was to engineer commercial interactions in ways that would somehow create inflation and thereby drive the economy out of depression. In the specific case that the Supreme Court had ruled on, *A.L.A. Schechter Poultry Corp. v. United States*, the federal government had brought a long list of charges against a small New York company for how it slaughtered and sold chickens and treated its employees. The rules that Schechter had allegedly violated had been published as the Live Poultry Code of the NIRA.

The Court found that the president did not have authority to establish such rules in the first place, and that even if he did, Schechter was simply too small and too local for any such federal rules to apply. The NIRA as a whole thus represented a dangerous centralization of power in the federal government. Not only was the Court's decision unanimous, but Brandeis—whom Roosevelt worshipped—was adamant that the NIRA betrayed the vision of political economics

Wilson and he had promoted in the New Freedom. And, for that matter, what the founders had established in the earliest days of the Republic.

Of all the myths in American history, none is stronger than that the New Deal was mainly a project to impose top-down, command-and-control systems on American society. To be sure, the American people did ask the federal government to assume new responsibilities, such as providing old-age insurance and—for a short period of time—temporary jobs for unemployed men. (Roosevelt's predecessor, the Republican Herbert Hoover, had experimented with similar programs, albeit implemented at the state level.)

In fact, *Schechter* marked the end of almost any real effort by the administration to concentrate economic power or control. From this point on, Roosevelt directed the New Deal to reinforce, expand, and complete the work that Wilson and Brandeis had begun in 1912, hence what the populists had begun in the 1890s. The true history of the New Deal, in other words, is of the *distribution* of power, opportunity, and property, on a plan almost entirely in keeping with the principles of the New Freedom and the founding. As in the first days of the Republic, citizens had no qualms about using government to regulate corporations, banks, financial and commodity markets, even land use. But they did so in ways designed to promote the liberty of the individual and the independence of the local community.

Tugwell, in the mid-1950s, still bitter over his failure, took a last swipe at his opponents. Roosevelt, he wrote, had rejected "modernism" in favor of an "atomism" based on the antique idea that "make them all little and all would be safe."[5] Yet it would be a mistake to see Brandeis's stance, or Roosevelt's, as in any way shaped by a romantic view of some better past. It was based, instead, on a highly realistic appraisal of human nature, directly in the tradition of James Madison. Brandeis and his allies, just as in their 1912 fight against Teddy Roosevelt's corporatism, saw the combination of private monopoly and public power as a direct threat to democracy. As Schlesinger put it, the populists believed that it was Tugwell and his allies who were "hopelessly naïve."[6]

Once again, the American System of Liberty had been put to the test, and once again the American people withstood the challenge of concentrated power. Even at this most desperate moment in the worst economic crisis in the nation's history, citizens retained full faith in the American System of Liberty, with its checks and balances and careful distribution of power. And for 50 years to come, right through a series of new challenges—posed by a cataclysmic Second World War, the nuclear threats of the Cold War, and a racial and social crisis at home—the foundations would hold.

THE TRUE NEW DEAL

Franklin Roosevelt is often described as a pragmatist, a leader who did not so much wield an ideology as simply exhibit a willingness to test one idea after another until something worked. And certainly, compared to Woodrow Wilson—who published five scholarly books, including major studies of constitutional government—Roosevelt did not fit the mold of a traditional intellectual.

Unlike Wilson, however, Roosevelt had been extensively schooled in real-world power and policy. This included an intimate knowledge of American finance and American financiers. Much of this was from personal experience. Roosevelt could trace his mother's family to the *Mayflower*, and his father's to 1650s New Amsterdam, and the great wealth he inherited came from banking, shipping, sugar growing, Manhattan real estate, and trade with China.[7]

Roosevelt's knowledge also came—after he opted not to go into any of the family businesses or his own original plan to work in admiralty law—from extensive public service both in the federal government and in New York state politics. He served as assistant secretary of the Navy through the entire Wilson administration, overseeing a vast workforce and complex contracting procedures during the First World War. Then as governor of New York he ran America's largest and most complex state government in the days and months immediately after the devastating crash of 1929.

To the extent Roosevelt had developed a practical vision of political economics by the time he entered the White House, it was the traditional democratic republican belief that banks and corporations exist ultimately to serve the public interest.

Indeed, Roosevelt had already proved highly adept at bending the actions of corporate executives to the will of the people. He did so most dramatically in 1919 when, in order to develop a modern radio system for the U.S. Navy, he forced General Electric, Westinghouse, and AT&T to combine their radio patents with those of the American Marconi Corporation in a new enterprise known as the Radio Corporation of America, or RCA.[8] During his time in Washington, Roosevelt was also exposed to many other experiments in the use of the federal government to harness and neutralize the power of business without destroying all the incentives that led private people to invest money in a particular venture. This included the wartime nationalization of America's railways and telephone system and the use of the War Industries Board to force businesses to modernize and expand their factories and sometimes to coordinate their activities with one another.[9] Later, in Albany, it included a close education in the ways that utility monopolies price electricity and restrict the development of new generation and distribution systems.[10]

While in Washington, Roosevelt also came to know many of the main actors in both the New Freedom and the New Nationalism camps.[11] In part, this was due to the fact that Wilson himself, during the 1916 election, had welcomed many of the veterans of Theodore Roosevelt's Bull Moose Progressive campaign of 1912, with its focus on centralization of the political economy, into the Democratic Party. Even though many retained their centralizing instincts, without the autocratic and self-admiring Teddy Roosevelt riling them up, these intellectuals seemed far less dangerous to the Republic.

By 1933 Franklin Roosevelt was also intimately familiar with the practical uses of populism. This was true of the intoxicating political qualities of the 190-proof "soak-the-rich" language of men like Louisiana governor Huey Long. And it was true of the more sober structural policies of Wright Patman, a congressman from rural Texas who in addition to fighting for the pensions of soldiers and impeaching Herbert Hoover's treasury secretary Andrew Mellon helped to draft some of the more complicated antitrust legislation in American history (as we will discuss shortly).

When Roosevelt entered the White House in 1933 he brought both groups in tow, along with a reputation for giving both a lot of rope. Indeed, even as Roosevelt was signing off on what would become the NIRA, he was also siding very dramatically with the populists on how to deal directly with the money power itself.

We see this perhaps most dramatically in the very first days of his presidency. The Hoover administration had recently bailed out many bigger banks, and the office that Hoover had created to oversee that task—the Reconstruction Finance Corporation (RFC)—now proposed the permanent closure of more than 2,000 smaller banks that remained shuttered, mostly in rural areas. Jesse Jones, the Texas banker whom Roosevelt had appointed to run the RFC, said it would be more "efficient" to allow "larger bank chains with more capital to establish branches in their place."[12]

Roosevelt, however, forced Jones to develop a plan to bail these smaller banks out as well.[13] And this model almost immediately became a main part of the New Deal. In the years to come, even at the height of the NIRA's power, the RFC would provide emergency loans to small credit unions, building and loan associations, industrial banks, land banks, farm cooperatives, and insurance companies.[14]

Early on, Roosevelt made other high-profile decisions to expand and federalize control over certain activities, such as by creating the Civilian Conservation Corps and the Civil Works Administration to improve on Hoover's work programs. But the list of actions we normally associate with the New Deal is made up mainly of efforts to carry the basic principles of the New Freedom into specific sectors of the American political economy. All were passed in tandem with a Democratic Congress generally loath to embrace any idea from the command-and-control wing of the administration. Most used the power of the federal government to structure markets in ways that helped the independent businessperson and farmer rather than the speculator and financier, and generally in ways that shifted power away from Washington to regulators in the state capital and the town hall.

Their resolutions include the Glass-Steagall Act to separate investment banking from commercial banking, the Securities Act of 1933 and the Securities Exchange Act of 1934 to govern trade in stocks, and the Commodity Exchange Act of 1936 to govern trade in agricultural futures. They include the Public Utility Holding Company Act of 1935, which broke up the entire electrical industry of the United States along state lines, and the Rural Electrification Act of 1936, which provided loans to the new cooperatives now able to compete. They include the Agricultural Adjustment Act of 1933, which introduced a system of supply management into farming and much stronger enforcement of antitrust law against slaughterhouse corporations and grain traders.[15] And they include the Motor Carrier Act of 1935 and Civil Aeronautics Act of 1938 to promote constructive competition in the trucking and airline industries. They include the Communications Act of 1934 to rein in the power of private broadcasters and to promote locally controlled and locally oriented news and information. And they include the National Housing Act of 1933, with its aim to protect the mortgage of the independent homeowner. They also include the National Labor Relations Act of 1935 to make it easier for workers to form unions and to protect their skills and to win better pay and benefits.

Perhaps most tellingly, they include increasing the number of antitrust lawyers at the Justice Department from 60 to more than 600.[16]

Importantly, the list also includes the adoption of more inflationist monetary and fiscal policies, such as those widely associated with the famous British economist John Maynard Keynes, who strongly urged governments to spend their way out of the Depression. "The second New Deal," Arthur Schlesinger Jr. later wrote, "was eventually a coalition between lawyers in the school of Brandeis and economists in the school of Keynes."[17]

Tugwell, looking back from the 1950s, believed Roosevelt had decided to follow the New Freedom model of Wilson and Brandeis even before the Democratic convention in the summer of 1932.[18]

If any doubts lingered in Roosevelt's mind about the wisdom of the New Freedom approach, the *Schechter* decision resolved them and unleashed his inner populist.[19] In his July 1936 acceptance speech at the Democratic National Convention in Philadelphia, the president eagerly and expertly wielded the old American language of liberty. "The privileged princes of these new economic dynasties, thirsting for power, reached out for control over Government itself," he said. "They created a new despotism and wrapped it in the robes of legal sanction. In its service new mercenaries sought to regiment the people, their labor, and their property. And as a result the average man once more confronts the problem that faced the Minute Man."

By mid-October of 1936, Roosevelt was speaking lines straight from the pages of Wilson and Brandeis. This "concentration of economic power in all-embracing corporations does not represent private enterprise as we Americans cherish it and propose to foster it. On the contrary, it represents private enterprise which has become a kind of private government, a power unto itself—a regimentation of other people's lives . . . The struggle against private monopoly is a struggle for, and not against, American business. It is a struggle to preserve individual enterprise and economic freedom."[20]

Thus did Roosevelt's New Dealers work with Congress to complete the New Freedom of Wilson and Brandeis. Or rather, thus did the American people force the Roosevelt administration to complete their efforts to restore the American System of Liberty, albeit carefully updated to account for the fantastic new technologies of the late nineteenth and early twentieth centuries.

THE PRICING OF LIBERTY

Antimonopoly law is not merely about preventing mergers or breaking big companies into smaller pieces. It is also, as the Interstate Commerce Act demonstrates, a matter of setting clear rules on whether one company can charge other companies different prices for the same service. And it is about determining who along a chain of commerce has the right to price a good or service.

When Franklin Roosevelt took office, America's pricing laws were in chaos. This was due to a series of highly contradictory decisions by the Supreme Court. In the first, from 1911, a drug manufacturer named Dr. Miles sued a retailer named John D. Park & Sons for violating a sales contract that required the drug to be sold at a particular price. In deciding against Dr. Miles, the Court shifted much of the pricing decision away from the actual maker of the good or provider of the service to the retailers, traders, wholesalers, and other middlemen who handled or represented the good or service on its way to market.[21]

The command-and-control pricing policies of the NIRA had only complicated the debate. Whereas in their *Dr. Miles* decision the justices had accepted the argument that a prime goal of competition policy should be to drive prices down, the New Dealers, as we have seen, in the years before their discovery of Keynesian economics, aimed to use NIRA to drive prices up.

To the extent there was clarity anywhere on pricing, it was the Interstate Commerce Act's outright prohibition against price discrimination. In 1910 Congress had fortified this most fundamental of antimonopoly regimes by passing the Mann-Elkins Act, which formally extended common carrier rules to the telegraph, telephone, wireless industries, and pipelines.

But the reach of the Interstate Commerce Act (ICA) was limited, and first-degree discrimination in pricing and terms remained a big problem within the rest of the political economy. Although the railroads and other network monopolists covered by the ICA could not engage in such practices, many other powerful intermediaries—such as retailers, distributors, and wholesalers—still could. And even though many of these corporations were quite small compared to the great national monopolists, they could be just as vital to the lives of individuals and businesses in a particular community. Similarly, powerful manufacturers were also free to use first-degree price discrimination to manipulate smaller retailers and other providers of services.

One of the most important outcomes of the New Deal years would be to clarify U.S. pricing policy and to restore the traditional requirement that middlemen charge every seller who relies on their services, no matter how small or powerless, the same price in exchange for the same service. A closely related outcome was to force big manufacturers to treat all retailers—no matter how small—the same and not to use price discrimination to buttress their power and control within a market. In doing so, citizens essentially restored the open market structures established in the first years of the nation.

As we have seen, the citizens who first structured the American System of Liberty spent almost all their time thinking about how to protect individual liberty and democracy, not how to drive prices lower. Their basic thinking on pricing was essentially the same as that of Adam Smith, who held that if you structure markets in ways that prevent concentration of power, by either a producer or a trading company, the competition that would result would take care of pricing all by itself.

In a famous passage in *The Wealth of Nations*, Smith had written: "The market price of every particular commodity is regulated by the proportion between the quantity which is actually brought to the market, and the demand of those who are willing to pay the natural price of the commodity, or the whole value of the rent, labour, and profit, which must be paid to bring it thither."

This price, Smith went on, is "not always the lowest at which a dealer may sometimes sell his goods, it is the lowest at which he is likely to sell them for any considerable time; at least where there is perfect liberty, or where he may change his trade as often as he pleases."[22]

This same line of thinking clearly guided Senator John Sherman, who believed that casting all monopolists from the marketplaces would restore this basic interaction between supply and demand. In a Senate resolution, Sherman wrote that his antitrust law "will tend to preserve freedom of trade and production, the natural competition of increasing production, [and] the lowering of prices by such competition."[23]

Then in his speech defending his bill, Sherman made clear he strongly opposed the idea that price should ever be the result of "dictates" of "terms" by one company to another. And he bluntly rejected the argument that monopoly led to efficiencies that lowered prices. "It is sometimes said of these combinations that they reduce prices to the consumer by better methods of production, but all experience shows that this saving of cost goes to the pockets of the producer. The price . . . depends upon the supply, which can be reduced at pleasure by the combination."[24]

During these same years, Americans also developed a third way of preventing middlemen from exercising arbitrary power over the companies and people who actually grow and make the goods and services we use. In addition to the more traditional tactics of simply preventing concentration where possible and imposing common carrier laws where concentration was more or less "natural," the new rules aimed to prevent any middleman from interfering in the act of pricing that product, so as to leave the job of setting prices to the producer of that product. Such rules are often referred to as resale price maintenance, or RPM, and we can trace them, and court decisions defending such practices, to the middle of the nineteenth century.[25]

In combination with common carrier rules on middlemen, such pricing laws—by carefully placing the decision on how to price a product squarely in the hands of the creator and manufacturer of the good—helped to achieve six fundamental aims, each of which buttressed the overall goal of preventing concentration of power and control. These were to:

- **Ensure that the competitive market system functions across the entire nation**. When the producers of a good control the pricing of their own product, everywhere, it means that their competition with rival producers of that good is the same in Arizona as in Pennsylvania, in Florida as in Oregon. The fact that no middleman in any of these places can interfere in that competition ensures that citizens in every corner of the country will have access to the best quality goods, at fair market prices.
- **Greatly reduce the ability of financiers and bankers to use chain stores and other middlemen to concentrate power**, by making it difficult or impossible for them to load up one chain store system with capital and then use that pile of money to undersell their rivals—through predatory pricing—to the point of bankrupting their competitors.
- **Drive information, in the form of prices set by the actual**

producer of a good or service, into the public sphere, so citizens can better identify political or natural threats to the wide supply of a particular good or service and can use their political power to address those threats.

- **Greatly increase the incentive for retailers to provide a greater variety of goods and higher-quality services**, and more information to their customers, and to devise more efficient systems for the handling and distribution of goods. The incentive here is simple. If retailers are barred from competing on price, they must then find other ways to compete.

- **Greatly increase the opportunities for manufacturers and producers—no matter how small—to find an outlet for their goods**, and to test their product and prices in the marketplace. More retailers mean more competition to find and display new products and services.

- **Ensure true price competition between producers of similar goods**. As long as there are no barriers to entering the market, such "inter-brand" competition will result in the lowest possible price at any moment and a perpetual incentive to find ways to further lower the price, exactly in the manner envisioned in *The Wealth of Nations*.[26]

As we will see in chapter seven, one of the main goals of the academics who in the 1970s and 1980s helped to overthrow the American System of Liberty was to recharacterize the nature of predatory pricing. Rather than an aggressive effort by a monopolist to use a pile of capital to buy up or bankrupt all competitors, they contended that predatory pricing by banker-backed corporations promoted the "welfare" of the "consumer."

But the pro-monopoly academics did not invent this line of reasoning about the intersection of capital, pricing, and monopoly power. On the contrary, monopolists more than a century ago used these same basic arguments to sway the majority of the Supreme Court in the *Dr. Miles* case, thereby shattering the whole carefully structured system of using pricing rules to help limit the concentration of power.

The *Dr. Miles* decision did provide Justice Oliver Wendell

Holmes with an opportunity to deliver one of the most eloquent and blunt attacks on price predation and manipulation in U.S. history. "I cannot believe," Holmes wrote in his dissent, "that in the long run the public will profit by this Court permitting knaves to cut reasonable prices for some ulterior purpose of their own, and thus to impair, if not to destroy, the production and sale of articles which it is assumed to be desirable that the public be able to get."[27]

By 1919 the Court had begun to backtrack on *Dr. Miles*. But the string of contradictory decisions left American pricing law riddled with great ambiguities. In response, citizens began to use their state governments to pass their own versions of RPM laws, which they called "fair trade" laws, in the 1920s and 1930s.

Then in 1936, Congress stepped into the debate. It did so first by passing the Robinson-Patman Antitrust Act, which in essence extended common carrier pricing principles to powerful middlemen other than railroads—such as retailers, wholesalers, distributors, and other trading companies. Co-sponsored by Wright Patman and Senate majority leader Joseph T. Robinson of Arkansas, Robinson-Patman is the single most important amendment to antitrust law after the Clayton Antitrust Act.

Its main aim, in the words of Patman, was to prohibit "unfair price discriminations in their various forms."[28]

Congress returned to the subject a year later with the Miller-Tydings Act, which legalized fair trade laws and state-level RPM agreements, after a Supreme Court decision had held that states could not engage in such regulation. The overall effects of this law were mixed at best. As one historian of the era has explained, "sloppy draftsmanship" of the bill meant Miller-Tydings ended up applying only to commerce that took place entirely within a single state and did not affect commerce across state borders.[29] The overall result was to generally prevent manufacturers from using fair trade statutes and to make them "of quite limited usefulness for most manufacturers."[30]

But Robinson-Patman did work exactly as intended. One of the main architects of the overthrow of antitrust law in the late 1970s and early 1980s was the legal scholar Robert Bork. We will look at Bork's thinking and the influence of his book *The Antitrust Paradox* in more depth in later chapters. But for now, it's worth noting that although Bork despised Robinson-Patman more than perhaps any other law, he readily admitted that its effects on American commerce were extensive and profound. "[E]very antitrust practitioner knows," Bork wrote in 1978, "that tens of thousands, perhaps hundreds of thousands, of pricing decisions every year are altered through fear of Robinson-Patman."[31] Bork then went on to lament how the law had taken away all the many discriminatory tools that retailers and manufacturers used to extract cash or kindnesses, political and economic, from companies subject to their power.[32] Which was, of course, exactly the intent of the law's authors.

In short, by the mid-1930s, the American people had—after a poorly reasoned and destructive decision by the Supreme Court— fully restored a pricing system that had proven remarkably effective in protecting both the independent manufacturer and the independent retailer from the predations of the capitalist while also keeping prices as low as possible.

Americans during the Great Depression were, in anything, far more sensitive to high prices than Americans are today. Yet in writing antimonopoly law, citizens did not ever aim specifically to lower prices. Instead, they believed that if they got the market structures and corporate behaviors right, the competition that resulted would ensure that prices would be as low as they reasonably could be.

And thus it proved. Market structures designed to protect the liberties and well-being of every American as a producer, worker, grower, seller, and thinker also forced citizens to compete to bring higher-quality goods and services to market, for ever-lower real prices. The result, over the next half century, was the world's first true consumer paradise, created by the freest makers and creators in the world, for themselves.

Adam Smith would have been very proud.

THE RULE OF 160 RESTORED

Wright Patman's law was more than a way to ensure that bigger companies treated smaller companies fairly. It also marked the culmination of a popular rebellion against chain stores that had been growing for years. In tandem with the more generalized rebellion against concentration in the U.S. political economy, and the more specific efforts to protect the ability of the independent farmer to make a living on a compact plot of land, the new law helped to restore the American community envisioned at the founding, in which business would be conducted mainly by residents of the community itself.

In the 1920s, Woolworths, the A&P, and other chain stores had greatly expanded their hold on American commerce and on the storefronts of America's Main Streets. By the 1930s individuals across the country had come to view these chain stores as direct threats not only to the ability of citizens to compete but the ability of local communities to govern themselves and to ensure that the money of local citizens stayed within the community.[33]

One of the more widely read books of the period was called *The Forgotten Man*. In it, Ernest G. Shinner, who ran a small meat business in Michigan, condemned "the many evils of excessive capitalization and over-centralization" and demanded "a federal law forbidding monopoly in every form."[34]

But with the Republican Party in control of the White House and both houses of Congress through the entire decade, there was little interest in protecting Main Street. If anything, the opposite was true. In 1927, for instance, Congress pushed through the McFadden Act, which made it easier for many banks to create branch systems, and allowed banks to own subsidiaries.[35]

In the years before the New Deal, citizens were sometimes able to use state law to battle the giants. Floridians, for instance, passed a law that taxed chain stores at a higher rate than independent stores, and in January 1933 the Supreme Court held the law to be constitutional.[36] Over the next two years, 15 more states imposed new chain store taxes.[37]

Patman's main political aim with the Robinson-Patman Act was to speed this process along. For a sense of Patman's thinking, consider these words from a speech he gave a few years later. "The small business men and women of America are essential to our democratic way of life," he said. And sounding like a dustbowl Madison, he went on, "They are necessary to our social order. They [are the] bulwark [of] our greatest institutions, around which all civilization is built— the home, the church and the school."[38]

Of the Robinson-Patman Act specifically, Patman wrote that Congress had passed the law "in the belief that it was in the public interest to keep trade and industry divided among as many different parties as possible and to protect the weak against the strong."[39]

Robinson-Patman—and to a lesser extent Miller-Tydings—had a revolutionary effect on America's communities, both small and large. The banning of both predatory pricing and first-degree price discrimination eliminated two of the main tools the big financier had traditionally used to bankrupt and displace the local retailer and trader. By the late 1930s the financiers and their chain store model were in sharp retreat across the country.

For the next half century, the great majority of America's retail businesses—groceries, drugstores, general merchandise stores, gas stations, garages, restaurants, clothing stores, department stores, book stores, electronics stores, stationers, banks, car dealerships, movie theaters, shoe stores, tire stores, hardware stores, music clubs—would be owned and operated by individual proprietors.

So too doctors and dentists, optometrists and opticians, insurance agents, plumbers, and services such as warehousing, distribution, trucking, bottling, printing, ice making, music and book publishing, and tree trimming. So too most light manufacturing and food processing, such as bottlers, bakeries, tool and die shops, lumber mills, paper mills, textile mills, and clothing manufacturers. So too most of the businesses that supplied farmers with inputs such as seeds and machinery or bought their crops, produce, and livestock on the open market.

The magnitude of this revolutionary shift of power to local citizens has been somewhat obscured by the practice of franchising. Under such arrangements, a successful company expands not by direct ownership of new stores, restaurants, or other business outlets but through a symbiotic partnering with local families who provide much if not all of the capital and much of the labor in exchange for branding, stock and supplies, and coaching in business and sales practices.

By 1950, almost 100 companies were using franchising to some extent to expand either regionally or nationally. By 1960 the number had exploded to more than 900, engaged in a total of some 200,000 cooperative arrangements. Top brands in the early days of franchising included Tastee Freez, Dairy Queen, Dunkin' Donuts, McDonald's, Burger King, Kentucky Fried Chicken, Lee Myles, Midas, 7-Eleven, and Orange Julius. During these years many service-oriented businesses also began to use the franchise model, including H&R Block, Holiday Inn, and Roto-Rooter. Then there was the fact that national brand corporations like Coca-Cola and Holsum Bread relied on local bottlers and local bakeries to manufacture and distribute their products.

The Robinson-Patman law and taxation were not the only tools that supported this revolution. Trustbusters at the Justice Department and Federal Trade Commission also helped, for example, by bringing antitrust cases against the A&P in the 1930s and again in the 1950s. Some of the most dramatic instances of enforcement took place at the local level; in 1962 the Supreme Court upheld a decision that blocked a Los Angeles grocery merger that would have brought just under 9 percent of the local market under the control of one owner.[40]

These efforts to distribute ownership and control over business were further supported by the New Deal's focus on ensuring that every citizen and every community (again, with the marked exception of black Americans) enjoy reasonably fair access to all basic networked services like electricity, telephones, air and bus travel, freight carriage, and roads and highways.

One result was a phenomenally modern and prosperous America, with individual entrepreneurs competing with one another to provide cleaner, brighter, better staffed, and more efficient stores. Trustbusters did not try to prevent local entrepreneurs from setting up bigger and more modern stores, such as supermarkets and department stores. They just limited the total number of big stores that any one person or corporation could own.

Another result was an incredibly wide distribution of prosperity.

This was true in terms of the types of manufacturing and retail businesses that were headquartered in smaller cities and towns.[41] And it was true in terms of what individuals in those communities earned for a day's work, with incomes across the nation converging dramatically between 1929 and 1979.[42]

There were, to be sure, huge flaws in the political economy of this era, as well as in the larger American society of these years. Government development policy, backed by powerful private interests, promoted sprawling suburban developments and energy-intensive transportation systems that needlessly destroyed farmlands, emptied cities, locked millions into hours-long commutes, locked millions more into urban ghettos, and unnecessarily released vast amounts of hydrocarbons into the atmosphere.

But in terms of the actual distribution of power over any particular community, industrial activity, or corporation, the overall result of this highly coordinated use of federal, state, and local law amounted to something very close to a full reestablishment of the American System of Liberty. As in the days of the Northwest Ordinance, citizens consciously used their government to carve properties into citizen-sized portions and then acted to ensure these independent businesses were distributed among as many individuals and communities as possible, in as fair a way as possible. As also in the Northwest Ordinance, citizens then buttressed this effort with the subsidization of education and basic communications and transportation services. Their main reasons for doing so were the same as those of the founders—to engineer a particular type of independent, self-regulating citizen and a particular form of self-governing community.

It was during these years that America's citizens engineered the Bentonville that in 1950 would welcome and sustain Sam Walton and his family. These same antimonopoly measures also ensured that the commercial systems in thousands of similar towns in America were geared to promote the well-being of the owners of America's independent farms, stores, and small factories, and also of the individuals who worked as employees in these businesses.

But this was not merely a remaking of small-town America. The effects of this renewed democratic republicanism were also felt even in the biggest of America's cities, where most businesses would also continue to be owned by families within the community.

In 2016, Brian Feldman from our Open Markets team published an article in the *Washington Monthly* on the political economy of St. Louis from the end of the Second World War into the 1980s. Our goal in that article, in focusing so closely on the business structure of a single city, was to give readers a sense of the complexity and robustness of the American political economy of that time. We chose St. Louis specifically mainly because it provided such a perfect snapshot of midcentury middle America.

For one thing, St. Louis has a character that is neither of the East nor West, neither of the South nor the North, neither mainly white nor mainly black. Rather St. Louis is a purple city in a populist state and the home of many of the most quintessentially American voices of the twentieth century, including Maya Angelou, Josephine Baker, Yogi Berra, Chuck Berry, Miles Davis, T. S. Eliot, Walker Evans, Redd Foxx, Joe Garagiola, Betty Grable, Al Hirschfeld, Vincent Price, Phyllis Schlafly, Dick Gregory, Tennessee Williams, and William Burroughs, all of whom were born there or moved there as children.

For another, St. Louis well into the 1980s combined a robust community of small- and medium-sized businesses with some of the nation's most advanced industrial activity. Yes, St. Louis was the city of "shoes, booze, and blues," the home of the International Shoe Company, Southern Comfort, and a style of piano based on jump blues that was very popular in the 1940s. But it was also a city of steel mills, the second-largest manufacturer of automobiles after Detroit, and the home to electronics pioneers like the Burroughs Corporation and Emerson Electric.[43]

Post-war St. Louis was a center for the farming and food industries, the home to Monsanto, Ralston Purina, and Anheuser-Busch. It was a city of powerful banks like Boatmen's and Mercantile, which did business across the South and Southwest, as well as many community banks.[44] St. Louis was home to one of the best-known department stores in the nation, the May Department Stores Company, with its Famous-Barr store downtown. And its citizens led the way in retailing investment services to independent citizens through such brokerages as A. G. Edwards, Edward Jones, and Scottrade. St. Louis also helped lead the way in creating America's modern advertising industry. Not only did the city birth such agencies as Fleishman-Hillard, D'Arcy, and Gardner, which for many years stood as peers of even the strongest of Madison Avenue companies. It was thanks to a St. Louis ad agency that Santa Claus grew fat and happy while drinking Coca-Cola. And it was thanks to a St. Louis agency that Americans first learned that "this Bud's for you."[45]

Finally, there were TWA and Ozark Airlines, which helped to pioneer the modern airline system. And McDonnell Douglas, which developed and built such key early airliners as the four-engine DC-8, the twin-engine DC-9, and the wide-body DC-10.

McDonnell Douglas also made fighter jets. And in January 1975 the pilot of a brand-new F-15 turned the aircraft's nose directly up and, on twin Pratt & Whitney F100 turbofan engines, accelerated, the first time ever that a jet-powered aircraft was able to gain speed while climbing.[46]

The main lesson of our close study of the St. Louis political economy? That the American people, living in checkerboard fields within a checkerboard economy, their minds and hands unshackled from Wall Street, had responded by building not only the most prosperous and free community of communities in history but also the most powerful.

AN EMPIRE OF LIBERTY

In 1944, the Roosevelt administration invited delegates from 44 allied nations to meet in the Grand Hotel in Bretton Woods, New Hampshire, to structure the international system that would exist after the war. With Europe, China, and Japan in ruins, it was clear the United States had become the world's main financial and manufacturing power, and the main question for attendees was how would Americans use this power in the years to come.

The two main institutions established during the meeting—the

World Bank and the International Monetary Fund—both gave the United States a great deal of sway over the economies of other nations. As a result, the Bretton Woods system has long been criticized for being overly colonial in nature. Increasingly, with the rise to power of China, India, and other nations, it is also seen as simply no longer necessary.

Yet at the time, the idea that the United States might impose a new international order was not especially controversial. After the trauma of two industrialized world wars, not only America's allies but even most neutral nations simply wanted a restoration of peace and predictability—and some reasonable degree of rule of law. Indeed, the Second World War itself was often interpreted as the result of the failure by the Wilson administration to impose precisely such an order in 1919, at the end of the First World War.

Among many Americans, the belief that the United States would have to impose such a system dated to well before the German invasion of Poland. In 1937, for instance, Walter Lippmann, who had long since abandoned his youthful embrace of socialism, had written of the need to impose a system able to "conserve the existing order of things in the field of ultimate power."[47] The question was not whether America should impose its own rules on the nations of the world but how truly "liberal" those rules should be. Should they aim at centralizing control over industry in ways that made other nations dependent on the United States, much in the style of the British imperial system, with its careful closing off of such Commonwealth economies as India, Australia, and Canada? Or should the aim be something more like what Americans had built at home, in which every individual should have as much freedom as possible to trade with every other individual?

Lippmann, for one, believed that Americans, once they had established the basic rules of the system, must then "concede an increasing equality of rights in all other fields" to the people of other nations.[48]

From the first days of the United States, Americans had viewed trade policy as a form of antimonopoly policy. The immediate practical goal of 1776, and of the Embargo Act of 1807, and of the War of

1812, was, after all, independence of both the nation and of individual Americans from the concentrated power and control of the British imperial trading system.

The intimate interconnection between trade policy and antitrust policy was made clear by John Sherman himself. In a resolution in the Senate in 1888, Sherman said that the law that now bears his name would help ensure that citizens enjoy "the full benefit designed by and hitherto conferred by the policy of the government to protect and encourage American industries by levying duties on imported goods."[49]

Add to this history the degree to which the Franklin Roosevelt, Truman, Eisenhower, and Johnson administrations were guided by antimonopoly principles, and it is hardly surprising that in the years after the war Americans ended up building a world system designed not to monopolize power in the hands of Americans but to share out, to a truly remarkable degree, prosperity and opportunity with other peoples.

As we saw in the first chapter, Truman and Eisenhower used America's position as the dominant power in both occupied Germany and occupied Japan to impose on those two nations the most robust antimonopoly regimes in the world, outside the United States. This included strong antimonopoly language in the Potsdam Declaration with the Soviet Union as well as the famous "four D" policy for Germany: "denazification, demilitarization, democratization, and decartelization."[50] And it included the adoption in Japan, under the occupation government overseen by General Douglas MacArthur, of a far-reaching and mature antimonopoly law in April 1947, more than two weeks before the new democratic constitution was adopted.[51]

The American focus on antimonopolism is even more clear in the competitive and open market systems the U.S. government engineered—in tandem with allies—during and immediately after the war. We see much of the basic thinking in the plans for the International Trade Organization (ITO)—the projected third institution of Bretton Woods—which was designed to enforce a non-discriminatory global trade system within a multinational framework.[52] This included mechanisms to establish aggressive antimonopoly powers, close restrictions on the actions of private investors, and strong labor standards.[53]

But after the Senate voted in 1950 to reject the ITO, the Truman and Eisenhower administrations responded by using the Marshall Plan and their powers as occupiers to engineer an even more deeply integrated industrial system spanning the world from Western Europe to East Asia. Or rather, they engineered two different systems, which they then linked together.

The first was a system of liberal trade within Europe and across the Atlantic. This centered on the vision of an integrated European political economy first fully delineated in the process of creating the European Coal and Steel Community in 1951. The other was a system of relatively liberal trade that the United States engineered initially with Japan, Taiwan, and South Korea, beginning at roughly the same time. As I wrote in *End of the Line*, this Pacific-centric effort amounted to "a sort of mini–Marshall Plan." In the case of Taiwan, for instance, U.S. officials helped that country "rewrite its laws regulating business, structured trade agreements to promote imports from the island, funded efforts to lure American companies to invest in Taiwan, arranged for the transfer to Taiwanese electronics firms of radar, avionics, and other advanced technologies developed in the United States, and paid to educate thousands of Taiwanese engineers and scientists at American universities."[54]

America's trustbusters also played a huge role in building this new and open international system, with enforcers actively encouraging patent-rich corporations like AT&T and RCA to transfer technologies not only to U.S. competitors but to their European and Japanese rivals. One of the more famous instances took place in 1952 when AT&T, facing an antitrust suit by the Justice Department, licensed the technology for a device it called an "electronic transistor" to 25 U.S. corporations and 10 foreign corporations.[55] Nowadays we call this device the semiconductor. The U.S. government during these years similarly worked closely with allies to structure open, neutral, and stable international systems for communications, transportation, banking and finance, trade in food and energy, and ultimately, the Internet.

The result was a world system based largely on the same anti-monopoly principles Americans had been advocating both at home and around the world since 1776. It was a system that was as open as possible, not just in terms of trade but in terms of technology and the componentry of complex networks.

It was a system protected with great care by every U.S. administration, right through the Reagan administration, which despite its radical libertarianism in the domestic area eagerly used traditional antimonopoly tools in the international political economy. Indeed, one of the best examples of the American vision of international commerce came in the mid-1980s, after IBM responded to an antitrust suit by the government by opening up the technologies within its personal computer. When the Japanese subsequently sought to capture control over DRAM and EPROM chips and other key computer components, the Reagan White House responded with tariffs and quotas. But the Reagan administration also made clear that its goal was not so much to transfer production from Japan back to the United States as it was to transfer production from Japan to South Korea, Taiwan, Malaysia, and Singapore. Put another way, the U.S. government's goal was not to hoard the technologies and industrial capacities within the borders of the United States but to ensure the safe distribution of these capacities among many nations.[56]

The overall result of America's post-war trade policy was the greatest burst in prosperity and the longest period of major-power peace in the history of the world.

Time and again during the twentieth century the world had intruded into the lives of Americans. Time and again some in America had responded to these threats and crises with calls to close the border and to concentrate power in monopolies at home. But even as other nations responded to the shocks of world war and depression by embracing fascism and communism and other forms of command-and-control industrialism, Americans went in the exact opposite direction.

Not only did Americans move to protect their system of liberty in the 1930s, they expanded it and made it stronger. Then after the Second World War, even while facing new forms of existential threats, citizens exported our system of liberty to our allies and friends.

THE FIRST PAGE—REDEEMED AT LAST?

On New Year's Eve 1964, in the Hotel Teresa in Harlem, Malcolm X spoke to 37 teenagers from McComb, Mississippi, about the promise of America. "Imagine that," he said. "A country that's supposed to be a democracy, supposed to be for freedom, and . . . they want to draft you and put you in the army and send you to Saigon to fight for them, and then you've got to turn around and all night long discuss how you're just going to get a right to register and vote without being murdered. Why it's the most hypocritical government since the world began."[57]

A half century had passed since W. E. B. Du Bois, in the early days of American involvement in the First World War, demanded that President Wilson address this fundamental hypocrisy, of a nation fighting for democracy abroad while denying the right to vote to millions of citizens at home. Now, the fundamental contradictions of American society had again become impossible to ignore.

The problem was not only that most African Americans in the South were effectively barred from the polling place and from many basic public services. There was also the raw rankling racism and segregation in the North, if not on public buses then certainly by neighborhood, school, and job. America, the great classless society, had a very obvious second-class population—millions of Americans barred from full citizenship for no reason other than the color of their skin.

President Truman in 1948 had desegregated both the military and the federal workforce. But in the decade before Malcolm X spoke, Dwight Eisenhower had done little to promote civil rights, and John Kennedy not much more. Woodrow Wilson's great summary statement in the New Freedom, that "America was created to break every kind of monopoly, and to set men free, upon a footing of equality, upon a footing of opportunity," read less as unmet promise than outright fraud.[58]

As we saw in the last chapter, American citizens, both black and white, had made many efforts over the years to join hands across the race line. Famously this included the early days of Reconstruction. And it included, even more dramatically, black and white populists marching side by side in many parts of the South in the 1890s.[59] Yet as we also saw, the white man's grip on the better jobs and privileges of the nation had held strong, sometimes with the help of the demagogue but just as often without.

All this while another great revolution in America was growing. It was a revolution that stood on the same footing as every previous successful battle in America for true liberty.

In the early twentieth century Du Bois had helped to set clear goals. The aims of the struggle for black Americans included the full independence of the individual, according to the basic rules of the American System of Liberty. Every citizen, Du Bois wrote, must have "land," "learning," and "liberty." The aims also included full integration. In 1935 Du Bois had made clear that without full integration, there could be no true liberty or democracy. "This the American black man knows: his fight here is a fight to the finish. Either he . . . will enter modern civilization here in America as a black man on terms of perfect, and unlimited equality with any white man, or he will not enter at all. Either extermination root and branch, or absolute equality. There can be no compromise."[60]

Over the next two generations, African Americans—as well as citizens of other oppressed races—used the same understanding of American liberty that had guided white Americans, the same arguments and the same intellectual tools, to fight for true and complete equality and liberty.

This included members of a rising cohort of African American professionals, such as Thurgood Marshall. Born in Baltimore, Marshall grew up working in the grocery stores of his grandparents as well as for other shopkeepers in his integrated middle-class neighborhood. Later, as chief counsel at the NAACP, it was Marshall who developed a sophisticated legal strategy that included using antimonopoly law to win equal access to businesses and services.

But it was also a matter of ordinary citizens using their properties and what independence they had thus far won to concentrate sufficient power to fight for more. For decades, segregationists were able to threaten African Americans who stood for civil rights with dismissal from their jobs or eviction from their tenant farms. But those African Americans who owned their own businesses and lands had much greater liberty to speak out and act in public. It was these "independent" citizens who were most free to fight to make more "independent" citizens.

And thanks to the same antimonopoly laws and policies that had been designed to protect America's white citizens against concentrated capital and corporate monopoly, the number of independent black-owned businesses had also grown rapidly. Between 1935 and 1939, for instance, the number of African American retail stores increased by 31 percent. As a coalition of black wholesale grocers put it, in reference to a 1947 New York fair trade law that prohibited loss leading, the law "will afford additional protection to the small businessman, be he Negro or white."[61]

Across the South it was independent black citizens who often led the fight for liberty. In Biloxi, Gilbert R. Mason, owner of a drugstore, fought to integrate a public beach. In Tallahassee, Daniel Speed, who owned a grocery store, allowed black leaders to meet in his shop, then financed a boycott of the local segregated bus service. This was nowhere more true than in Selma, Alabama, where a "strong community of black business owners offered critical logistical, financial, and other forms of support," and where the great march east to Montgomery was made possible by the ability of marchers to camp on freehold farms along state highway 80.[62]

Many citizens other than Marshall also used antimonopoly policy as a tool to win civil rights. In 1961, the black owners of ten independent medical practices in Chicago used the Sherman Antitrust Act against 61 local hospitals and medical organizations that barred African Americans from the medical staff.[63]

Many factors played on the minds of America's white and black citizens during these years and helped to shape their attitudes about racism and segregation. The general prosperity of these years made many white Americans less anxious about black prosperity. And the competition for world leadership with the Soviet Union made many Americans feel embarrassed by the fundamental hypocrisies highlighted by Du Bois and Malcom X. But another psychological effect may also have been at play. As we saw in chapters three and four, a main goal of the founders of the American System of Liberty was that true independence would result not only in individuals who feel secure in their liberty and prosperity, as they stand squarely on their properties, but who to some extent come to be "enlightened" and "liberal." The great success of the second American economic revolution, of the New Freedom and New Deal, may have helped open hearts as well as minds, much as happened in the run-up to the Civil War.

This is all, of course, mere speculation. And the fact remains that the full weight of the fight to break segregation and win true equality was carried by African Americans.

History books, for instance, tell us that the great civil rights bills of the 1960s were hammered through Congress by the Texas-born populist Lyndon Johnson, working in close alliance with Martin Luther King Jr. And there is no doubt Johnson fought hard, consciously aiming to outdo even Lincoln. Indeed, as Thurgood Marshall later recalled of Johnson's work on civil rights, his "ambition was, 'That history must show that compared to me, Lincoln was a piker.'"[64]

But Johnson himself made clear he understood who was responsible for winning these battles. In his speech in support of the Voting Rights Act of 1965, just before the Selma march, Johnson said that what was happening in Selma "is part of a far larger movement which reaches into every section and State of America. It is the effort of American Negroes to secure for themselves the full blessings of American life. Their cause must be our cause too. Because it is not just Negroes, but really it is all of us, who must overcome the crippling legacy of bigotry and injustice. And we shall overcome."[65]

Yet again in America, to those who sought liberty nothing was given. Again in America full civil rights was a case of liberty taken by the people who would have it. And now finally African Americans, a small minority in an overwhelmingly white nation, were in a position to take their liberty, using the same tools as every previous generation of citizens.

Time and again, over the course of two centuries, as soon as an African American family grasped some property or other, whites would often take that property away. Other times, they simply destroyed those properties, as in the Tulsa, Oklahoma, race riot and massacre of 1921 in which white men killed hundreds of black citizens and burned down 35 square blocks of that city's Greenwood neighborhood, then the most prosperous black community in America.[66] But the final destruction of Jim Crow and of government-sanctioned segregation and property theft in America did finally come close to redeeming the promise on our nation's first page. For the first time, every American—white as much as black—was truly free, if not yet in the eyes of every other citizen, or yet in every town, at least under the law and practice of the federal government.

In 1965, President Johnson named Thurgood Marshall to the Supreme Court to protect the system of civil rights, much in the way Wilson had named Brandeis to the Court to protect the New Freedom. In the years to come Marshall would serve that purpose—and many others—exceedingly well. But his career proved to be more than that; Marshall was the last justice on the Court who fully understood the role that citizen-sized property holdings had played in protecting American democracy and liberty.[67] In one of the last great defenses of antimonopoly law before Bork and his allies wiped such thinking from the Court, Marshall wrote that antitrust laws "are the Magna Carta of free enterprise. They are as important to the preservation of economic freedom and our free-enterprise system as the Bill of Rights is to the protection of our fundamental personal freedoms."[68]

In the dark days of the mid-1930s, a time when Jim Crow still lounged on the porch of almost every police station in the nation, W. E. B. Du Bois had dared to dream of this day. In that greatest of all cries for American liberty, the book *Black Reconstruction*, he distilled the American System of Liberty into words more eloquent perhaps even than those of Madison and Brandeis. America's great contribution to the world, Du Bois wrote, is "a vision of democratic self-government: the domination of political life by the intelligent decision of free and self-sustaining men."

And then, after a beat, Du Bois concluded: "What an idea."[69]

SEVEN

NEW LIBERTIES FOR THE MASTER

FROM CITIZEN TO CONSUMER

In 1987, President Ronald Reagan nominated Robert Bork to serve on the Supreme Court. Bork, who had served as solicitor general in the Nixon and Ford administrations, had been the target of public ire once before, for his role in firing Archibald Cox, the special prosecutor charged with investigating Richard Nixon's involvement in the Watergate break-in. But nothing prepared him for what now awaited in the Senate.

Senator Ted Kennedy led the attack, in what would become the most contentious nomination fight up to that time. "Robert Bork's America," Kennedy charged in a speech, "is a land in which women would be forced into back-alley abortions, blacks would sit at segregated lunch counters, rogue police could break down citizens' doors in midnight raids, schoolchildren could not be taught about evolution, [and] writers and artists could be censored at the whim of the Government."[1]

Bork later ruefully claimed that not a single line in Kennedy's speech was true. But it worked. The Senate voted 58 to 42 to reject Bork, who soon also quit his judgeship on the U.S. Court of Appeals for the District of Columbia Circuit. And the man himself would be transformed into a verb. The Oxford English Dictionary now defines "bork" as "to defame or vilify (a person) systematically, esp. in the mass media, usually with the aim of preventing his or her appointment to public office."

Yet Bork ended up having a far more revolutionary effect on the political and social structure of the United States than even the most influential of justices. And it was due to a subject that did not appear in Kennedy's speech—antimonopoly law. In 1978, while teaching at Yale, Bork had published a book titled *The Antitrust Paradox*, and it was this work more than any other that would be used to reshape how Americans not only regulate markets and corporations but understand the purpose of competition within society.

In that book, Bork made a long, intentionally arcane, often contradictory, and historically erroneous argument. But what would change America, and the world, was a four-point assertion early on in the text.

First, Bork held that "history" teaches that the sole goal of antimonopoly law is to promote the "welfare" of the "consumer."

Second, the one clear means to achieve this end of consumer welfare is to promote "productive efficiency" that results in a lowering of the price of goods and services.

Third, antitrust law, like economics, is "a science."

Fourth, the only way to understand how to enforce the law "with logical rigor" is to use economic "science" to understand the purpose of the law and to judge behaviors.

A more radical restatement of American antimonopoly law is hard to imagine.

For two centuries, Americans had used a vision of the liberty and independence of the citizen to guide their use of antimonopoly law. The result, as we have seen, was a wide and systematic distribution of power where possible, and where concentration was necessary, a reining in and neutralization of power. But Bork's line of reasoning led in almost the exact opposite direction. The logic of consumerism, after all, goes like this: What do consumers want? Bigger piles of stuff. How do we get bigger piles of stuff? More efficient production. How do we produce more efficiently? Bigger manufacturers, bigger distributors, and bigger retailers. Who, ultimately, is the best friend of the consumer? The big monopolist.[2]

Autocrats like Louis XIV and Joseph Stalin have often used the concept of efficiency to defend the concentration of power and control in their own hands. So too America's slave masters and, later, the monopolists of America's plutocratic age. But such celebrations of efficiency never captured sway over the thinking of America's citizens. Opposition tended to be immediate, absolute, and unrelenting.

One of the clearest statements of the basic American understanding of the dangers posed by aiming foremost at "efficiency" was by Louis Brandeis, in 1926, while he was serving on the Supreme Court. "Checks and balances were established in order that this should be 'a government of laws and not of men,'" he wrote. The goal is "not to promote efficiency but to preclude the exercise of arbitrary power. The purpose [is] not to avoid friction, but, by means of the inevitable friction incident to the distribution [of power], to save the people from autocracy."[3]

Bork's work in *The Antitrust Paradox* was anything but innocent intellectual wildcatting. On the contrary, it was the culmination of a carefully planned overthrow of fundamental structures and strictures put in place in the early years of the Republic, an overthrow funded generously from the 1950s on by some of the richest and most powerful corporations and individuals in America.[4]

In the years since Ronald Reagan and Margaret Thatcher were first elected to power in the United States and Britain, many progressives and liberals have told the same basic story of decline and fall. According to this account, the reactionary forces centered their efforts on the overthrow of labor unions and the privatization of properties and activities that had been owned by, and managed by, the public.

What we see in the work of Robert Bork is that the reaction also had a third primary goal—or rather a much more fundamental goal. This was to lift all restrictions on the right of capitalists to concentrate their power, not merely in the form of banks and investment funds but especially in the form of the monopoly corporation, the capitalist's main tool for exercising power within the political economy.[5]

Depending on the audience, Bork and his allies also spoke of how their work promoted individual liberty. Of course, this was not the liberty of the individual citizen to master one's own self but rather the liberty of which Lincoln had warned so eloquently, in which it is the master who is loosed to lord over the individual.

And yet the efficiency argument ultimately won the day. In 1981, a mere three years after Bork published *The Antitrust Paradox*, the Reagan administration's first antitrust enforcer, William Baxter, said the Justice Department would rely on an "efficiency test" to guide its response to concentrated economic power. Three years after that, Reagan's second antitrust enforcer, J. Paul McGrath, in his first speech in office, declared that the main goal of antitrust enforcement would be "consumer welfare."[6]

At a stroke, the main body of law that had undergirded the American System of Liberty was overthrown, not piecemeal but all at once, by this adoption of an entirely new set of guidelines and principles by which to interpret the law. It was a true coup, the single most dramatic reversal in political economic regulation in American history.

The ease of the success astounded even Robert Bork himself. In the introduction to a 1993 reissue of *The Antitrust Paradox*, he was able to report that over the previous 15 years "what has happened to antitrust amounts to a revolution." He then admitted that he had not seen it coming. "I failed to anticipate the rapid improvements that were about to occur."

Finally, Bork shared the main lesson he had learned. "My pessimism," he concluded, had "resulted from a serious underestimation of the power of ideas."[7]

FROM CITIZENRY TO MOB

It is a truism of American thought that our nation does not have a hard right or a hard left, or that these movements at most play a marginal role in our political life.

If we define hard right and hard left as openly advocating the complete overthrow of one-person, one-vote democracy, and the imposition of political dictatorship, be it of the "proletariat" or the oligarchs, then this belief is correct. But if we define hard left and hard right as advocating the complete overthrow of America's open and democratic *economic* system of one person, one property, and the imposition of commercial and industrial dictatorship, be it by the private estate or the state, then this belief is false.

As we saw in chapter five, America's hard right and hard left were on full display in the election of 1912. The hard right was exemplified by the banker J. P. Morgan's tight control over most of America's vital industrial sectors, as wielded through his financial control over the monopoly corporations that directed these activities. The hard left, with its vision of a dictatorship by the state over the actions of these monopoly corporations, was best exemplified by Teddy Roosevelt himself, as we saw in his Osawatomie speech.

It was this American left of the early twentieth century that first developed the concept of "consumer" as it would be understood over the next 100 years, and as Robert Bork and his allies would wield it politically beginning in the late 1970s. Although we can trace the origins of the concept to late nineteenth-century Germany, for a mature vision of the political purpose of the concept, we can turn to the 1914 book *Drift and Mastery* by Walter Lippmann, who was then Roosevelt's close ally.

Lippmann's basic argument can be boiled down to five short quotes:

- "Bad as big business is to-day, it has wide promise within it, and . . . the real task of our generation is to realize it."
- "Where there is centralization [in business] the solidarity of the consumer is made possible."
- "There is a need for . . . creating in the consumer a knowledge of what he wants and of the different ways there are of getting it."
- The immediate task of the intellectual, and of the enlightened leader, is "the organization and education of the consumer for control."
- "Collectivism or state socialism is . . . the chief instrument of the awakened consumer."[8]

What we see reflected in Lippmann's reasoning is a fundamentally new claim about the nature of the American public and of how the public operates within the American political system.

The traditional view of how Americans come together—be it within the town square or legislature—was expressed by James Madison in "Federalist 51." In discussing how to protect the interests of minorities against dictatorial majorities, Madison wrote of the natural separation of the public "into so many parts, interests and classes of citizens." In this, Madison meant not merely differences in wealth but differences in profession, as he believed that farmers and mechanics, merchants and carters, craftsmen and sailors, all viewed the world in slightly different ways and hence sought different outcomes through their political activities.

Such distinctions, Madison wrote, will ensure "that the rights of individuals, or of the minority, will be in little danger from interested combinations of the majority . . . In a free government the security for civil rights must be the same as that for religious rights. It consists in the one case in the multiplicity of interests; and in the other in the multiplicity of sects."

Lippmann himself does not take on Madison's view directly, but his friend and colleague Walter Weyl did, in a book published at roughly the same time, called *The New Democracy*. "The producer," Weyl wrote, "is highly differentiated. He is banker, lawyer, soldier, tailor, farmer, shoeblack, messenger boy. He is capitalist, workman, money lender, money borrower, urban worker, rural worker. The consumer, on the other hand, is undifferentiated. All men, women, and children who buy shoes . . . are interested in cheap good shoes."[9]

This common interest, in turn, Weyl wrote, provides an immense political opening. "The consumers of most articles are overwhelmingly superior in numbers to the producers," Weyl wrote.[10] The "common hostility" to getting ripped off is what allows the individual, viewing the world through the eyes of a "consumer," "to compromise conflicting interests within the group [and] to secure a united front against a common enemy."[11]

In Madison's view, the aim is to prevent the formation of a mob.

In that of Lippmann and Weyl, the aim is precisely the opposite—to forge a mob that would in turn help to empower a strongman, in this case Teddy Roosevelt, to hammer "enemies"—in this instance the people who grow and make what we consume—into submission.

In the thinking of Lippmann and Weyl and their allies, we also see a new claim about the nature of the individual, one that has had important political and psychological effects. As we have seen, the American System of Liberty was based in fundamental ways on a conception of the citizen as a producer, maker, thinker. The citizen's primary responsibility, according to this line of reasoning, is to fight for the liberty to sell or otherwise share what she has created, without restriction, at fair market prices.

The concept of "consumer," by contrast, reinforces the idea that the individual, rather than desiring more liberty to create, really desires only more stuff. Over time, this alternative vision of the individual affects how we understand market and corporate structures and our place within them. As we cease to view ourselves as producers, we also cease to fight for the liberty to freely sell and share what we create. This in turn means we spend less time guarding against the concentration of power within the political economy and increasingly lose our ability even to recognize the clenching of the fist that will be used to beat us down. Having been transformed into mere subjects of another's power, rather than stand and fight, we cower and whine.

Not surprisingly, Brandeis fully understood the danger of the concept of the consumer. In 1913, in an article in *Harper's Weekly*, he belittled the idea that consumers could ever act as a coherent political group. All the capitalist had to do, Brandeis said, was dangle the promise of lower prices in their faces, and the army would collapse.

"Americans should be under no illusions as to the value or effect of price-cutting. It has been the most potent weapon of monopoly— a means of killing the small rival to which the great trusts have resorted most frequently. It is so simple, so effective. Far-seeing organized capital secures by this means the co-operation of the short-sighted unorganized consumer to his own undoing. Thoughtless or weak, he yields to the temptation of trifling immediate gain, and, selling his birthright for a mess of pottage, becomes himself an instrument of monopoly."[12]

THE "EXPERTS" PLAY FOR CONTROL

The idea that the Reagan administration would attempt to radically weaken or even overthrow America's antimonopoly laws was not surprising in 1981, and it's not surprising now. The Republican Party of Ronald Reagan was not the party of Dwight Eisenhower and Richard Nixon, both of whom operated within the policy framework provided by the New Freedom and the New Deal. The philosophy of Reagan's Republican Party, by contrast, had been shaped by the libertarian musings of Milton Friedman, Ayn Rand, and Barry Goldwater. Reagan's team came to power armed to fight for more liberty for the master. Their goal was not to capture power over the American System of Liberty; it was to destroy that system.

The big question, for Reagan officials, and for the American people, was how Democrats would react. Members of the Democratic Party had been the main architects of the modern antimonopoly regime and had long been its most staunch defenders. And indeed, the antimonopoly fires had burned hot right through the 1970s, fueled by leaders as diverse as Lyndon Johnson, Robert Kennedy, Teddy Kennedy, and Michigan senator Phil Hart.[13]

Yet when Baxter announced that henceforth antimonopoly enforcement would be subjected to an "efficiency test," the outrage was limited.

In the Senate, the Ohio Democrat Howard Metzenbaum accused Baxter of breaking the law and wrote that he had shown "disdain" for "the entire political and social dimension" of America's antimonopoly policy.[14] Many moderate Republicans joined in opposition, with Pennsylvania senator Arlen Specter calling Baxter's plan "a most unusual and extreme situation."

What was far more noticeable, however, was the approval that came from across the aisle. Less than a month after Reagan took office, the *New York Times* ran an article about how big business "breathes easier" thanks to the new approach to antitrust. The article included a quote from Lester Thurow, identified as "a liberal economist" at the Massachusetts Institute of Technology. "Realistically, the Reagan Administration can only focus its deregulation efforts in one or two key areas," Thurow said. "If I had to choose one, I'd get rid of antitrust."[15]

The revolution in thinking in the Republican Party, in the years leading up to Reagan, has been well documented. Thanks to such works as Matt Stoller's *Goliath* and Angus Burgin's *The Great Persuasion*, we know the names of the main intellectuals who promoted liberty for the master.[16] In addition to Bork, this list includes the economists Milton Friedman and Alan Greenspan, and the legal scholars Aaron Director and Richard Posner (whom we will discuss in more depth in the next chapter). We also know what think tanks and other institutions were enlisted in selling this idea, including the Heritage Foundation, the American Enterprise Institute, the Cato Institute, and *Reason* magazine. And we know who paid the bills; among them, in the early years, the Walgreen family and, in more recent times, the Koch brothers.[17]

Far less well understood is that a very similar intellectual and political revolution also took place in the Democratic Party during these same years, one that was in many ways very closely tied to the libertarian revolution in the Republican Party.

It's important to recognize the role played by Ralph Nader, whose pioneering campaigns in the 1960s against unsafe automobiles and other products had jump-started the long-moribund consumer rights movement. Nader and other members of his team understood that concentration of power led to "many forms of injustice," including lower productivity, less innovation, greater pollution, and corruption of the political system. Nevertheless, Nader and his team strongly embraced the idea that the prime goal of antitrust should be "consumer welfare," as measured not only by safety and quality but also price.[18]

But Nader and his "raiders" were mainly activists, their influence more a matter of concentrated numbers than concentrated thought. The radical change in the Democratic Party's approach to antitrust during these years, on the other hand, was mainly a product of a deeper and more substantive change in philosophy that was driven largely by an economist named John Kenneth Galbraith.

The story here leads directly back to that same great election of 1912. Even though that vote brought Woodrow Wilson and Louis

Brandeis to power, it did not destroy the statist vision of Teddy Roosevelt and his friends. On the contrary, the basic ideas of Roosevelt's campaign—that competition was wasteful, consolidation was efficient, and the state should direct the economy—were passed from generation to generation of progressive thinkers. One of the most important was Thorstein Veblen, whose books included *The Engineers and the Price System.* Another—as we saw in the last chapter—was the Columbia University economist Rexford Tugwell, who carried this line of thinking into the early days of New Deal.

By the 1970s, however, the single most important influence was Galbraith, who, in the words of the historian Sean Wilentz, "was the most renowned and, arguably, most influential liberal economist in the United States during the decades after the Second World War."[19]

In some respects, Galbraith was a hero. A passionate opponent of the Vietnam War, he was also a pioneering environmentalist and an insightful critic of the effects of mass advertising. But like Teddy Roosevelt and the other statists of that line, Galbraith promoted a fundamentally materialistic and deterministic understanding of economics. And although his prose is often elegant and witty, Galbraith delivered his drolleries in an intentionally passive language designed to present certain political economic outcomes as all but inevitable.[20]

The one great exception to this rule came when Galbraith spoke of antitrust. Here his hatred was virulent. "The antitrust laws are . . . a blind alley along the path to reform . . . a cul-de-sac in which reform can safely be contained." Their main purpose, he wrote, was to provide lawyers with "a rewarding pecuniary return," much "in the manner of traditional automobile insurance."[21]

The overarching economic effect of antitrust law, Galbraith added, was to keep many industries "in a limbo of nondevelopment or primitive development."[22] By contrast, the workers and executives in big business were doing just fine. "In the planning system," he wrote, "workers are defended by unions and the state and favored by the market power of the employing corporation which allows it to pass the cost of wage settlements along to the public. Workers in this part of the economy are, relative to those in the market system, a favored caste."[23]

Galbraith long feared being vilified as a Communist, and through the 1950s and 1960s he had hidden the centralizing, statist, command-and-control nature of his thinking behind vague observations about the similarity of the U.S. and Soviet political economies. But in the wake of the social revolutions of the late 1960s and early 1970s, Galbraith finally felt confident enough to dare to reveal his ultimate goal, which he did with a carefully constructed two-step argument toward the end of his 1973 book *Economics and the Public Purpose.*

Of America's independent retailers, farmers, and light manufacturers, he wrote, "The only answer for these industries is full organization under public ownership. This is the new socialism which searches not for the positions of power in the economy but for the positions of weakness."[24]

Galbraith then turned his eye toward big industry. "But the story is not yet complete," he went on. "The case for socialism is imperative in the weakest areas of the economy. It is also paradoxically compelling in the parts of exceptional strength. It is here the answer, or part of the answer, to the power of the planning system that derives from bureaucratic symbiosis."[25]

In retrospect, standing in the America of today, within a political economy characterized by such vast concentrations of private and unaccountable power, in a society so deeply warped and twisted by the pro-monopoly policies of Ronald Reagan, Bill Clinton, and Donald Trump, the naïveté of Galbraith's thinking is as bright as Death Valley at noontime.

Yet the influence of Galbraith's work spread far beyond the influence of those like Thurow, who joined in advocating for the complete overthrow of antitrust laws. We see it in the thinking of Nader and his team, who adopted large parts of Galbraith's analysis and openly advocated for breaking the power of America's independent businesspeople and unionized working people.[26] We see it in the thinking of many of the progressive antitrust scholars of Galbraith's day. This includes Alfred Kahn, an economist who—as Jimmy Carter's "inflation czar" in the 1970s—played a major role in taking apart the market structures of the New Deal. Kahn had somehow concluded that the wealth and power of flight attendants, truck drivers, assembly-line workers, and other middle-class union members was the main factor driving prices in America up, rather than the OPEC oil cartel and unsettled debt from the Vietnam War. "I'd love the Teamsters to be worse off. I'd love the automobile workers to be worse off," Kahn said in 1981, soon after Carter had lost his bid for reelection. "[T]here's no way of making improvements for the consumer without limiting the monopoly profits of either the workers or the laborers."[27]

Even more importantly, the influence includes Donald Turner, a legal scholar who headed the Justice Department's Antitrust Division under President Johnson. After being bullied by the imperious Galbraith in a Senate hearing, Turner would drift from the Brandeisian structuralist approach to antitrust to a reliance on economics, thereby helping to lay the groundwork for Bork's success in the early 1980s.[28]

In other words, some of the leading progressives of the 1960s and 1970s consciously strove to break three of the main constituencies of the Democratic Party of the twentieth century—the unionized worker, the independent business owner, and the farmer. And they used the same concept of "consumer welfare" employed by Bork to help construct corporations powerful enough to smash individual American workers, farmers, and entrepreneurs into complete and abject submission.

For our purposes, however, it is the career of Robert Reich that is perhaps most important, not merely to illustrate what went wrong but also to illustrate how it can be made right again. Reich today is known as one of the most energetic fighters for the economic and political well-being of the American people. This includes speaking out strongly against efforts to concentrate economic power. Yet from the mid-1970s to the mid-1990s few people did more to pave the way for the monopolist's takeover of America. This is due, in large part, to the fact that Reich, more than any other American intellectual of the last 40 years, fused the thinking of Galbraith to that of Bork.

Reich's debt to Galbraith is mainly as a teacher. Like other young scholars of his generation, Reich viewed Galbraith as the master explainer of political economics. And we see Galbraith's influence throughout Reich's body of work, from his early books of the 1980s right through *Saving Capitalism* in 2015, which Reich dedicates to Galbraith, and in which he includes a resoundingly clear call to "Restor[e] Countervailing Power," a nod to what was perhaps Galbraith's single most important concept.[29]

Reich's debt to Bork is more personal. At Yale Law School in the early 1970s, where he was in the same class as Bill and Hillary Clinton, Reich studied antitrust law with Bork. He soon followed Bork to Washington, where he worked for Bork in his new position as solicitor general in the Ford administration. Then in the late 1970s, Reich carried his hybridized mix of Galbraithian and Borkian competition thinking into a stint as the head of the Office of Policy Planning at the Federal Trade Commission, having been appointed by Jimmy Carter.

Most importantly, in 1991 Reich would publish a book he titled *Work of Nations.* Written in the immediate aftermath of the collapse of the Soviet Union, the book is perhaps the single most libertarian political economic work ever published by a self-described progressive. The power of both the business corporation and the nation-state had all but vanished, Reich wrote. The idea that people should regulate either the national political economy or international trade was, Reich contended from his perch between the statism of Galbraith and the estatism of Bork, a "naively vestigial" albeit also somewhat "charming" belief.[30]

During the 1992 presidential election, *Work of Nations* would be called the single best "primer" for understanding Bill Clinton's approach to political economics. And indeed, given the radical promonopolism of the Clinton administration, this proved, sadly, to be all too true.[31]

Acknowledging mistakes is rare. But it is important to do so. And perhaps the single best reason to accept Reich's work today at face value is that, in 2015, as I noted in the introduction, he did precisely that. In an article titled "The Political Roots of Widening Inequality" in the *American Prospect*, Reich admitted that he had been wrong to blame "globalization and technological change" for the sharp decline in the wealth and well-being of the working people of America and around the world.

"While the explanation I offered a quarter-century ago for what has happened is still relevant," Reich wrote, "indeed, it has become the standard, widely accepted explanation—I've come to believe it overlooks a critically important phenomenon: the increasing concentration of political power in a corporate and financial elite that has been able to influence the rules by which the economy runs. And the governmental solutions I have propounded, while I believe them still useful, are in some ways beside the point because they take insufficient account of the government's more basic role in setting the rules of the economic game."

"Most fundamentally," Reich concludes, "the standard explanation for what has happened ignores power."[32]

Yes, here again, we see the highly passive language that helped get us into the mess in the first place. Yes, Reich still largely ignores his own role in greasing the skids that carried us toward autocracy. But at least Reich's acknowledgment of his role in creating the "standard explanation," which for a generation helped to hide the slow-motion political catastrophe of monopolization from his fellow progressives, allows us to understand what happened.

Reich in recent years has worked enormously hard to make amends. In doing so he provides a fine model for so many others of the "libertarian" generation—from both parties—who sold out their fellow citizens, perhaps to fatten their bank accounts or maybe just for a few hours in the flickering spotlight of fame.[33]

THE AMERICAN SYSTEM COLLAPSES

In the early 1980s, under assault by the combined forces of the right and the left, both wielding their freshly burnished concept of "consumer welfare" and their promise of lower prices achieved through the corporate dictatorship over particular sectors of the political economy, the American System of Liberty collapsed.

First to fall was the simple "bright line" system for structuring markets and divvying out property and opportunity. Put into place in the earliest days of the Republic, this system was perhaps best exemplified in the 160-acre rule for divvying up America's farmlands.

The battle over this system of bright-line rules took place far from public view, within the walls of the Antitrust Division of the Justice Department. The field of battle was a relatively short document—called the "Merger Guidelines"—published by the Antitrust Division to ensure that law enforcers, the courts, and the business community all clearly understood the exact goals of America's antitrust laws.

According to the guidelines published in 1968 by the generally populist administration of Lyndon Johnson, the main goal of antitrust enforcement was "identification and prevention of those mergers which *alter market structure* in ways likely now or eventually to encourage or permit non-competitive conduct."[34] And what was acceptable market structure? According to the Justice Department in 1968, it was that the top four companies within a market could together control no more than 75 percent of that market. The guidelines then made absolutely clear that the U.S. government would challenge any merger whatsoever if pursued by any corporation that already controlled 25 percent of any market.

Further, the guidelines emphasized that this simple rule would hold fast even if the corporations pursuing the merger could absolutely prove that the deal would result in efficiencies in the production and distribution of goods and services. On this issue, the guidelines were blunt. "[T]he Department will not accept" any such efficiency argument "as a justification for an acquisition."[35]

Reagan administration officials published new guidelines in 1982, then again in 1984. At a glance, the guidelines don't read all that differently than those published by the Johnson administration in 1968. But on close inspection, two changes stand out. First, the prime goal of enforcement became the promotion of "efficiencies" within the economy. Or as the 1984 guidelines put it, "The primary benefit of mergers to the economy is their efficiency-enhancing potential." This meant henceforth, that the Justice Department would "allow firms to achieve available efficiencies through mergers without interference."[36]

Second, the Justice Department now intended to measure such efficiencies by studying the potential effect of any particular merger on the price of the good or service being produced. To make this clear, Reagan administration officials wrote the words "price" and "pricing" 117 times in the 1984 guidelines. By contrast, in the 1968 guidelines, the words "price" and "pricing" appear but eight times.[37]

In practice, the change could not have been more radical. From this moment on, as long as executives could make the most rudimentary case that a merger would result in efficiencies that might eventually lower the price of some good or service, they had a license to consolidate, no matter what the political or social effects of the deal. And in case anyone chose to challenge the merger, rather than judges deciding the case based on simple rules, such as the percentage of a market controlled by each corporation, the decision whether to approve the deal would now be handled mainly by economists. These "experts" were expected (as we will discuss in more detail in the next chapter) to "scientifically" measure the "price effects" of a particular deal so as to be able to deliver a firm conclusion about the theoretical efficiencies it would create.

The second pillar of traditional antimonopoly law to fall was the regime designed to prevent price discrimination at the national, regional, or local level.

Here again, it was Bork, in *The Antitrust Paradox*, who made the key arguments in favor of changes that would clear the way for the radical concentration not merely of power within the political economy but also of direct control over the lives and livelihoods of individual citizens and businesses.

Bork began his attack on the laws designed to prevent price discrimination by first nodding recognition to the idea that price discrimination might indeed pose a big problem. "[T]he question remains whether antitrust should try to deal with price discrimination in some other fashion," he wrote. "This is a more difficult question."

Then, in the same sentence, Bork proceeded to dismiss this "difficult question" based on nothing more than personal whim. "[T]he better guess, it seems to me, is that antitrust policy would do well to ignore price discrimination."[38]

A few pages later, Bork went much further and delivered a straightforward defense of price discrimination from the point of view of the seller. "The basic theory of price discrimination is quite simple," he wrote. "When the demand elasticities of customers are different, no single price can extract the maximum return from each. If they can be segregated ... the monopolist can charge them different prices and so extract the maximum return from each class."[39]

Bork then used the same sleight of hand he wielded throughout *The Antitrust Paradox* and claimed that what was good for the monopolist was also good for the public. "There is more to the argument than this, however," he wrote. "The case for allowing discrimination freely is strengthened by the observation that the more a monopolist is able to discriminate, the more likely becomes the favorable outcome of an increase in output."[40] Translated into the language of Brandeis, Bork was saying, in essence, that in exchange for your traditional liberty from manipulation and exploitation by all-powerful monopolists, at least we promise you a mess of pottage.

The actual subversion of the body of U.S. law designed to prevent personalized discrimination in pricing and terms, hence the centralized private control and manipulation of the flow of commerce and information in America, came in three blows.

First, a coalition led by Ralph Nader and other progressives in 1975 convinced Congress to pass the Consumer Goods Pricing Act, which overturned the Miller-Tydings Act and dealt a fatal blow to the flawed system of state-level fair trade laws and resale price maintenance.

Second, and far more important, in the 1980s the Reagan administration essentially ceased to enforce the Robinson-Patman law against price discrimination. In the 1960s the government brought 518 cases under the law. In eight years in office, the Reagan administration brought five.[41]

The third and most dangerous change would not be clear until the last years of the twentieth century. This was the decision by first the Clinton administration and then the administration of George

W. Bush—both of which were fully under the influence of Bork's pro-monopoly philosophy—to exempt communication monopolists, such as cable and mobile phone corporations and Internet platforms like Google and Amazon, from any and all laws prohibiting such discrimination.

THE DICTATORSHIP OF THE CAPITALIST—REBORN

When Edmund Burke used the floor of Parliament to assail the British East India Company in 1783, he focused both on the corporation's immense political power and on how it used that power in ways that destroyed the economy and shattered social balances across wide regions of India.

"The East India charter is a charter to establish monopoly, *and to create power*," Burke said. The problem was that there were no checks, no limits, on that power, which left the corporation free to extract all it could from the people and places under its control, to the point of absolute destitution.[42]

For the next 200 years, as we have discussed in depth, a prime goal of American antimonopoly policy was precisely to protect the citizen as a creator and producer of goods and services from the brute extractive power of such trading monopolies. Americans understood that the threat posed by these institutions was not only the potential loss of control over the production of goods vital to the independence of the nation. They understood the threat also to be the capture, manipulation, and ultimate destruction of the companies and individuals made subject to the power of monopolists who controlled the gate to the market. Hence, the practical aim became, as we have seen, to use antimonopoly to protect the liberties and properties of the citizen as creator by breaking or neutralizing any and all dangerous concentrations of private power over the market.

But the overthrow of the bright-line approach to making markets in the early 1980s, combined with the overthrow of the even more ancient rules against price discrimination and predation, cleared the way for the return of monopoly trading companies on a scale as grand and terrifying as the East India Company of the eighteenth century.

Even before the Reagan administration had published its new merger guidelines, American capitalists had begun to dust off corporate models that had sat on the shelf since the days of the New Deal and New Freedom. Foremost was the use of the chain store to capture control over entire systems of retail and production.

In some instances, capitalists would provide a retail corporation piles of cash big enough to allow them to undersell and bankrupt most rivals. This was the basic approach of Walmart, Target, and Staples. In other instances, the capitalists would provide a retail corporation with sufficient money to buy up all their rivals. One such effort brought nearly 1,000 department stores, in just about every city across the nation, under the banner of Macy's by 2005. Another such effort brought most of the retail eyeglass market under the banner of EssilorLuxottica by 2019, either through direct control of the retailers themselves or through control over the manufacturing of frames and lenses.

For years, politicians and writers assured America's citizens that the new trading company monopolies were a great boon for which they should be enormously grateful. No such celebration of "consumerism" and "discounterism" was more influential than Robert Reich's. In 2007, even as America's heavily monopolized economy was beginning to collapse into the Great Recession, Reich in his book *Supercapitalism* explained how it was we, the consumers, who were the true masters of America's political economy, not the financiers who were concentrating these powers.

"[E]conomic power has shifted to consumers and investors, and away from large corporations and unionized workers," Reich wrote. And what had we demanded, with our new power? Efficiency. "We as consumers have threatened to take our business elsewhere unless they do things as efficiently as possible," Reich explained. It was via "consumer intermediaries like Wal-Mart," he said, that we applied our pressure and delivered our threats to the companies and people who actually supplied us with goods and services.[43]

Today it is clear that, rather than carry out the diktats of the all-powerful consumer, the masters of Walmart and Amazon and other market-bestriding trading monopolies chose instead to use their gatekeeper power to impose a series of taxes, and economic levies and social revolutions, on the rest of us.

Consider, for instance, the personal properties that for 200 years served to ensure the economic self-sufficiency and political independence of millions of American families. Over the last generation, capitalists from America and around the world were left largely free to use massive trading companies simply to seize millions of these properties—in the form of the family farm, family store, and family manufacturer—for themselves. They did so largely by driving these enterprises out of business. Indeed, since the early 1980s, the American people have been the victims of perhaps the greatest seizure of personal properties in history, other than in the early years of Soviet Russia and Maoist China.

This mass expropriation of independent farms and businesses by capitalists wielding trading companies, in turn, has been the single most powerful driver of the degradation of democratic community in America. For two centuries, Americans used antimonopoly to ensure that the businesses that served the cities and towns of America would be run by the people who lived in them. Today, it is the masters of these globe-spanning corporations who increasingly control our communities as distant—and largely absentee—landlords.

Even more immediately dangerous are the effects of the brute extractive power of such trading monopolies on the people, and systems of human industry, over which they exercise control. Exactly as was true of the East India Company, trading monopolies like Walmart and Amazon today use their gatekeeper power to regulate and govern, through increasingly autocratic means, the people who depend on them to get to market. One result has been the steady extortion of wealth and power from the people who actually make the goods and services we buy. As I detailed in my last book, *Cornered*, this extraction often continues to the point—exactly as was true of the East India Company—of their complete destruction.

Importantly, this trading company model can be applied beyond retail. Over the last generation, corporations as diverse as Boeing, General Electric, Monsanto, and the BNSF railway have reorganized their operations in ways designed to enable the financiers who "own" these institutions to exercise greater control over, and to extract ever more wealth from, the people and companies who actually create the products and services these corporations sell. Often they do so to the point of destroying even the most vital of skills and capacities, such as the ability to develop safe software for airliners like Boeing's 737 MAX.[44]

It is natural to believe that the main harm of monopolists is that they charge citizens ever more for the same good or service. And today's monopolists certainly do, for everything from drugs to milk to airline seats to hospital beds to eyeglasses to syringes.[45] But as Americans well understood for the first two centuries of our nation, the far bigger danger posed by trading monopolists comes from their power to pay the citizens and companies under their sway ever less for the same work.

And indeed, just about every ill in our society today is the result of, or has been greatly worsened by, the destruction of America's open market systems and the concentration of power by these immense trading companies over the American people in their roles as the creators, makers, growers, and providers of the goods and services we then consume.

The executives of these corporations have used concentrated power to drive down wages and benefits, which makes it often vastly harder to change jobs. They have used that power to drive manufacturing offshore and to drive down the quality and variety of even basic products and services. They have used that power to drive farmers off their land and to drive livestock into industrial warehouses. They have used that power to drive fossil fuels into our cars and homes and hydrocarbons into our atmosphere. They have used that power to drive newspapers into bankruptcy and to drive foreign propaganda into our elections. They have used that power to drive musicians and book authors and scriptwriters out of business. They have used that power to block us from placing the most simple of renewable technologies in our own homes and to destroy vital systems of technological innovation, including the human skills needed to address the disruption of climate change.[46]

Perhaps most outrageously, the executives of these corporations have taken advantage of their monopoly power to strip many of our most vital industrial and financial systems of the most basic forms of redundancy and resiliency. This has created existential threats to both the United States and the world as a whole. This was made shockingly clear when the Covid-19 crisis revealed that the United States had come to rely on Chinese factories for our supply of even the most simple facemasks and cotton swabs, and that entire systems of production depended on single factories on the far side of the world.

A generation ago, there were multiple sources of supply in the United States and around the world for almost every imaginable industrial product and for every imaginable component of those products, including every important metal, chemical, and electronic device. As a result, it was all but impossible for any individual nation-state or corporation to be able to threaten the basic well-being of the American people through any action short of war.

Since then, however, the executives and financiers who control our trading monopolies have used their power to shut down vast portions of the industrial capacity of the United States and our closest allies in Europe and Asia, in the theory that doing so would result in more efficient systems of production.

One result has been to open the United States to entirely new forms of coercion, as actors ranging from the Chinese state to Kim Jong-un to democracy protesters in Hong Kong can now plausibly threaten to disrupt the manufacture and transportation of goods that are vital to the well-being of the American people.

Another result has been to open the United States, and indeed the whole world, to the threat that these vital systems of supply might suddenly collapse, perhaps in catastrophic fashion. The concentration of essential industrial capacities in single locations has created numerous "single points of failure" within these systems. This means, as I detailed in my first book, *End of the Line*, that a wide variety of events—not only political conflict but earthquakes, financial crashes, and epidemics—can today disrupt the normal flow of trade even to the point of triggering complete social collapse.[47]

Under the "consumer welfare" model of economic organization, in other words, in exchange for the theoretical benefit of a few pennies in savings, a few financiers and their C-suite allies constructed systems of autocratic corporate control over us, then used their new power to strip us of our wealth, our liberty, our dignity, and our most basic forms of security.

THE DISCRIMINATION MACHINE PERFECTED

In 2001, a Berkeley economics professor named Hal Varian co-wrote a paper titled "Conditioning Prices on Purchase History." Varian was already a highly successful author of what are now standard microeconomics textbooks for the information economy.

Although the paper may seem highly arcane, Varian was very clear about his purpose. He wanted to examine whether the technologies and structures of online commerce made it easier for sellers to charge different people different prices for the same product, or to charge different people the same price for different-quality versions of the same product.

"The rapid advance in information technology now makes it feasible for sellers to condition their price offers on consumers' prior purchase behavior," Varian and his co-author wrote. "In this paper we examine when it is profitable to engage in this form of price discrimination."

Varian's conclusion? Yes, it is absolutely profitable if you are an online seller. "[I]f enough customers are myopic, or the costs of anonymizing technologies are too high, sellers will want to condition pricing on purchase history."

And for the buyer, Varian included a warning. "[P]urchasing at a high price is not the best strategy, since it guarantees that [you, the consumer] will face a high price in the future."[48]

In other words, online sellers can study you and use what they learn about you to manipulate you and fleece you, by providing you with prices, terms of service, and information tailored specifically to exploit your personal weaknesses and needs. And there's almost nothing you can do about it.

Within a year of his paper, Varian would head in an entirely new direction in his career. In 2002, two years before Google went public, CEO Eric Schmidt hired Varian as a consultant to help the corporation develop its new business plan. By 2007 Varian had risen to the position of chief economist within Google. Today Varian is, by almost any measure, immensely successful. Not only is he relatively rich, he can correctly claim that his economic vision is at the center of the most awesome and sophisticated systems for manipulating human behavior ever built by private enterprise—namely Google and Amazon.

What made the work of Varian and his co-author so especially valuable was that he was able to show how corporations could apply first-degree price discrimination to buyers. Until the Internet, retailers had largely lacked any real ability to engage in routine price discrimination, whether they believed the practice to be legal or not. Varian, however, was able to describe in very simple terms that in the online world then fast emerging, in which essential platform monopolists were able to study you, the buyer, in a myriad of ways, first-degree price discrimination was not only feasible but could also be highly profitable.

For most of American history, when citizens fought against price discrimination, the danger they saw was that a gatekeeper would use such tools to manipulate and exploit citizens in their capacity as sellers of goods and services. Citizens viewed such discrimination as essentially political in nature. Not only was it a way to extort the seller unto his last penny but it was a way to capture control over the seller and manipulate the actions and words of the seller not only in the commercial realm but in the political. The danger they saw, in short, was that the gatekeeper would use his power to turn the seller into a stooge.

As we saw earlier in this chapter, thanks to the writings of Robert Bork and his allies, over the last generation most traditional restrictions on price discrimination have been taken down or blithely set aside and ignored. As a result, corporations such as Walmart, Comcast, Google, and Amazon are now largely free to treat you, as a seller of goods or work or ideas, differently than they treat your competitors.

Nowhere is this truer, or more important politically, than in those parts of the economy controlled by the online platform monopolists.

As we saw in chapter two, it is the collapse of traditional antidiscrimination laws that provides Amazon with its license to manipulate the actions of book publishers. And that provides Uber with its license to arbitrarily manipulate the actions of drivers. And that provides Tyson with its license to arbitrarily manipulate the actions of farmers.

The stoogification of America, in other words, is already well under way. It is trained on you and your neighbors, in your capacity as producers and creators.

Thanks to the work of Varian and other thinkers, the world's biggest corporations have now perfected the ability to apply these same basic manipulative tools to you as a buyer. As Varian understood two decades ago, Google and similar digital platforms can gather and store vast amounts of information about you, then use that information to deliver you different prices and different services than they deliver to your neighbor, your partner, your co-worker, your rival. Their goal is not only to extract more money from you. It is to learn how to manipulate your behavior ever more perfectly, day after day after day.

And today Google, Amazon, and a growing number of other online platforms do precisely that. Even old-line retailers like Walmart do so, right in their stores, through the use of such tools as personalized coupons. Such discrimination is also becoming common in sectors of the economy far from the consumer realm where we spend most of our time. Monsanto, for instance, routinely prices its seeds and chemicals based on its knowledge of how much a particular farmer earned selling last year's crop. If the farmer had a bumper year, she must pay Monsanto more.

In the case of Google, the license to deliver different pricing directly actually does not matter all that much. The corporation simply does not sell that many goods or services directly to you. Instead Google makes almost all its money off the sale of advertising to companies that do aim to sell something directly to you.

What makes Google so attractive to these buyers of advertising is not that it has a license to price differently but that it has a license to deliver you a different service than it delivers to other people, in the form of different information. Google may provide you different search results. Or a different route on a map. Or different music on

YouTube. Or different news or political information. In other words, Google is selling its ability to manipulate you.

The fundamental danger lies not in the algorithms these corporations use. Nor does it lie in the vast tranches of data they collect. Nor even, necessarily, in the monopoly nature of their business structures.

None of these things, on their own, make Google and Amazon and Facebook—and a few other similar corporations—so especially dangerous. What makes them dangerous is their license to manipulate you in ways designed to alter your behavior, to alter your purchases, to alter your pathway through the world, to alter your vote, to alter your thought.

That's why, time and again in American history, citizens have required every essential intermediary to treat everyone the same and banned personalized discrimination in pricing and in terms of service.

The most terrifying of all of Robert Bork's legacies was to create the legal license that allows Google, Amazon, and Facebook to discriminate among individual sellers and buyers, hence to manipulate these people and these companies. The legacy of Hal Varian was to identify the intellectual tools that enable Google, Amazon, and Facebook to understand how to discriminate in ways that have been not merely profitable but enormously so, and that give these corporations increasingly terrifying powers over the individual.

The practical immediate effects of this concentration of power and control are far too many to list here. But three especially stand out:

The collapse of open market systems, as online platforms like Amazon use their knowledge of the citizen as both seller and buyer to determine not merely the pricing and terms of transactions but even who gets to deal with whom.

The collapse of open democracy, both at home and in some of our closest allies around the world. This results from the practice by Google and Facebook of renting out their manipulation machines to almost any comer, in ways that degrade and destroy the systems designed to provide citizens with reasonably trustworthy news and information. It results also from the exploitation by Google, Facebook, and Amazon of their license to open and close the gate to the market as they alone see fit, which in turn gives them effective political control over anyone who depends on them to sell their services and wares.

The collapse of the public, and of society itself. As pricing and other forms of information are personalized for each individual by corporations engineered to know every financial and psychological secret, citizens are fast losing their ability to identify common interests and to concentrate their thinking in the ways necessary to concentrate their will.

Here in America, the license that Google and Amazon and Facebook enjoy to deliver different prices and different information to each of us is license to shatter our society into 320 million individuals, every one of whom now orbits separately around these immense centralized powers, every one of whom is now directed individually from afar, a tiny satellite drifting outside any real community in cold dark space.

But then again, maybe it's all for our own good. As Varian wrote in that pioneering paper so many years ago, personalized manipulation by the monopolist of the individual may ultimately "have positive effects on *consumer welfare.*"[49]

Thank goodness. More pottage, for the enthralled.

EIGHT

OTHER PEOPLE'S GODS

OF POWER AND IDEAS

Iᴍᴀɢɪɴᴇ ʏᴏᴜ ᴀʀᴇ ɪɴ Gʀᴀɴᴅ Cᴇɴᴛʀᴀʟ Tᴇʀᴍɪɴᴀʟ ɪɴ Nᴇᴡ Yᴏʀᴋ during evening rush hour. You stand on the western balcony looking down. At any moment, many hundreds of commuters scurry across the marble floor to ticket machines, information counters, subway entrances, train platforms.

People enter the great room from dozens of points. They push through doors from 42nd Street and from Lexington and Vanderbilt Avenues. They descend the two great stairways and escalators from office buildings. They bound up subway stairways and pop from the doors of stores. From the Oyster Bar they step, and the food market. And from the Apple Store, the MetLife Building, the Grand Hyatt Hotel, the Yale Club, and the Vanderbilt Tennis Club.

The numbers are phenomenal. The Metro-North commuter railway alone carries more than 71 million passengers in and out of the station each year. Then there are the visitors. On any day more than 60,000 tourists come take a look around. This adds up to some 750,000 people passing through Grand Central on any workday.[1]

Once inside, all these thousands of people separate out to their destinations. These include 44 active train platforms, split between the main floor and a lower level, handling trains from the Metro-North Railroad's Harlem, Hudson, and New Haven lines. They include the East Side IRT, which carries the 4, 5, and 6 subway trains, the crosstown shuttle to Times Square, and the number 7 to Flushing. They include buses and taxis on the streets outside. And the stores and restaurants inside.

From your perch, above the floor, you watch all these hundreds and thousands of people weaving left, cutting right, as they make their way past one another to their destinations. Each makes decision upon decision, often many in a moment, as they tilt, twist, dodge, slow, and sidestep their way past people who cross their paths at almost every conceivable angle. Some talk intensely, to companions or into their phones. Others seem in a trance as they listen to music or podcasts. Others stare at screens, flipping and sorting though their online selves. And yet only rarely do any two people collide, only rarely does anyone even clip someone else with a shoulder, elbow, or handbag. Instead all swiftly get where they wish to go, while just as swiftly, others follow.

You drift in your perception, outward. You no longer see individuals but rather the crowd, the mass. It can seem, almost, as you allow all these hundreds and thousands of people to blur together, that some sort of mechanism is at work here, some overarching force, shaping and directing the movements of all these people, sorting them all toward their destinations. So you ask yourself: Are these individuals fully in control of their own actions? Of their particular movements? Or are they in some fashion directed? By some sort of machine? Some sort of power? Then you break the spell and laugh. What a silly thought.

Each individual is not, of course, entirely free to go absolutely anywhere they wish. They are, on the contrary, very much guided, by signs, by walls, by carefully placed obstacles, by the location and width of staircases, by the tilt of the floor and the direction of escalators, by the placement and intensity of lights, by all the techniques an architect can use to shape human movement. Look carefully and you can see all these tricks of the designer's trade. They are transparent. There to be interpreted and judged in how well they function. There to be admired and copied. There to be adjusted or even rebuilt if they are not working well.

Grand Central itself, you realize, is just a smart, human-made structure designed to empower individuals, hundreds and thousands at any moment, to get where they need to go, based on their own desires, at their own speeds, in their own ways, according to their own decisions, using their own senses.

But if, on the contrary, you were to conclude that some sort of active mechanism is at work, helping to control the movement of people across the Tennessee marble of Grand Central, you would actually find yourself in very good company. In recent years many of our most influential leaders have told us that exactly such mechanisms, such forces, are somehow in control of big parts of the world around us, somehow responsible even for some of the greatest changes within our society.

Consider, for instance, what Alan Greenspan said in 2007, after serving almost 20 years as chairman of the Federal Reserve: "It hardly makes any difference who will be the next president. The world is governed by market forces." Or consider what former German chancellor Gerhard Schröder said in 2003. The German economy, he said, must modernize or it would "be modernized" by the "forces of the market" and by "storms of globalization."[2]

Much the same is true today of many of our intellectual and political leaders. Even insightful researchers and thinkers like Shoshana Zuboff, author of the smart book *Surveillance Capitalism*, write of the "nature" of capitalism and of the intrinsic and highly limiting tendencies of certain essential technologies.[3]

"Determinism" is a fancy word to describe when someone believes that forces outside human control dictate largely—or entirely—what happens in our economy, society, and even our politics. It is tempting to dismiss the question of whether any one person believes in such powers as being of no more importance than whether or not that person believes in God.

But before we can begin to rebuild the American System of Liberty for the twenty-first century, it is vital to understand what has blinded us for so long to the efforts to overthrow antimonopoly law in the first place and to the many, sometimes existential, threats that have been created by this monopolization. We must understand why we perceive and react to certain threats and not others, why we aim at certain goals while failing to identify vast opportunities.

Many of those who hold that some force outside human society limits or determines what takes place within human society mean well. They truly believe that mechanisms and natural powers shape our lives. They truly believe they are providing a vital service by helping us see and understand the little demigods they imagine at work all around us.

Others, however, intentionally preach such ideas knowing full well they are nonsense. They do so because they want to use such beliefs to hide the actual architecture of America's political economy, as it has been rebuilt over the last 40 years, so we don't see all the ways in which it is designed to take power and properties away from us and concentrate them in the hands of the few. These people do so because they and their friends want to continue to use this existing architecture to drive us through tunnels and down alleys, into windowless warehouses and confinement pens, into harnesses and yokes, and ultimately into a noose, tied just so, to fit the particular shape of each and every one of our necks.

Which is why our most pressing task is to truly master our own thoughts and perceptions, truly liberate ourselves to interpret the plain facts before our eyes using our own powers of reason.

CREATING THE MIND FREE

In early 1777 Thomas Jefferson began to sketch out what, in many senses, amounted to the second part of the Declaration of Independence. He began with a statement as resounding as any in the great document of the year before. "Almighty God," he wrote, "created the mind free."

Jefferson then moved swiftly to the threat. This was posed not by the British Parliament or the Crown, nor by any commercial monopoly, but by the established church and its buttresses in the state. Or as Jefferson put it, "the impious presumption of legislators and rulers, civil as well as ecclesiastical, who, being themselves but fallible and uninspired men have assumed dominion over the faith of others, setting up their own opinions and modes of thinking as the only true and infallible, and as such endeavouring to impose them on others."

The problem, Jefferson held, was that the churchmen and their allies in government had succeeded. These "fallible" men had in fact "established and maintained false religions over the greatest part of the world." And these false religions, by threatening the ability of people to exercise their reason in the management of their own lives and communities, threatened not only true "religious liberty" but the "rightful purposes of civil government."

"Truth," Jefferson wrote, "is the proper and sufficient antagonist to error and has nothing to fear from the conflict, unless by human interposition disarmed of her natural weapons, free argument and debate." The time had therefore come to liberate the human mind from all arbitrary religious constraints so individuals could argue the facts of human life as they found them.[4]

It took until 1786 for the Virginia General Assembly to approve Jefferson's statement, in the form of a "bill for establishing religious freedom," called the Virginia Statute for Religious Freedom. In doing so, the citizens of this new society helped to frame the First Amendment to the Constitution, with its strong protections for freedom of religion, speech, the press, assembly, and petition.[5] Jefferson himself was so proud of this statement that he later instructed his family to list it on his tombstone, along with his authorship of the Declaration and his founding of the University of Virginia, as one of his three greatest accomplishments.[6]

The American Revolution, as we have seen, was in many respects as much an intellectual as a political revolution. And America's first citizens understood that to create true liberty to think, they had to do more than free the individual from top-down political and commercial rule and excessive toil. They also had to free the individual from belief in any one church's version of God and, if possible, for those who so chose, from belief in any god whatsoever. Their aim was not to destroy religion or belief in God. On the contrary, most of America's first citizens very much believed in some god. But they also believed that after their particular god gave human beings the power to reason, it was up to humans to use that gift actively and responsibly.[7]

The thinking, the hopes, in Jefferson's statement and in the minds of those who embraced it were not in any way new to Americans of the late eighteenth century. They were, in fact, the culmination of a centuries-old battle to think and believe as one alone desired. In the British-centric thinking of America's colonists, it led to John Locke and John Milton and Isaac Newton and Sir Francis Bacon, among many others. In part, as with Newton and Bacon, the desire was to freely engage in scientific speculations that might—such as through the revelation of certain "natural" laws—disturb prevailing religious interpretations of how the universe and human society worked. In part, as we see with Milton, the aim was to freely engage in political and economic speculations—and to promote changes in political and economic structures—that might disturb the interests and positions of those who held the levers of the state-backed religion.[8]

Importantly, this fight for religious liberty was also very much a result of the religious ferment that swept through the American people before and after 1776. We see this in such facts as the explosion in the number of Baptist churches in America in the early 1770s.[9] We see it especially in what historians have come to call the Second Great Awakening, a period of almost chaotic religious evangelism and debate that began around 1790 and continued into the 1830s.[10] The "fundamental impetus of these movements was to make Christianity a liberating force," Nathan Hatch wrote in *The Democratization of American Christianity*. "[P]eople were given the freedom to think and act for themselves rather than depending upon the mediations of an educated elite."[11]

This period of religious excitement, in turn, fired popular political ferment in America. The very act of separating religion from politics strongly reinforced the democratic republican belief that it was up to each individual citizen to help protect liberty and to make the world right. As Gordon Wood has put it, Americans for the first time in history "saw that their culture was exclusively man-made. They alone were responsible for what they thought and believed and for what would be thought and believed in the future by those they often called the 'millions unborn.'"[12]

Still, in 1777, Jefferson believed a simple statement was necessary to reinforce the idea that all was in our power to shape, to master. Not only our economy, not only our politics, but our souls. And the people embraced this idea as their own.[13]

Unfortunately, most Americans did not enjoy this new freedom for long.

If there is a fundamental tragedy in American history, it is that Jefferson and many of his contemporaries to the end of their lives remained subject to perhaps the single most insidious form of deterministic thought—the belief that biology, that race, can limit the dreams, thoughts, and achievements of individuals and even entire groups of people.

Over the coming two centuries, Americans would use this belief—often buttressed by state power—to structure society and community and to limit the lives and thoughts not just of enslaved African Americans but to some extent of every individual in the nation, to the point of determining caste and status and fate as crudely as any state religion was used to structure any eighteenth-century European society.

To further complicate matters, Jefferson and the other citizens of the new nation failed entirely to understand how ingenious the masters of men would prove in thinking up entirely new metaphysical systems with which to awe and manipulate the people, systems entirely unconnected to any traditional—or, for that matter, any newfangled—church. Although the "historical" determinism of Hegel and Marx never gained much hold in America, citizens of this nation have proven to be especially susceptible to the idea that some particular technology, or some structure in capitalism or "the market," has the power to shape the action of human individuals and communities.

In other words, much as the last 250 years have been the story of monopolistic efforts to overturn the economic and political achievements of the Revolution and to recapture control over the properties of the individual and the democratic institutions in which we protect them, so too have the last 250 years been the story of efforts to over-turn the intellectual achievements of the Revolution and to recapture control over the individual mind.

Jefferson's contribution, as imperfect as it may have been, was to understand how economic and political liberty depended on intel-lectual liberty. And in his statement on religious freedom, he did leave us with a tool we can use today to understand how these twin counterrevolutions reinforce one another.

A SOCIOLOGIST FOR THE MONOPOLIST

In the 1850s, the Virginia lawyer and painter George Fitzhugh published two of the most opprobrious books in American history, *Sociology of the South* and *Cannibals All*. A virtuoso provocateur, Fitzhugh gleefully made the case that not only should most blacks be kept in slavery because of a fundamental inability to compete in free society, but most whites as well, for the same reason, as was proved by their growing degradation under systems of "wage slavery" in the North. "It is the duty of society to protect the weak," Fitzhugh wrote. And since true protection requires control over those who are protected, "It is the duty of society to enslave the weak."

And who was to do the enslaving? Roughly 1 in every 20 people, Fitzhugh wrote, "are as clearly born or educated or some way fitted for command and liberty."[14]

Fitzhugh's writings can be viewed as little more than a glib re-sponse to the growing threat to planter rule in the South posed by increasingly radical democratic republican arguments, such as the Free Soil movement of the 1850s, against all forms of concentrated power. Fitzhugh simply flipped the basic assumptions of America upside down. All men are not created equal, he wrote. The American system was a lie, for whites as well as blacks.

But there was more than mere glibness at work here. What made Fitzhugh's contribution especially powerful was that he helped to pioneer the importation of a variety of arguments and tropes from the new European "sciences" of sociology and anthropology. He used these to buttress his efforts to *prove* the superiority of a select few individuals and their natural ability—hence right—to rule over others. Put another way, Fitzhugh took the fundamental flaw in Jefferson's thinking, his belief in race determinism, and built it into a system that not only destroyed arguments against slavery but also destroyed all arguments for "Jeffersonian" democracy built on the idea that "all men are created equal."

Though Fitzhugh's effort to destroy democracy for the white man failed, his efforts to buttress racist arguments with the new sciences worked magnificently well. As Du Bois later put it, "For the average planter born after 1840 it was impossible not to believe that all valid laws in psychology, economics and politics stopped with the Negro race."

Much the same would also prove true after the war, not only in the South but increasingly also in the North. It was easy, Du Bois wrote, "to believe the accusations of the South and to listen to the proof which biology and social science hastened to adduce of the inferiority of the Negro. The North seized upon the new Darwinism, the 'Survival of the Fittest,' to prove that what they had attempted in the South [through Reconstruction] was an impossibility; and they did this in the face of the facts which were before them, the examples of Negro efficiency, of Negro brains, of phenomenal possibilities of advancement."[15]

White Americans, in all corners of the country, continued to use these false sciences to bolster discrimination for a whole long century more, especially against African Americans but also against all people of color. Indeed, many white Americans continue to use these false sciences straight through to today.

But these false sciences were not used only against people of color. In the years after the Civil War, the effort to use crude biological determinism to reinforce the rule of the rich and powerful *within* white America also continued.

Here the key intellectual was Herbert Spencer, the English philosopher who, after reading Charles Darwin's *On the Origin of Species*, coined the term "survival of the fittest."

Described by one historian as a "British railway engineer turned evolutionary cosmic philosopher," Spencer, while working as an editor at *The Economist*, became fascinated with the idea that human behavior was largely or entirely the function of "natural law."[16] He then published numerous books in which he claimed to prove that human thought was shaped by physical structures and forces and that human societies and behaviors are shaped by natural biological competition.[17]

A good example of Spencer's thought is found in his essay "The Morals of Trade," published in 1857: "It has been said that the law of animal creation is—'Eat and be eaten,' and of our trading community it may be said similarly that its law is 'Cheat and be cheated.' A system of keen competition, carried on, as it is, without adequate moral restraint, is very much a system of commercial cannibalism. Its alternatives are—use the same weapons as your antagonists, or be conquered and devoured."[18]

By the early 1870s Spencer's efforts to reduce human commercial and political behavior down to certain forms of natural—hence fundamentally unchangeable—law had won him wide renown almost everywhere except in America, where the original democratic republican antagonism to deterministic systems continued to hold strong.

For those Americans who wished to exploit Spencer's philosophy for political ends—for instance, to justify rule by the rich and already powerful—the challenge now became to get the American people to embrace the philosopher's theories. The person who came up with the solution was none other than Andrew Carnegie, the steel magnate who would in time become the wealthiest American, in relative terms, in the history of the nation.[19] Carnegie's solution was simple—import the great metaphysician and then parade him and celebrate him in front of the American people.

Although, as his biographer Joseph Frazier Wall put it, "There was no prize that Carnegie sought more eagerly than Herbert Spencer," the task did not prove easy, even for a man as charming and powerful as Carnegie. Not only was Spencer in extremely high demand in Europe, but he hated travel. It was not until 1882 that Carnegie's "long, patient courting of his hero" paid off. Spencer agreed to cross the Atlantic, and Carnegie was able to arrange to dine with him on each of the nine nights of the ocean passage.[20]

When Spencer did get to see the American version of dog-eat-dog in action—at Carnegie's steel mills in Pittsburgh—he recoiled in horror and told his American hosts to go easier on their workers. But Carnegie's aim was not so much to win Spencer's approval as to be able to "[s]how off his prize," which he was able to do most dramatically at a famous banquet at Delmonico's steak house in New York.[21]

In his autobiography, Carnegie described his feeling of first reading Spencer in terms of rapture. "[L]ight came as in a flood and all was clear. Not only had I got rid of theology and the supernatural, but I had found the truth of evolution. 'All is well since all grows better' became my motto, my true source of comfort."[22]

It is by no means clear Carnegie fully understood Spencer's work, at least as Spencer believed it should be understood. More to the point, it's not clear Carnegie ever bothered to try.[23] His goal was simply to buttress his own political position in the upper firmament, high above America's egalitarian and somewhat chaotic republican democracy. And in the outlines of Spencer's theories Carnegie found the rough argument he needed to provide an intellectual and moral justification for his own predatory behaviors, and for the private systems of power he had constructed.[24]

After all, as Hans Thorelli succinctly put it, in his history of American antimonopoly law, "the logical outcome of 'survival of the fittest' thinking was monopoly."[25]

For the rest of his life Carnegie would be "a Social Darwinist *par excellence*."[26] In the 1889 article "The Gospel of Wealth," he wrote: "While the law [of competition] may be sometimes hard for the individual, it is best for the race, because it insures the survival of the fittest in every department. We accept and welcome, therefore, as conditions to which we must accommodate ourselves, great inequality of environment; the concentration of business, industrial and commercial, in the hands of a few."[27]

Other monopolists gladly joined in Carnegie's crude parroting of Spencer's not-much-less-crude theories. John D. Rockefeller, for instance, reportedly once said, "The growth of a large business is merely a survival of the fittest . . . This is not an evil tendency in business. It is merely the working out of a law of nature and a law of god."[28]

So too many politicians, most notably Teddy Roosevelt. In a December 1904 speech, with more than a dollop of self-regard mixed in, Roosevelt declared that "Great corporations are necessary and only men of great singular mental power can manage such corporations successfully, and such men must have great rewards."[29]

By 1909, some Americans had evolved Spencer's thinking far beyond simply helping to justify monopoly and rule by plutocrat. Herbert Croly, in the book in which he shaped much of the thinking that would animate Roosevelt's campaign in 1912, and which thereby shaped much of the thinking of the command-and-control wing of the progressive movement in the twentieth century, proposed to use the state to speed the process of selection. In doing so Croly helped to point the way toward the state-backed eugenicism and racial fascism of the future.

"The Hamiltonian principle of national responsibility recognizes the inevitability of selection," Croly wrote. "And since it is inevitable, is not afraid to interfere on behalf of the selection of the really fittest."[30]

AN ECONOMICS BEYOND POLITICS?

Walter Bagehot is one of the few nineteenth-century journalists remembered today. In part it's because his book *Lombard Street: A Description of the Money Market* is still cited by bank regulators, mainly for his dictum that in times of panic large banks should lend "freely, and generously." In part it's because *The Economist*, which Bagehot edited for 15 years until his death in 1877, still runs a column that bears his name.[31]

I use Bagehot to open this section because of the title of one of his books that is only rarely recollected nowadays. This was *Physics and Politics*, from 1872, in which Bagehot claimed to have discovered a "doctrine" able to describe "a physical cause of improvement from generation to generation" and a "continuous force which binds age to age."[32] Bagehot in this title and in these words captured one of the main aims of the generation that established the framework of "modern" economics. This was to supply, in place of the somewhat sweaty biological mechanisms of Fitzhugh and Spencer, a vision of a machine, coldly clicking, physically, according to Newtonian laws, within and around the economy and society.[33] And further, to then claim to have developed a "science" capable of understanding the workings of this mechanism.

The actual credit for establishing the "science" of economics is often given to Léon Walras, a French mathematician whose 1874 book *Elements of Pure Economics* is regarded as the main foundation for what we now call "neoclassical economics." Walras's partner in the effort was the engineer and sociologist Vilfredo Pareto, the scion of a noble Italian family exiled to Switzerland and a sworn enemy of democracy.

To the extent that Walras and Pareto were able to set a practical goal for their new "science," it was to get people to believe that political economies are characterized by a state of "perfect competition" governed by laws that ensure that the supply of a product would always equal demand for that product, in a state they termed "equilibrium." Their closely related goal was to concoct a mathematics that would allow them to claim they could study such mechanisms and such equilibriums "scientifically."

Importantly for the future of economics, Walras, Pareto, and the other self-anointed experts who helped to create what we now know as "neoclassical" economics were not content merely with obscuring the exercise of power behind their descriptions of "natural" mechanical systems. They also aimed to develop theories that would allow them to *prescribe* certain best economic and political practices.

As we have seen, the basic approach of Adam Smith and almost all early American political economists was to carefully assemble a set of facts, then attempt to make an argument based on those facts either for or against some potential change in policy: a lowering of the tariff perhaps, or a new regulation on bankers. Walras, Pareto, and the other new "scientists," however, not only abandoned such evidence-based methods of political economics for mathematically based "deductive" methods, they then elevated theory over observation in the sketching out of policy.

In his book, Walras describes their intentions with some clarity. "[T]he physic-mathematical sciences, like the mathematical sciences, in the narrow sense, do go beyond experience as soon as they have drawn their type concepts from it. From real-type concepts, these sciences abstract ideal-type concepts which they define, and then on the basis of these definitions they construct a priori the whole framework of their theorems and proofs. After that they go back to experience not to confirm *but to apply their conclusions.*"[34]

Put another way, rather than treat political economics as the application of observation, debate, and inspiration to the setting of social rules and human laws designed to govern cooperation and conflict, the new "scientists" aimed instead to treat societies as data-generating mechanisms whose deep structures can be deduced from the data but not to any important extent altered through politics.

Not surprisingly, innocent scientific speculation alone does not explain this sudden explosion of interest in turning economics into a "physic-mathematical" science. Part of the explanation for this lies in two great political events that had shaken the political and economic hierarchies of Europe just before Walras and Pareto published their project. One was the triumph of the Union in the Civil War, an event widely read to mean that republican democracy—with its core focus on economic and political power—would continue to inspire liberal and socialist revolutionaries in Europe for years to come. The other was the lightning victory of Germany over France in the Franco-Prussian War of 1871 and the popular rebellion known as the Paris Commune. During the more than two months before the French army brutally suppressed the "communards," middle- and lower-class Parisians embraced such reforms as abolishing child labor, suspending certain debts, and socializing some properties.

Hence the goal of Europe's new "scientific" economists was also, quite intentionally, to depoliticize political economics by replacing the power analysis of the American and French revolutions with a vision of a system largely if not entirely "mechanical" and "self-regulating" in nature.[35]

In the years since, numerous thinkers have tried to bring this system into better alignment with actual human society.

One of the most sophisticated attacks from inside the academy would be mounted in the 1930s by the British economist Joan Robinson and the American economist Edward Chamberlin. In separate books, they attempted to take Walras's concept of perfect competition and replace it with a concept they called "imperfect" or "monopolistic" competition, which they believed better captured the actual ways in which the large corporations of the time competed with one another.[36]

Although their own highly abstract system still falsified actual political economics in fundamental ways, and still hid much of the blunt exercise of power, the vision of Robinson and Chamberlin was less abstract than the prevailing approach, and perhaps over time could have been used to steer mathematical economics toward a somewhat closer focus on actual market structures and corporate behaviors. By 1950, however, the economist George Stigler had managed to largely destroy Robinson and Chamberlin's rebellion.[37] Stigler later gained renown as one of the masterminds of the neoliberal revolution in economic thinking.

Sophisticated critics of "neoclassical" economics also launched attacks from outside the academy.

Perhaps the most damning was mounted by Karl Popper, a Vienna-born philosopher and historian of ideas, in a two-volume work published in 1945 called *The Open Society and Its Enemies*. Popper described deterministic thinking like that of Walras and Pareto, or what he called "historicism," as an intentional "revolt against freedom." The idea that the social sciences must be prophetic, he wrote, "must lead to a rejection of the applicability of [true] science or of reason to the problems of social life—and ultimately, to a doctrine of power, of domination and submission."[38]

Perhaps the most eloquent attack on such deterministic thinking was made by Du Bois. In the conclusion of *Black Reconstruction*, the historian and political economist devoted a long section to the work of the economic historian Charles Beard, who in 1913 had published *An Economic Interpretation of the Constitution of the United States*, and then in 1927 published *The Rise of American Civilization*. Beard's work, which had become highly influential, especially among progressives, much in the manner of Walras and Marx presented politics mainly as a function of the mechanical workings of economic and political forces.

Or as Du Bois now described it in terms that anyone could understand, Beard had reduced the Civil War to a simple tale of a "difference of development" between "North and South," a simple "working out of cosmic social and economic law." Beard's approach to history, Du Bois wrote, promoted the "comfortable feeling" that the Civil War had little to do with "right or wrong." Instead, things just happen. "Manufacturing and industry develop in the North; agrarian feudalism develops in the South. They clash, as winds and waters strive, and the stronger forces develop the tremendous industrial machine that governs us so magnificently and selfishly today."

Then Du Bois stuck the individual, complete with the power to reason and the urge to dream, back into the picture. "In this sweeping mechanistic interpretation, there is no room for the real plot of the story, for the clear mistake and guilt of rebuilding a new slavery of the working class in the midst of a fateful experiment in democracy; for the triumph of sheer moral courage and sacrifice in the abolition crusade; for the hurt and struggle of degraded black millions in their fight for freedom and their attempt to enter democracy. Can all this be omitted or half suppressed in a treatise that calls itself scientific?"[39]

When faced with such attacks, the "scientific" economists usually responded simply by closing their circles that much tighter and by inventing new ways to prove "their own opinions and modes of thinking as the only true and infallible" faith, such as by awarding well-endowed and widely publicized prizes to one another.

The fundamental fraudulence of their "science," however, is perhaps best revealed by the fact that so many leading "economists" in the years since Walras and Pareto have repeatedly turned to biological determinism to buttress their "physic-mathematical" contentions.[40]

This approach was pioneered by the British economist Alfred Marshall, who more than any other actor is responsible for establishing twentieth-century economics on the foundations laid by Walras and Pareto. As one historian has put it, Marshall, "while taking care to state his economic principles as reflections of mathematics," routinely adopted "the evolutionary rhetoric of biology."[41]

No writer, however, would prove more adept at using biological determinism to prop up "physic-mathematical" economics than the Austrian-born Joseph Schumpeter, a onetime Marxist whose work was revered by economists from across the political spectrum, from John Kenneth Galbraith to Alan Greenspan, from Paul Sweezy to Robert Solow.[42]

There is perhaps no better example of how Schumpeter wove such thinking into his economics than in the paragraph from his 1942 book *Capitalism, Socialism, and Democracy* that contains his single most famous statement—that capitalism is a process of "creative destruction."

"The opening up of new markets, foreign or domestic, and the organizational development from the craft shop and factory to such concerns as U.S. Steel illustrates the same process of industrial mutation—if I may use the biological term—that incessantly revolutionizes the economic structure *from within*, incessantly destroying the old one, incessantly creating a new one. This process of creative destruction is the essential fact of capitalism. It is what capitalism consists [of] and what every capitalist concern has got to live in."[43]

In other words, even as economists claim that their "science" represents an escape from metaphysics, "modern" economics actually continues to *depend* on belief in the myth that human economic life is controlled by some sort of metaphysical *forces*.

Most economists today will strongly deny that they believe in fairies, sprites, and angels. And yet, it's not hard to find evidence that they do. In their recent book *Radical Markets*, for instance, the economists Eric Posner and Glen Weyl argue that the way to solve inequality is to unleash "market forces." Indeed, a quick search of Google Scholar shows that the term "market forces" has been used in academic articles more than 30,000 times just since 2015.

This is an impressively large number. Perhaps the time has come for bright young mathematically inclined students of human society to provide us with an economics of this false science.

FROM JUSTICE TO EFFICIENCY

Through most of the twentieth century, the various fashions, factions, fights, and faiths within economics did not much affect the American System of Liberty. This was not because the democratic republicans were not aware of the debates of the economists. It was because they saw little use for work they believed was overly abstract at best, and downright corrupt at worse.

This basic approach to economics was clear from the first. As Hans Thorelli described the foundational era of modern antimonopoly law, "in accordance with legislative custom at the time, rooted in traditional American distrust of experts, Congress itself considered one antimonopoly bill after another without ever, insofar as is known, calling on the advice of professional economists."[44]

Woodrow Wilson then reinforced this line of thinking during the 1912 campaign. Even as Teddy Roosevelt proposed that scientists be put in charge of the economy, Wilson declared, "I don't want a smug lot of experts to sit down behind closed doors in Washington and play Providence to me. There is a Providence to which I am perfectly willing to submit. But as for other men setting up as Providence over myself, I seriously object."[45]

Brandeis was even more vigorous in ignoring or outright rejecting the work of economists. In the words of Gerald Berk, "Like the pragmatists of his time and the legal realists after him, [Brandeis] thought efforts to match facts to deductive categories elusive." Antitrust must instead always focus, he believed, on "the distribution of economic power in [an] industry."[46]

Not that Brandeis was against science. On the contrary, he was fascinated with the potential of scientists, and especially engineers, to develop better ways to manufacture goods and to deliver services. This included celebrating the work of the engineer Frederick Taylor, whom Brandeis helped make famous for his close studies of ways to improve the efficiency of factories and railroads.[47]

Over time, Brandeis was able to build this distrust of "scientific" economics both into the work of institutions such as the Interstate Commerce Commission and into the law itself. For instance,

Brandeis worked closely with engineers to radically change account-ing practices within railroads and utilities, away from approaches favored by economists toward approaches favored by engineers. The ultimate effect was to keep neoclassical economics at the margins of competition policy for most of the twentieth century. As Berk ex-plains, Brandeis "deepened the chasm between the way engineering and economics approached the construction of knowledge."[48]

Franklin Roosevelt's administration largely hewed to this same line of thinking. As Roosevelt himself said of economists in 1935, "Two things stand out: The first is that no two of them agree, and the other thing is that they are so foggy in what they say that it is almost impossible to figure out what they mean. It is jargon; abso-lute jargon."[49] Most officials in the Truman, Eisenhower, Kennedy, and Johnson administrations generally agreed.[50] During these same years we do see the elevation of the economist as "primary expert" in many of the debates over monetary and fiscal policy—for example, the raw free-silver inflationism of William Jennings Bryan and the tobacco-spitting farmers was carefully dressed up in a lab coat of Keynesian mathematical "macroeconomics." But for many decades, Americans largely kept the economist out of the debates over how to structure the American System of Liberty.

Thus, in the early days of the twentieth century, did the Amer-ican people reclaim their liberty from the theorist. The American System of Liberty, as designed by the first citizens, was now run by Louisville-born lawyers and Texas and Missouri farmers. The simple squares of land of the Northwest Ordinance, and the simple rules of corporate behavior imposed in the years of direct legislative charter, were now renewed for an era of electricity, internal combustion, and mass manufacturing. It was a commonsense system run by and for the common citizen.

And it was a system that had been engineered, overtly, to protect the work of the engineer and scientist from the predations of the financier, while still maintaining an important role for the private investor.

Which brings us to my last key player in the subversion of the American System of Liberty over the last generation—Richard

Posner. Although Posner would serve more than 35 years on the U.S. Seventh Circuit Court of Appeals in Chicago, and would publish more than two dozen books on law, policy, and politics, it was his first book, published in 1973 when he was a professor of law at Stanford, that would have the greatest effect. This was called *Economic Analysis of Law*, and not only did it clear the path that Bork followed a few years later with *The Antitrust Paradox*, it led to an even wider rethinking of the purpose and practice of law within society.

In the book, Posner contended he had discovered something new and yet fundamental in the law. As he explained in a greatly expanded version of the book, published in 1986, this was that "the logic of the law might be economics."[51] And further, that the law itself had "been shaped by *economic forces*."[52]

To explain his thinking, Posner wrote, "Law embodies and enforces fundamental social norms, and it would be surprising to find that those norms were inconsistent with the society's ethical system." Then Posner asked a rhetorical question that allowed him to nudge law out of the realm of justice and into that of the production and distribution of material goods. Wielding a Pareto-inspired concept that economists sometimes use to measure the distribution of "welfare" in a society, Posner wrote, "is the Kaldor-Hicks concept of efficiency really so at variance with that system?"[53]

This line of reasoning allowed Posner to unfurl his plan, his project, which was nothing short of "the application of economics to law" so that "judges might be *led to use efficiency to guide decision*."[54]

Early on, Posner took care to protect his flank against attacks on his efforts to reduce all of human life and politics to this one theory. "[T]here is more to justice than economics," he wrote, "a point the reader should keep in mind in evaluating normative statements in this book."[55] But then Posner immediately makes clear that what he intends is, indeed, a fundamental redefinition of the nature of law, justice, and morality.

"A second meaning of justice, perhaps the most common, is efficiency," he writes. "We shall see, among many other examples, that when people describe as unjust convicting a person without a trial, taking property without just compensation, or failing to make a negligent automobile driver answer in damages to the victim of his negligence, this means nothing more pretentious than that *the conduct wastes resources*. Even the principle of unjust enrichment can be derived from the concept of efficiency."[56]

Then, with more than a dash of audacity, or sloppiness, of thinking, Posner concludes that same paragraph with an unmoored assertion. "[W]ith a little reflection, it will come as no surprise that in a world of scarce resources waste should be regarded as *immoral*."[57]

Only a few years earlier, the idea that any legal scholar would attempt to reorient the law away from justice and toward a pursuit of efficiency would have been met with howls of laughter. And in the 1986 edition of his book, Posner did in fact write of the "outrage" of his critics, many of whom found his ideas to be "repulsive" and who believed that "it is inconceivable that the legal system would . . . embrace them."[58]

But in that same edition, published five years after Ronald Reagan had taken office, Posner was able to report that his thinking had in fact given birth to a "movement that challenges not only the methodological but also the political predispositions of many traditional legal scholars as well as many law students, lawyers, and judges."[59]

It is hard to overstate the radicalism of the argument Posner makes in *Law and Economics*. It is also hard to overstate its success within the law, economics, society, and politics.

Many aspects of this intellectual revolution have been documented by other writers, including Thomas Frank, Matt Stoller, Angus Burgin, Quinn Slobodian, and Nancy MacLean. The specific efforts to reconstruct antimonopoly law on the intellectual foundations laid by Posner and Bork were especially well planned and closely coordinated. One result, supported by enormous contributions by corporations and from the personal funds of monopolists, has been the at least partial embrace of this basic philosophy by every important school of law, school of economics, and school of business in the United States. Which means that millions of Americans have been trained—or perhaps more accurately, indoctrinated—to at least some degree to this way of thinking.

The biggest effect, however, came from simply building economic analysis directly into the institutions and processes we use to enforce the law. Or put another way, to build economists into the process of delivering justice to the American people.

A good guide to how exactly this was accomplished is the book *Antitrust and the Triumph of Economics* by the political scientist Marc Allen Eisner. As Eisner notes, the Antitrust Division in the Justice Department did not even establish an economics office until the mid-1970s, and throughout the decade the "only power" of economists "was that of persuasion."[60] Into the 1980s, he writes, decision making in the agency continued to be "monopolized by attorneys."[61]

The big change took place almost immediately after Ronald Reagan took office in early 1981. Reagan officials moved swiftly to overturn the traditional structure, in which the economist served the lawyer, first in the Justice Department and then at the Federal Trade Commission. This included doubling the relative number of economists within the division, to nearly three for every ten lawyers, by 1986.[62] And it included the decision to elevate the division's chief economist to the role of deputy assistant attorney general.[63]

The actions had a profound effect on how the law itself was enforced. By the mid-1980s, Eisner writes, economists at the Justice Department were able to exercise "what amounted to veto power in the enforcement process."[64] The law, as passed by Congress, was simply ignored. "Even if there were evidence that the law had been violated and reason to believe that the division could triumph before the courts," Eisner wrote in the 1991 edition of his book, "a case would not be approved unless economic analysis revealed that enforcement would be economically beneficial."[65]

Thus was the sword of justice placed into the hand of the false scientist, who was more or less directly in the pay of the monopolist, of the autocrat. And there it has remained, thanks to the often conscious efforts of high officials working in the administrations of Bill Clinton, George W. Bush, Barack Obama, and Donald Trump.

Indeed, one of the few accomplishments in competition policy of the Trump administration has been to further extend the sway of the economist over political economics. President Trump's Federal

Communications Commission chairman Ajit Pai is best known for overturning, in June 2018, the Federal Communications Commission's 2015 net neutrality order.

Importantly, Pai also managed to finally create an office of Economics and Analytics within the Federal Communications Commission just like those the Reagan administration established decades ago in the Justice Department and the Federal Trade Commission.[66] Who better than Donald Trump to expand the realm of a regime of lies.

THE BLIND LEADING THE LOBOTOMIZED

Even before the French economist Thomas Piketty's book *Capital in the Twenty-First Century* was published in the United States in April 2014, it had been hailed for months as an "event." "Marx 2.0" has arrived, *Time* magazine declared. But it wasn't only socialists like Britain's Paul Mason who praised Piketty's work for demonstrating—in great detail—how extreme inequality had become across Europe and the United States. So too did Larry Summers and Paul Krugman.

Even though *Capital* ran to almost 600 pages and included long discussions of such topics as "Rastignac's dilemma," the "Kuznets Curve," and the "Kotlikoff-Summers thesis," Piketty's work struck home far outside the economics academy or even the wider realm of policy experts. Not only did *Capital* hit number one on the bestseller lists of the *New York Times*, the *Wall Street Journal*, and Amazon, it went on to play a role in American politics, helping fuel the 2016 campaigns not only of Bernie Sanders but of Donald Trump.

To be clear, Piketty in *Capital* did develop statistical methods that provide a far more detailed understanding than any previous scholar of how income and wealth have been concentrated over the last century. For American readers, Piketty also confirmed that the top 1 percent had indeed doubled their share of the nation's wealth between 1980 and 2014, to about 20 percent of the total, bringing inequality levels more or less exactly back to where they were when Woodrow Wilson took office in 1913, at the peak of the age of the plutocrat.[67]

Yet Piketty's work is also flawed by a set of fundamental contradictions.

For instance, Piketty acknowledges the role of policy in making inequality worse, writing that the "resurgence of inequality after 1980 is due largely to the political shifts of the past several decades, especially in regard to taxation and finance." Yet in the same paragraph, he writes that the decline in inequality between 1910 and 1950 "was above all a consequence of war and of policies adopted to cope with the shocks of war." At no point does he devote a sentence to instances in which policies enacted in relatively peaceful times[68]—for instance in the first 18 months of the Wilson administration or the early years of the Johnson administration—reduced inequality.[69]

Piketty speaks strongly against economic determinism and warns the reader that "The history of the distribution of wealth has always been deeply political, and it cannot be reduced to purely economic mechanisms." Yet throughout *Capital* he writes in a passive voice and tells the reader that "capitalism" all but "automatically generates arbitrary and unsustainable inequalities." Or as the journalist and author Rana Foroohar put it, "According to Piketty," inequality is "the natural order of things."[70]

Piketty, to his credit, warns readers not to believe in "economic science" and instead to reembrace the term "political economics."[71] But he then admits he personally is almost completely ignorant of corporate power and the actual structure of markets. "To be frank, I know virtually nothing about exactly how Carlos Slim or Bill Gates became rich, and I am quite incapable of assessing their relative merits."[72]

Finally, Piketty writes that "historical experience remains our principal source of knowledge."[73] Then he admits that he knows almost nothing about the two great periods in American history—after the Revolution of 1776 and after the New Freedom and New Deal—during which wealth and power were widely redistributed in a largely peaceful fashion.[74]

Piketty concludes his work by declaring that the only way to fix inequality is to impose a "global tax on income." Then he immediately characterizes this solution as a "utopian idea" that would "require a very high and no doubt unrealistic level of international cooperation." Meaning, it would seem, there is nothing to be done.[75]

Over the course of Piketty's immense book, there are a total of three mentions of the word "monopoly." In two instances, Piketty writes about local monopolists who could have no great effect on the larger structure of wealth and power in society. The other is his glib speculation about how Bill Gates and Carlos Slim may have actually amassed their fortunes, already mentioned above. In short, Piketty in *Capital* all but entirely ignores many of the subjects he says are key—including the concentration of power, the structures of markets, the behaviors of corporations, the structures of complex systems, the effects of monopsony, and the effects of first-degree price discrimination.

Indeed, there are few better proofs than *Capital* of how the intellectual structure, language system, and investigative tools of modern economics can make it hard for even the brightest and most well-meaning of economists to understand what is actually happening in our society.

The real importance of *Capital* lies in the fact that, even as Piketty personally displays many of the greatest weaknesses of modern economics, he also mounts one of the most powerful critiques of the academy by any scholar in recent times.

Piketty starts by recounting a three-year stint in the United States in his early twenties as an assistant professor at the Massachusetts Institute of Technology. "I quickly realized that there had been no significant effort to collect historical data on the dynamics of inequality since [the early 1950s], yet the profession continued to churn out purely theoretical results without even knowing what facts needed to be explained. And it expected me to do the same."[76]

In the 20 years between his time in Boston and the publication of *Capital*, he says that little changed. "[T]he discipline of economics has yet to get over its childish passion for purely theoretical and often highly ideological speculation," Piketty writes early in the book. "This obsession with mathematics is an easy way of acquiring the appearance of scientificity without having to answer the far more complex questions posed by the world we live in." Such mathematical models, he concludes, "are frequently no more than an excuse for . . . masking the vacuity of the content."[77]

Piketty concludes by assailing mainstream American economists for "their absurd claim to greater scientific legitimacy, despite the fact that they *know almost nothing about anything*."[78]

It's a scene from *Lear*, the blind man cursing the lobotomized.

In Piketty, we have a scholar who has dedicated his career to creating the most important set of data on inequality and the tools to understand that data. And yet he has no ability to offer useful policy. But at least he appears to understand, as he grasps impotently at the empty air, that his eyes have been gouged out. More important, Piketty knows who did the gouging.

And so in the end we are left with a two-part problem.

First, belief in the "market as machine" or the "market as biological being" radically shrinks or even destroys much of our ability to see power, hence to protect ourselves from the political and economic effects of concentrated power. Second, this positing of a mechanism, or organism, that does not exist also means we lose our understanding of how the real systems, and the real machines, work.

At one and the same time, we lose our simple human politics, simple human morality, and our capacity for true engineering and true science.

For more than 800 years, we battled to bring law into alignment with justice.

For more than 200 years, we battled to bring law into alignment with liberty.

For a century, we battled to bring law into alignment with the building and running of complex financial, communications, transportation, and industrial systems, in ways that promote not merely our basic safety but a wide prosperity and even peace.

It is now clear that—over the course of but a few years—the subjugation of law to the idea of efficiency, and to a false science designed to promote and measure efficiency, directly threatens all justice, all liberty, and the most basic forms of human security.

What we have witnessed this last generation is the destruction of law, of science, of reason. What we have witnessed is a form of barbarism by men in white shirts and silk ties.

But maybe it's all for the best. Maybe this gives us the opportunity to simply surrender ourselves to the new "meta" physics just now emerging, in which the human being and human society are increasingly directed—in what we buy, where we walk, what we think, how we vote—by Google, Amazon, and a few other immensely powerful corporations armed with vast caches of information and licenses to discriminate in the information they deliver to us. Corporations that control machines are increasingly able to guide our course through Grand Central Terminal, and through all the other rooms and plazas and cities and debates and markets through which we pass, without us having even to bother to exercise our own senses or thoughts, without us having to bear that great burden of being masters over our own lives.

Were the messiah to appear, would we be able to see her? Even if we did, would we be at liberty to follow?

NINE

THE SWORD IN YOUR HAND

WHO ARE YOU?

ARE YOU A CITIZEN? OR A CONSUMER? A PERSON WHO USES REASON to judge fact? Or a parroter of rumors, lies, and hate? Are you the master of your own fate? Or another dog's body?

In America today, we talk all the time of how we are defined by others. We understand that when others name us, they aim to manipulate us, to exploit us, to discard us.

And so we rebel, and we create new labels for ourselves. And in the process, sometimes new liberties and rights. We are good at it. We should be proud.

Yet in America today, we have largely lost this ability to define our own selves within the political economy. We have largely lost the ability even to see how others shape us and the world around us.

For two centuries in America we fought—as individuals, as communities, as a people—to win and keep power. Our aim was not simply a voter's share of some distant national sovereignty. Our aim was the liberty to make our own selves and our own society. The liberty to make our own worlds and our own world.

To that end we developed a language to illuminate the power in the corporation and the power in concentrations of capital, and we designed systems to master that power. We used this language also to define ourselves absolutely as wielders of power, as creators, growers, makers, thinkers, citizens.

But a generation ago, we let others develop a bastard version of this language to label and categorize us in ways designed to take all such power, and all such liberties, away. They did so by defining us as simple buyers, eaters, button pushers, voyeurs.

And with mouths agape, and eyes vacant, we have stared and watched them, passive spectators of our own debauchment.

At what point—exactly—do you lose ownership of your self?

The ideas in your head? At what point do they become another's tool to exploit and manipulate you?

The liberty you seek? Do you even know what exactly that is anymore?

This ignorance—of who you are and how others shape you—is license to use your own secrets to farm you, to harrow you.

This ignorance—of who you are and how others shape you—is license to use your own appetites to degrade you.

This ignorance—of who you are and how others shape you—is license to strip you of your skills, your intellectual tools, your confidence as a thinker and creator.

This ignorance—of who you are and how others shape you—is license to use your fears to lure the fiend up within you. And thereby enthrall you not only to their structures of power but to their ability to manipulate the grossest of your passions.

This ignorance—of who you are and how others shape you—is why we now face the gravest threat to liberty and democracy in America, and to equality and individual dignity, since the days of the slave power.

WHERE IS YOUR WORLD?

Our grandparents and great-grandparents, in building America, made it so that all society would be public society, except for what took place in our homes and in our minds.

They built America so that important decisions would be common decisions and structured the political economy so our minds could wander freely anywhere, so we could deliberate fully together everywhere.

Nowhere was such freedom more important than in the realms of technology and industry. The goal was to keep all such intellectual and commercial systems open and common. So we could work with one another to think up and to make whatever we needed to survive and thrive. So we could participate freely, plug in freely, within these "technological commons."[1]

It took millions of Americans, working together, thinking together, to make our railroads and electrical and telephone networks and automobile and airplane and computer networks, so we could more easily connect with one another, and communicate with one another, and build a better world with one another. On our farms, millions of Americans adapted their seeds and animals to the particularities of land and moment so we could better clothe and feed one another.

But today vast reaches of our world have been cut off from us. As we walk the streets and drive the highways and till the land, as we go online to do business with one another and communicate with one another, we pass along walls and fences that enclose entire realms of life and mind that used to be largely or entirely open to us.

Today, our energy systems, transportation systems, health systems, education systems, communications systems, news systems, agricultural systems, entertainment systems, and security systems were not made by us to serve our needs. All these systems were made by others to serve their needs. These systems are not open to our ideas. They are designed to impose the ideas—and will—of others on us.

This affects us as individuals. It's one reason we find ourselves standing even outside our own jobs and families, our own businesses and farms, gazing numbly through little windows smeared with thumbprints, watching others run our lives.

It also affects all of us together. Climate change is the greatest challenge humans have ever faced, together, as a species. To survive and keep our dignity, we must figure out all over again how to feed and house ourselves, how to warm and transport ourselves, and how to protect ourselves against disease and despair in a world going through extreme and unpredictable change.

We have every power of mind, every moral capacity necessary to succeed, and to succeed in ways that result in a far more just distribution of well-being and opportunity among all people.

What we don't have today are the keys to any of the technological commons that have been enclosed by the monopolists. Which means we no longer have an ability to study and see what is needed or to share and refine better ideas with one another.

And so with mouths agape, and eyes vacant, we look on silently as others loot and break the systems that we built, and that our parents and grandparents built, and the lives and communities and worlds that depend on them.

We are free to wander in the shadows of other people's walls, along other people's fences, down other people's corridors. While the world that was ours—now unowned, untended, unconsidered—falls to ruin.

Our world is dying because we can no longer put our hands to it, can no longer put our thoughts to it, can no longer dream better ways to make and mend it. Because in every direction we look, a monopolist stands in our way.

WHERE ARE YOUR LEADERS?

You and 100 million others stand, fretful, alarmed, agitated. And you have loitered so for more than a decade, since the days of the Tea Party and Occupy. You and 100 million others have been waiting, calling, for a leader, a savior.

But thus far all our saviors have failed. And all our rebellions have guttered, their molten energies carefully redirected away from the powerful, perhaps into some harmless and sterile amusement, increasingly into hatred of some other because of their race, or where they were born, or simply because of their political party.

I remember when we first stood up after the financial crash of 2008, suddenly impoverished, terrified, outraged. I wrote my last book, *Cornered*, in part to help us understand who had broken our lives and what we must demand from those who would lead us.

But no one ever really answered us.

First came President Obama, with his promises of pragmatism and his coterie of meritocratically selected technocrats. But he failed. In part, President Obama failed because he never mastered the political machine that had elected him, never established clear lines between the people's government and the Wall Street financier and Silicon Valley mogul.[2]

But President Obama's failure was also one of philosophy, of vision. He failed because he and most of his meritocrats did not really understand political economic power. And their inability to see that power made them unable to project power, hence to protect America's citizens from those "who store up violence and robbery in their palaces."[3]

Even though President Obama and his team imagined themselves to be "realists," able to direct the interests of Goldman Sachs and Google toward the common good, their view of how the world works was in many respects strikingly naïve, based as it was on a belief in "rational" man and "rational" markets and other mythical beasts.

Next came President Trump, with his nationalism and tribalism and spluttering fury, his one big idea to build a wall and bolt the doors to keep out the Mexican worker and the Chinese corporation and the "Wuhan virus." (Unless, of course, the Chinese corporation were to pay him, in the form of some personal political favor, for a license to enter.)

From the point of view of the American people, the Trump presidency has been an almost flawless catastrophe. Not only has President Trump failed to deal with the vast array of threats China poses to America's national security and sovereignty, he has also worked hard to further empower the oligarchs and autocrats, handing out grand favors to big ag, big oil, big pharma, big hospital, and especially big tech, and taking particular delight in sabotaging efforts to fight climate change.

In response to these failures, growing numbers of Americans today are working to create a people's movement able to force our leaders to make truly radical changes to our political economy, right now. This movement is to a great degree a product of the American people awakening to the dangers posed by extreme concentrations of economic power.

In but a few years, the movement has won many victories. This includes building real power within the Democratic Party and developing analyses and language that have intruded deep into the thinking of many Republicans and Independents. Thanks to the power of this movement, both Elizabeth Warren and Bernie Sanders published new visions for the enforcement of American antimonopoly law, based on principles and rules derived directly from the American System of Liberty.

Yet despite these striking advances, it is a movement that—if viewed through the eyes of Louis Brandeis or any of the millions of other Americans who built our original System of Liberty—still looks deeply flawed.

One problem is that the main energies of the movement are directed almost entirely toward the federal government. And a prime focus has been on massive plans, like the Green New Deal and Medicare for All, that would require the centralization of direction and control over vast swaths of the American economy and American life. It is a movement, in other words, that ignores the actual political structures in our country, which direct citizens to exercise power within each and every state, and each and every town. It's a movement that ignores the need to construct a story and a language that speaks to the people of every corner in America, no matter their color or party.

A second flaw is that the movement drifts every day further toward a sentimental and romantic vision of revolution. The American System of Liberty has proven methods for structuring markets and corporations and property rights, and for wielding the lure of profit to make a more just society and to radically speed up and redirect technological innovation. But growing numbers of people prefer instead to dream of utopia and content themselves with intellectually indolent calls for the "overthrow" of "capitalism," the walling off of "market forces," and the extirpation of the "profit motive"—and, apparently, all human selfishness—from our lives.

A third flaw is that the movement is still focused ultimately on finding and elevating some savior, who once in power is to somehow, miraculously, multiply loaves, fishes, and windmills and turn hydrocarbons into chardonnay.

The overall result is a vision profoundly disempowering of individual citizens, who rather than being encouraged to fight for themselves, in their own communities, in their own lives, in their own ways, are encouraged to gaze rapturously and passively at some glorious redeemer. It is vision also, not paradoxically, profoundly disempowering of the leaders themselves, whom we saddle with expectations impossible for any human to achieve.

It is a vision, even if its believers were to capture power, designed to fail.

Here again, the ultimate flaw lies in us. In our failure to understand that the foundation stone of the American System of Liberty is the citizen, is each of us individually.

Leaders are ultimately made by the people. Until we know who we truly are, we will never be able to make the leaders we need. Leaders who do not promise to do everything for us but who will help us win sufficient liberty to do all we must, for ourselves and one another, right at home.

WHO ARE YOUR PROPHETS?

In America, the line separating the prophetic visions of the Hebrew Bible and political debate has always been thin. Lincoln, Douglass, Anthony, Brandeis, Du Bois, Roosevelt, and King all invoked the prophets and often wielded their words and imagery. It came to them naturally, an inheritance from the Puritans and Baptists, and the King James Bible, a way of thinking and acting built directly into American language and literature, hence into the American soul.[4]

In America there is also a clear apocalyptic tradition even among those not wont to quote Scripture. Jefferson in his fight against

Hamilton's plan to enthrone the financier, Jackson in his "war" on the national bank, Kennedy in his warning of a missile gap with the Soviets, Gore in his alarms about climate change: all spoke the language of Armageddon.

There is even what we might call a faux-apocalyptic tradition in America, in which leaders depict relatively minor problems, or even imagined problems, in extreme terms so as to direct fear and anger toward particular ends or at particular people. Examples include McCarthy and communism, Wallace and integration, Reagan and welfare, Trump and immigrants.

We often call such apocalyptic prophecies jeremiads, after the prophet Jeremiah. I bring up the political jeremiad for three reasons.

First, it works. The jeremiad has been an essential part of American political culture, a proven way of standing people up to make change, from long before the Revolution, no matter their actual religion, no matter whether they believe in any god at all.[5] As Martin Luther King Jr. explained in 1968, "The Hebrew prophets are needed . . . because decent people must be imbued with the courage to speak the truth, to realize that silence may temporarily preserve status or security but to live with a lie is a gross affront to God."[6]

Second, the nature of the jeremiad teaches us that something more than simple material interest has repeatedly shaped the actions of large numbers of Americans time and again in our history. That love of justice and love of one's neighbor can at times actually lead us into the streets to fight for revolutionary ends. This in turn helps us to see how today, as we set about our next radical reconstruction of the American political economy, it is vital to admit that our ultimate goals are also intellectual and moral and spiritual in nature.

Third, the jeremiad helps us understand our own role, our own importance, as individuals. The essential role not only of our hands in the fight but of our individual thoughts and individual dreams, both to make the political change we seek and to build the world we must.

American revolutionaries over the centuries have used the jeremiad to target many evils, including slavery, racism, poverty, and the degradation of the earth. But the particular polemic that may best fit our needs today was published in 1644 by John Milton. In

Areopagitica, the poet railed against the choking off, by a system of official censorship, of the mind of the individual in society.

The true danger to society, Milton wrote, comes not from the outrageous word or wild notion but from those who would monopolize control over information and knowledge. It was they, he wrote, who threatened "to bring a famin upon our minds again, when we shall know nothing but what is measur'd to us by their bushel." Instead, Milton wrote, it is the people, all the people, who "should be disputing, reasoning, reading, inventing, discoursing, ev'n to a rarity, and admiration, things not before discourst or writt'n of."[7]

Not that Milton himself claimed credit for this vision of a democracy of thought. To make clear who had inspired his writings, Milton referred to a story in the Book of Numbers about a time when Moses learned that two men in his camp had begun to prophesy.[8]

According to that story, Joshua Son of Nun then pleaded with Moses to "forbid" the two men from prophesying. Moses responded not with any selfish effort to protect his precedence or profession but by delivering perhaps the most essentially democratic of laments in human history.

"[W]ould God that All the LORD'S people were prophets, and that the LORD would put His Spirit upon them!"

What these prophets mean to tell us, it would seem, is that the prophet must be each and every one of us. And that our fight today is not merely to restore our ability to govern ourselves and our world. Our fight is also, and perhaps mainly, to re-create a true democracy of thought and to bring all our ideas, all our capacities, together, so we can begin the work of repairing the world, together.

WHAT IS YOUR PLAN?

A decade ago, after the publication of my book *Cornered*, Phil Longman, Lina Khan, and I launched the Open Markets Institute at New America, a think tank in Washington. The goal of both *Cornered* and our work at Open Markets was simple. To use journalism, history, and commonsense arguments to help people see the Godzilla of monopoly and his fire. And to understand we have what with to slay him.

For five years, we made steady but slow progress. Then in 2016, we saw an explosion of interest in monopoly and of a courageous will to restore democracy. Today, with presidential candidates railing against monopoly on the campaign trail, with the attorneys general of our states and the Antitrust Subcommittee of Congress investigating Google and Facebook, and with a true movement rising to fight monopoly, we can honestly say this original mission has been accomplished.

Millions of Americans, and millions of people around the world, do see the threat posed by monopoly, and do see we have weapons.

I wrote *Liberty from All Masters* to help us move from awakening to victory. To the restoration of true liberty and true democracy in America through the destruction of all unregulated private power, most immediately the threat posed by Google, Amazon, and Facebook. And to the tearing down of all the walls and fences that exclude us from our technological commons and from true liberty to think and create with one another.

This book is fundamentally a work of history, an uncovering of the original principles of the American System of Liberty, and a recounting of the lessons of our nearly 250 years fighting for liberty, sometimes as individuals, often as a community, within these borders. My aim here has not been to detail what exactly to do in the years ahead. For that, you can turn to the website of our Open Markets Institute, where you will find a vast body of work on these issues.

And importantly, the Open Markets team is no longer the only keeper of this philosophy. Which means you can now turn also to the writings and actions of a fast-growing legion of allies and others who have rediscovered the rich array of laws, and the particular ways of seeing, of America's antimonopoly tradition.

In the early years of the nation, in the early days of the American System of Liberty, James Madison translated the prophetic voices of Moses and Milton into the more finely reasoned and drier language we associate with the Enlightenment. In doing so, he provided perhaps the single most concise expression in the American tradition of the intersection of power, democracy, and the mind of the individual.

"Although all men are born free, and all nations might be so, yet too true it is, that slavery has been the general lot of the human race. Ignorant—they have been cheated; asleep—they have been surprized; divided—the yoke has been forced upon them. But what is the lesson? That because the people may betray themselves, they ought to give themselves up, blindfold, to those who have an interest in betraying them? Rather conclude that the people ought to be enlightened, to be awakened, to be united, that after establishing a government they should watch over it, as well as obey it."

More than two centuries on, our challenge today is the same. Yes, the world today is—technologically, socially, culturally—profoundly different than that of the founding era. But the principles and language of those days remain as pertinent and potent and can be adapted perfectly to this moment. This, indeed, is precisely what the American people have done repeatedly over the years, every time some new technology or some new form of political thought and organization has threatened our lives, our democracy, our world.

For us today this means, at the most basic level, that our challenge is to resurrect the concept of the citizen for our twenty-first century and to define what it means to be a creator, grower, maker, thinker, and dreamer in the digital age. And it means using this concept of the citizen to rebuild our American System of Liberty to ensure it protects every one of our capacities as citizens, and every one of our human properties, as Madison would have understood the term, no matter the technologies of today or tomorrow.

It means banishing false economic sciences from our governing and judicial councils—and from our own thinking. And embracing again simple commonsense politics and simple bright-line rules of competition and justice.

It means structuring and regulating open markets designed to ensure an absolute liberty to share ideas and goods with one another, to protect our democracy through the careful distribution of power and opportunity, and to create public understanding and public power by pushing commercial information into the public realm through functioning systems for the pricing of all goods and services on which the public depends.

It means re-creating an open technological commons, designed to allow everyone to bring their ideas together, to bring new techniques and technologies to fruition, to empower us to better our lives, and to save our world.

It means using the state to ensure equality not just of opportunity but also of some real property in the American tradition of 160 acres per citizen.

It means using the state to make up, somehow, for our grotesque failure—even in the heart of the twentieth century—to provide African Americans with the same access to real properties as other Americans, or even to protect what properties African Americans were able to hammer into being.

Of most immediate importance in the age of Google and Amazon, it means taking from all powerful middlemen all license to discriminate in the delivery of their services, which is the only way to restore rule of law in our commercial and intellectual realms and ensure the protection of all personal property necessary for true liberty and democracy and for all true scientific advance.

Rarely in human history have we stood at such a fork. Down the road we now travel lies a future of degradation, depravity, and slow death. Yet we also see another path, one that leads to a world of technological and social wonders.

Which brings me to the fourth and last reason I brought up the subject of the jeremiad. Which is that all such prophecies always end with a vision of restoration. The purpose of the jeremiad, in the words of one scholar of the form, is to "direct an imperiled people . . . toward the fulfillment of their destiny, to guide them individually toward salvation, and collectively toward the American city of God."[9]

In 1968, Martin Luther King Jr., mere months before his death, in the midst of a war of mechanized murder in Vietnam, with the prospect of nuclear annihilation looming, in the early years of awareness of our environmental crisis, in the early days of his campaign against poverty, focused on the need to escape webs of ideological and institutional control over our physical and spiritual lives.

To survive, as individuals and as a society, King wrote, we must make ourselves master of all "that complex of devices, techniques, mechanisms and instrumentalities by means of which we live."[10]

American history, indeed, teaches that when the financiers are the masters of the technologies on which we depend, they will wield these technologies in ways designed to concentrate control over us, hence in ways that end up destroying our selves, our society, our world.

What American history also teaches is that the people, when we are truly masters of our own selves and our own communities, will create and wield technologies in ways that empower us—as a people—to achieve moral ends and to build a moral society.

And so we shall again, today.

THE SWORD IN YOUR HAND

Perhaps, one day soon, you will behold your own hands shining before you. Perhaps, one day soon, it will be your own eyes, sparking with inspiration, that you see in the mirror. Perhaps, one day, it will be an absolute love for all humankind that you feel glowing in your own soul.

But what about right now, today? Will you dare today to recognize, even without such signs, the glory within you?

Will you dare, today, to recognize that you already have the power to destroy and to create? The power to break what must be broken and to heal what has been torn?

Will you dare, today, to recognize how this spirit links you to all people everywhere? Who dream as you do? Fear as you do? Strive to understand as you do? Strive to hope as you do? Who live, in the words of King, in the same World House with you?

Are you ready yet to stand against the few men armed with immense machines designed to crush your life? And the lives of your children? And the life of your world?

Are you ready yet to stand against those few men, who in their actions if not their words mock the sacrifices of your grandparents and great-grandparents? Who mock the blood spilled by generation upon generation to get us here? Who mock your will and mock your mind and mock your dreams?

Are you ready yet to stand against those who have exiled you from your own capacity to gather facts and to reason? Who have exiled you from your own God-given existence as a complete human being, a thinker and creator?

Are you ready to "rebuild the ancient ruins" and to "raise up the age-old foundations"?

No one else will fix this for you. American democracy is not a gift of big men on thrones of power. American democracy is not something handed to us by Jefferson or Douglass or Lincoln or Anthony or Brandeis or Du Bois or Roosevelt. American democracy is made by the people imposing their will—and their own systems of control—on "big" men.

It's time to accept what we have lost. Our lives will never go back to normal. We have nowhere to retreat. Radical change, radical threat, are upon us.

Do nothing and our world ends. Do nothing and the songs of the temple shall all be howlings. Do nothing and our children and our children's children shall perish in fire.

We have but one way forward. Only the American System of Liberty provides us with the intellectual, institutional, psychological, technological, and spiritual tools that will enable us to break the powers that bind us and to build a world fit for our children and their children.

Only the American System of Liberty provides us with the tools to reestablish liberty in America for the next 100 years. To refit our world for the centuries. To remake a true World House of hope and trust and justice and love.

The sword is in your hand. See it. Know it. Use it.

ACKNOWLEDGMENTS

Figuring out who to thank after *Liberty from All Masters* is a different challenge than after my first two books. I wrote *End of the Line* and *Cornered* largely alone, composing chapters on long reporting drives across the country, refining sentences while strolling down the Mall. But for the last decade, I have helped to lead a debate on power and democracy that has cascaded from Washington to Silicon Valley to Brussels and elsewhere. The book in your hand was deeply shaped by the clashes of these years. It holds many lessons from friends, and some from foes.

One big change from ten years ago is I spend most days working to keep an organization alive. By the time I published *Cornered* in 2010, I knew that writing books was not enough. To counter the intellectual regime devised by George Stigler, Milton Friedman, Richard Posner, and Robert Bork, with its Orwellian repackaging of control as freedom, I knew we needed institutions as well as ideas. That's why in the leanest days of the Great Recession I set out to create an organization smart enough to counter the Federalist Society, Heritage Foundation, economics academy, and all other propagandists of monopoly and top-down control.

Building the Open Markets Institute was harder than writing any book. But it was worth it. From the first, our team of reporters, lawyers, historians, and organizers has served as the vital center for the ever-widening community of people dedicated to restoring the American System of Liberty. *Forbes* recently called Open Markets a "formidable counterweight" to the platform monopolists. And despite our modest size, we are formidable. That's because truth is cheap. What costs real money is to make a lie stick.

That's why, in thinking of whom to thank, my mind turned first to the folks who worked hardest to build and protect Open Markets. Four stand out—Phil Longman, Marcellus Andrews, Lina Khan, and Nidhi Hegde. Each has their own particular form of true genius. But what makes these four such heroes is that even during difficult times for Open Markets, they calmly focused on the well-being of the institution. Our team has won a lot of glory. But we've also had to figure out how to raise money, cooperate with allies, engage constructively with opponents, and work together in a grubby room in a WeWork. Not all teams survive this period. Thanks to Phil, Marcellus, Lina, and Nidhi, Open Markets has thrived.

Much the same is true of Joe Maxwell and Frank Foer, two other members of our board who devoted long hours to a fragile institution. My thanks also to Christy Hoffman and Laura Quinn, our powerful new board members. And to Beth Grupp, the best mind in the development business.

I am indebted to every member of Open Markets. My longtime friends Sandeep Vaheesan and Sally Hubbard are outstanding antitrust thinkers. This book is also infused with the spirit and ingenuity of Claire Kelloway, Kat Dill, Michael Bloom, Jody Brannon, Gina Salerno, Udit Thakir, Garphil Julien, Daniel Hanley, Beth Baltzin, Nikki Usher, and Mya Frazier. The same is true also for many former members of Open Markets, including Leah Douglass, Brian Feldman, Sidhartha Mahanta, Matt Buck, Laura Hitalsky, Stella Roque, Kevin Carty, Austin Frerick, Jonathan Tsoris, Sarah Miller, and Matt Stoller.

In writing *Liberty from All Masters*, I was thrilled to work again with Adam Bellow and Rafe Sagalyn. Adam and I have been conspiring to write this book for a long while. Rafe is the coolest agent in the business, and the most efficient; it took him all of three minutes to come up with the title. I have also very much enjoyed working with Pronoy Sarkar and the rest of the excellent team at St. Martin's.

I owe huge debts to Sabeel Rahman, Richard John, Gerald Berk,

Lina Khan, Marcellus Andrews, and Christopher Leonard for close readings of *Liberty from All Masters*. Their suggestions and reactions made the book richer and stronger.

Liberty from All Masters would not have been possible without the vision of the two great muckraker publishers of the early twenty-first century—Rick MacArthur of *Harper's* and Paul Glastris of the *Washington Monthly*.

The book also reflects the insights of many other friends and allies. This includes Bert Foer, Teddy Downey, Stacy Mitchell, and Tom Frank, all there at the beginning.

Other early leaders in the fight against monopoly, all close friends, include Doug Preston, Rana Foroohar, Alan Riley, Christian D'Cunha, Liza Lovdahl-Gormsen, Luther Lowe, Jonathan Kanter, Sascha Meinrath, Tim Wu, Mike Callicrate, Phillip Blond, Maurice Glasman, Alec Burnside, Zephyr Teachout, Roger McNamee, David Dayen, Tim Cowen, Jonathan Taplin, Maurice Stucke, John Kwoka, Ariel Ezrachi, Jonathan Sallet, Max Miller, Thea Lee, Jonathan Tepper, Tristan Harris, Marc Rotenberg, Ruth Vitale, Paul Pisano, Patrick Woodall, Patty Lovera, Zach Carter, Angela Huffman, Jonathan Rutherford, Paul Hilder, and Fred Stokes.

Cristina Caffarra, Bill Kovacic, Luigi Zingales, and Guy Rolnik deserve special credit. Not only are they experts on the dangers of monopoly, they do the hard work of organizing discussions.

Thanks also to the journalists who have led the way in addressing America's monopoly crisis. This includes Ken Vogel, Nancy Scola, Nick Thompson, David Streitfeld, David Leonhardt, Farhad Manjoo, Luke Mullins, Andy Kroll, Anya Bourg, Tony Romm, David McCabe, Gilad Edelman, and many others.

Ten years ago there was no market for our work on Capitol Hill. Senator Warren, Representative Cicilline, Senator Franken, and Representative Ellison changed that, by being the first to highlight the dangers of monopoly. Senator Booker, Senator Klobuchar, Senator Warner, Senator Sanders, Representative Khanna, Senator Rubio, Representative Nadler, Representative Ocasio-Cortez, and Senator Hawley have also all played hugely important roles. So too Tish James, Ken Paxton, and state attorneys general across America. Rohit Chopra showed us how to change the course of the FTC. Tom Perriello showed us how to change the course of a state.

I have been repeatedly inspired by the work of Andrea Dehlendorf, Lauren Jacobs, Nafisa Ula, Deb Axt, Jill Hurst, Maurice Weeks, and Dan Schlademan and many other members of the Athena coalition.

I am deeply grateful to Paul Krugman for giving us a huge boost by writing about our work in December 2012. Thanks also to Paul Romer and Ha-Joon Chang for critical support. And none of this would have been possible without the friendship of Reid Cramer, Mark Schmitt, and others at New America.

I want to especially thank the people who kept Open Markets up and running. This includes Vera Franz, Anamitra Deb, Allison Barlow, Herb Sandler, John and Laura Arnold, Alberto Ibarguen, Chris Hughes, Larry Kramer, Tom Kruse, Laleh Ispahani, Sam Gill, Lori McGlinchy, Jose Garcia, Gus Rossi, Jennifer Harris, Sharon Alpert, Laura Campos, Ila Duncan, John Sands, Stephen Heintz, Lance Lindblom, Peter Teague, Amber French, Jason Weins, Taylor Jo Isenberg, Richard DeWyngaert, Steve Daetz, and Dan Burger. Others I can't mention. You know who you are. You know how grateful we are.

One thing that has never changed is the support I've received from Anya, my wife. Until we create an asylum where authors can work through their madness in isolation, the burden of writing will fall hardest on the family. This is Anya's third walk through this valley. All I can offer in return is my love.

Last, thanks to my dad for making me ornery. And for showing me how to walk straight ahead, even in the hardest of times.

SELECTED
BIBLIOGRAPHY

Adams, Charles F., and Henry Adams. *Chapters of Erie and Other Essays*. Boston: James R. Osgood, 1871.

Adams, Henry. *The Life of Albert Gallatin* (1879). New York: Peter Smith, 1943.

———. *History of the United States of America During the Administrations of Thomas Jefferson and James Madison* (1891). New York: Library of America, 1986.

Adams, John. *Revolutionary Writings 1755–1775*, New York: Library of America, 2011.

Ali, Omar H. *In the Lion's Mouth: Black Populism in the New South, 1886–1900*. Jackson: University Press of Mississippi, 2010.

Amar, Akhil Reed. *America's Constitution: A Biography*. New York: Random House, 2005.

Angwin, Julia. *Dragnet Nation: A Quest for Privacy, Security, and Freedom in a World of Relentless Surveillance*. New York: Henry Holt, 2014.

Appelbaum, Binyamin. *The Economists' Hour: False Prophets, Free Markets, and the Fracture of Society*. New York: Little, Brown, 2019.

Appleby, Joyce. *Capitalism and a New Social Order: The Republican Vision of the 1790s*. New York: New York University Press, 1984

Bailyn, Bernard. *The Ideological Origins of the American Revolution*. Cambridge, MA: Belknap Press of Harvard University Press, 1967.

Bannister, Robert. *Social Darwinism: Science and Myth in Anglo-American Social Thought*. Philadelphia: Temple University Press, 1979.

Baradaran, Mehrsa. *The Color of Money: Black Banks and the Racial Wealth Gap*. Cambridge, MA: Harvard University Press, 2017.

Barry, Kathleen. *Susan B. Anthony: A Biography of a Singular Feminist*. New York: Ballantine, 1988.

Bean, Jonathan. *Beyond the Broker State: Federal Policies Toward Small Business, 1936–1961*. Chapel Hill: University of North Carolina Press, 2001.

Beckert, Sven. *Empire of Cotton: A Global History*. New York: Knopf, 2014.

Benton, Thomas Hart. *Thirty Years' View: Or a History of the Workings of the American Government, From 1820 to 1850* (1854). New York: Greenwood Press, 1968.

Bercovitch, Sacvan. *The American Jeremiad*. Madison: University of Wisconsin Press, 2012.

Berk, Gerald. *Louis D. Brandeis and the Making of Regulated Competition, 1900–1932*. Cambridge: Cambridge University Press, 2009.

Berman, Edward. *Labor and the Sherman Act*. New York: Harper & Brothers, 1930.

Blight, David. *Frederick Douglass, Prophet of Freedom*. New York: Simon & Schuster, 2018.

Boritt, Gabor. *Lincoln and the Economics of the American Dream*. Urbana: University of Illinois Press, 1978.

Bork, Robert. *The Antitrust Paradox: A Policy at War with Itself*. New York: The Free Press, 1993.

Bowen, Catherine Drinker. *The Lion and the Throne: The Life and Times of Sir Edward Coke*. Boston: Little, Brown, 1956.

Branch, Taylor. *Parting the Waters: America in the King Years 1954–63*. New York: Simon & Schuster, 1988.

———. *Pillar of Fire: America in the King Years 1963–65*. New York: Simon & Schuster, 1998.

———. *At Canaan's Edge: America in the King Years 1965–68*. New York: Simon & Schuster, 2006.

Brandeis, Louis. *Other People's Money and How the Bankers Use It* (1914). Boston: Bedford Books, 1995.

———. *The Curse of Bigness*. New York: Viking, 1934.

Brown, Christopher. *Moral Capital: Foundations of British Abolitionism*. Chapel Hill: University of North Carolina Press, 2006.

Burgin, Angus. *The Great Persuasion: Reinventing Free Markets Since the Depression*. Cambridge, MA: Harvard University Press, 2012.

Bushman, Richard Lyman. *The American Farmer in the Eighteenth Century*. New Haven, CT: Yale University Press, 2018.

Callahan, David. *The Givers: Money, Power, and Philanthropy in a New Gilded Age*. New York: Knopf, 2017.

Chandler, Alfred D. *Inventing the Electronic Century*. New York: The Free Press, 2001.

Chernow, Ron. *The House of Morgan: An American Banking Dynasty and the Rise of Modern Finance*. New York: Atlantic Monthly Press, 1990.

———. *Titan: The Life of John D. Rockefeller, Sr*. New York: Random House, 1998.

———. *Alexander Hamilton*. New York: Penguin, 2004.

———. *Grant*. New York: Penguin, 2017.

Connaughton, Jeff. *The Payoff: Why Wall Street Always Wins*. Westport, CT: Prospecta Press, 2012.

Croly, Herbert. *The Promise of American Life* (1909). Cambridge, MA: Harvard University Press, 1965.

Daniel, Pete. *Dispossession: Discrimination Against African American Farmers in the Age of Civil Rights*. Chapel Hill: University of North Carolina Press, 2014.

Darsey, James. *The Prophetic Tradition and Radical Rhetoric in America*. New York: New York University Press, 1997.

Dayen, David. *Monopolized: Life in the Age of Corporate Power*. New York: The New Press, 2020.

Deneen, Patrick. *Why Liberalism Failed*. New Haven, CT: Yale University Press, 2018.

Destler, Chester Macarthur. *American Radicalism 1865–1901*. New London: Connecticut College, 1946.

Douglass, Frederick. *My Bondage and My Freedom*. New York: Penguin, 2003.

———. *Selected Speeches and Writings*. Chicago: Chicago Review Press, 1999.

Douthat, Ross. *The Decadent Society: How We Became the Victims of Our Own Success*. New York: Simon & Schuster, 2020.

Du Bois, W. E. B. *The Souls of Black Folk*. New York: Dodd, Mead, 1961.

———. *Black Reconstruction in America, 1860–1880*. New York: Atheneum, 1992.

Eddy, Arthur Jerome. *The New Competition*. 4th ed. Chicago: A. C. McClurg, 1917.

Eisner, Marc Allen. *Antitrust and the Triumph of Economics*. Chapel Hill: University of North Carolina Press, 1991.

Ernst, Daniel. *Lawyers Against Labor: From Individual Rights to Corporate Liberalism*. Urbana: University of Illinois Press, 1995.

Ezrachi, Ariel, and Maurice Stucke. *Virtual Competition: The Promise and Perils of the Algorithm-Driven Economy*. Cambridge, MA: Harvard University Press, 2016.

Fehrenbacher, Don. *The Dred Scott Case*. Oxford: Oxford University Press, 1978.

Finkelman, Paul. *Slavery and the Founders: Race and Liberty in the Age of Jefferson*. Armonk, NY: M. E. Sharpe, 1996.

Fishman, Charles. *The Wal-Mart Effect*. New York: Penguin, 2006.

Fitzhugh, George. *Sociology of the South: Or, the Failure of Free Society*. Richmond: A. Morris, 1854.

———. *Cannibals All: Or, Slaves Without Masters* (1857). Cambridge, MA: Harvard University Press, 2006.

Flexner, Eleanor. *Century of Struggle: The Women's Rights Movement in the United States*. Cambridge, MA: Harvard University Press, 1975.

Foer, Franklin. *World Without Mind: The Existential Threat of Big Tech*. New York: Penguin, 2017.

Foley, Duncan. *Adam's Fallacy: A Guide to Economic Theology*. Cambridge, MA: Belknap Press of Harvard University Press, 2006.

Foner, Eric. *Free Soil, Free Labor, Free Men: The Ideology of the Republican Party Before the Civil War*. New York: Oxford University Press, 1970.

———. *Reconstruction: America's Unfinished Revolution 1863–1877*. New York: HarperCollins, 2014.

Forcey, Charles. *The Crossroads of Liberalism: Croly, Weyl, Lippmann, and the Progressive Era*. Oxford: Oxford University Press, 1961.

Foroohar, Rana. *Makers and Takers: The Rise of Finance and the Fall of American Business*. New York: Crown, 2016.

———. *Don't Be Evil: How Big Tech Betrayed Its Founding Principles and All of Us*. New York: Crown, 2019.

Fortune, Timothy Thomas. *Black and White: Land, Labor, and Politics in the South* (1884). Chicago: Johnson Publishing, 1970.

Frank, Thomas. *Listen Liberal: Or, What Ever Happened to the Party of the People?* New York: Metropolitan Books, 2016.

———. *The People, NO: A Brief History of Anti-Populism*. New York: Metropolitan Books, 2020.

Freyer, Tony. *Antitrust and Global Capitalism, 1930–2004*. Cambridge: Cambridge University Press, 2009.

Galbraith, John Kenneth. *The New Industrial State*. Boston: Houghton Mifflin, 1967.

———. *Economics and the Public Purpose*. Boston: Houghton Mifflin, 1973.

Gerber, David. *Law and Competition in Twentieth-Century Europe: Protecting Prometheus*. Oxford: Oxford University Press, 1998.

Ghent, William James. *Our Benevolent Feudalism*. New York: Macmillan, 1902.

Giridharadas, Anand. *Winners Take All: The Elite Charade of Changing the World*. New York: Knopf, 2018.

Goetz, Andrew. *Airline Deregulation and Laissez-Faire Mythology*. Westport, CT: Quorum Books, 1992.

Goodwin, Lawrence. *The Populist Moment: A Short History of the Agrarian Revolt in America*. Oxford: Oxford University Press, 1978.

Gordon-Reed, Annette. *Thomas Jefferson and Sally Hemings: An American Controversy*. Charlottesville: University of Virginia Press, 1997.

Gordon-Reed, Annette, and Peter Onuf. *Most Blessed of the Patriarchs: Thomas Jefferson and the Empire of the Imagination*. New York: W. W. Norton, 2016.

Gossett, Thomas. *Race: The History of an Idea in America*. Dallas: Southern Methodist University Press, 1963.

Green, Mark, Ralph Nader, and Beverly Moore. *The Closed Enterprise System: Ralph Nader's Study Group Report on Antitrust Enforcement*. New York: Bantam Books, 1972.

Grubbs, Donald. *Cry from the Cotton: The Southern Tenant Farmers' Union and the New Deal*. Chapel Hill: University of North Carolina Press, 1971.

Hadley, Arthur T. *Railroad Transportation—Its History and Its Laws*. New York: G. P. Putnam and Sons, 1885.

Hamilton, Alexander, John Jay, and James Hamilton. *The Federalist: A Commentary on the Constitution of the United States*. New York: Modern Library, 2001.

Hamilton, Thomas. *Men and Manners in America*. 2nd ed., 1843. New York: Russell & Russell, 1968.

Hammond, Bray. *Banks and Politics in America: From the Revolution to the Civil War*. Princeton, NJ: Princeton University Press, 1967.

Harris, Leslie. *In the Shadow of Slavery: African Americans in New York City, 1626–1863*. Chicago: University of Chicago Press, 2003.

Hatch, Nathan. *The Democratization of American Christianity*. New Haven: Yale, CT: Yale University Press, 1989.

Hawley, Ellis. *The New Deal and the Problem of Monopoly: A Study in Economic Ambivalence*. Princeton, NJ: Princeton University Press, 1966.

Hayek, Friedrich. *The Road to Serfdom*. Chicago: University of Chicago Press, 1994.

Heschel, Abraham. *The Prophets*. Peabody, MA: Prince Press, 1999.

Hicks, John D. *The Populist Revolt: A History of the Farmers' Alliance and the People's Party*. Minneapolis: University of Minnesota Press, 1931.

Hogeland, William. *Inventing American History*. Cambridge, MA: MIT Press, 2009.

Holton, Woody. *Unruly Americans and the Origins of the Constitution*. New York: Hill and Wang, 2007.

Horwitz, Morton J. *The Transformation of American Law, 1780–1860*. Cambridge, MA: Harvard University Press, 1977.

Hounshell, David. *From the American System to Mass Production, 1800–1932*. Baltimore: Johns Hopkins University Press, 1984.

Hume, David. *Essays: Moral, Political, and Literary*. Indianapolis: Liberty Fund, 1987.

Hundt, Reed. *A Crisis Wasted: Barack Obama's Defining Decisions*. New York: Simon & Schuster, 2019.

Huston, James. *Securing the Fruits of Labor: The American Concept of Wealth Distribution, 1765–1900*. Baton Rouge: Louisiana State, 1998.

———. *The British Gentry, The Southern Planter, and the Northern Family Farmer: Agriculture and Sectional Antagonism in North America*. Baton Rouge: Louisiana State University Press, 2015.

Jaffa, Harry. *Crisis of the House Divided: An Interpretation of the Issues in the Lincoln-Douglas Debates*. Chicago: University of Chicago Press, 1959.

Jefferson, Thomas. *Notes on the State of Virginia*. New York: Penguin Books, 1999.

John, Richard. *Spreading the News: The American Postal System from Franklin to Morse*. Cambridge, MA: Harvard University Press, 1998.

———. *Network Nation: Inventing American Telecommunications*. Cambridge, MA: Belknap Press of Harvard University Press, 2010.

Johnson, E. A. J. *The Foundations of American Economic Freedom: Government and Enterprise in the Age of Washington*. Minneapolis: University of Minnesota Press, 1973.

Johnson, Simon, and James Kwak. *13 Bankers: The Wall Street Takeover and the Next Financial Meltdown*. New York: Pantheon, 2010.

Kahn, B. Zorina. *The Democratization of Invention: Patents and Copyrights in American Economic Development, 1790–1920*. Cambridge: Cambridge University Press, 2005.

Katznelson, Ira. *When Affirmative Action Was White*. New York: W. W. Norton, 2005.

Kay, John. *Other People's Money: The Real Business of Finance*. New York: PublicAffairs, 2015.

Kazin, Michael. *A Godly Hero: The Life of William Jennings Bryan*. New York: Alfred A. Knopf, 2006.

Keane, John. *Tom Paine: A Political Life*. New York: Grove, 1995.

Kendi, Ibram X. *Stamped from the Beginning: The Definitive History of Racist Ideas in America*. New York: Bold Type Books, 2016.

Keppler, Jan. *Monopolistic Competition Theory: Origins, Results, and Implications*. Baltimore: Johns Hopkins University Press, 1994.

Ketcham, Ralph. *James Madison: A Biography*. Newtown, CT: American Political Biography Press, 1971.

King, Martin Luther, Jr. *Where Do We Go from Here: Chaos or Community?* Boston: Beacon Press, 1968.

Klein, Maury. *The Life and Legend of Jay Gould*. Baltimore: Johns Hopkins University Press, 1986.

Kwoka, John. *Mergers, Merger Control, and Remedies*. Cambridge, MA: MIT Press, 2014.

La Follette, Robert. *Robert La Follette's Autobiography: A Personal Narrative of Political Experiences.* Madison: University of Wisconsin Press, 1960.

Lamoreaux, Naomi. *The Great Merger Movement in American Business.* Cambridge: Cambridge University Press, 1985.

Lemann, Nicholas. *Transaction Man: The Rise of the Deal and the Decline of the American Dream.* New York: Farrar, Straus and Giroux, 2019.

Leonard, Christopher. *The Meat Racket: The Secret Takeover of America's Food Business.* New York: Simon & Schuster, 2014.

———. *Kochland: The Secret History of Koch Industries and Corporate Power in America.* New York: Simon & Schuster, 2019.

Lewalski, Barbara. *The Life of John Milton.* Oxford: Blackwell, 2000.

Lewis, David Levering. *W. E. B. Du Bois: Biography of a Race, 1868–1919.* New York: Henry Holt, 1993.

———. *W. E. B. Du Bois: The Fight for Equality and the American Century, 1919–1963.* New York: Henry Holt, 2000.

Link, Arthur. *Wilson.* 5 vols. Princeton, NJ: Princeton University Press, 1965.

Lippmann, Walter. *Drift & Mastery: An Attempt to Diagnose the Current Disease* (1914). Madison: University of Wisconsin Press, 1987.

———. *The Good Society.* New York: Little, Brown, 1937.

Locke, John. *Second Treatise of Government.* Indianapolis: Bobbs-Merrill, 1952.

Lowenstein, Roger. *America's Bank: The Epic Struggle to Create the Federal Reserve.* New York: Penguin, 2015.

Lynn, Barry C. *End of the Line: The Rise and Coming Fall of the Global Corporation.* New York: Doubleday, 2005.

———. *Cornered: The New Monopoly Capitalism and the Economics of Destruction.* Hoboken, NJ: Wiley, 2010.

MacLean, Nancy. *Democracy in Chains: The Deep History of the Radical Right's Stealth Plan for America.* New York: Viking, 2017.

Madigan, Tim. *The Burning: Massacre, Destruction, and the Tulsa Race Riot of 1921.* New York: Thomas Dunne Books, 2001.

Madison, James. *The Selected Writings of James Madison.* Edited by Ralph Ketcham. Indianapolis: Hackett, 2006.

Mann, Bruce. *Republic of Debtors: Bankruptcy in the Age of American Independence.* Cambridge, MA: Harvard University Press, 2002.

Mayville, Luke. *John Adams and the Fear of American Oligarchy.* Princeton, NJ: Princeton University Press, 2016.

McClenahan, William, and William Becker. *Eisenhower and the Cold War Economy.* Baltimore: Johns Hopkins University Press, 2011.

McCoy, Drew. *The Elusive Republic.* Chapel Hill: University of North Carolina Press, 1980.

McCraw, Thomas K. *Prophets of Regulation.* Cambridge, MA: Belknap Press of Harvard University Press, 1984.

McMath, Robert, Jr. *American Populism: A Social History 1877–1898.* New York: Hill & Wang, 1993.

Merritt, Leigh. *Masterless Men: Poor Whites and Slavery in the Antebellum South.* Cambridge: Cambridge University Press, 2017.

Milton, John. *John Milton Prose.* Edited by David Loewenstein. West Sussex: Wiley Blackwell, 2013.

Moreno, Paul. *Black Americans and Organized Labor: A New History.* Baton Rouge: Louisiana State University Press, 2006.

Morgan, Edmund. *American Slavery, American Freedom: The Ordeal of Colonial Virginia.* New York: Norton, 1975.

Morozov, Evgeny. *The Net Delusion: The Dark Side of Internet Freedom.* New York: PublicAffairs, 2011.

Morris, Edmund. *Theodore Rex.* New York: Random House, 2001.

Murphy, Sharon Ann. *Other People's Money: How Banking Worked in the Early American Republic.* Baltimore: Johns Hopkins University Press, 2017.

Nader, Ralph, Mark Green, and Joel Seligman. *Taming the Giant Corporation: How the Largest Corporations Control Our Lives.* New York: W. W. Norton, 1977.

Nash, Gary. *The Unknown American Revolution: The Unruly Birth of Democracy and the Struggle to Create America.* New York: Viking, 2005.

Novak, William. *The People's Welfare.* Chapel Hill: University of North Carolina Press, 1996.

Okrent, Daniel. *The Guarded Gate: Bigotry, Eugenics, and the Law.* New York: Scribner, 2019.

Olson, James Stuart. *Saving Capitalism: The Reconstruction Finance Corporation and the New Deal.* Princeton, NJ: Princeton University Press, 1988.

O'Neil, Cathy. *Weapons of Math Destruction: How Big Data Increases Inequality and Threatens Democracy.* New York: Crown, 2016.

Onuf, Peter. *Statehood and Union: A History of the Northwest Ordinance.* Bloomington: Indiana University Press, 1987.

Oubre, Claude. *40 Acres and a Mule.* Baton Rouge: Louisiana State University Press, 2012.

Pasquale, Frank. *Black Box Society: The Secret Algorithms That Control Money and Information.* Cambridge, MA: Harvard University Press, 2015.

Patman, Wright. *The Robinson-Patman Act: What You Can and Cannot Do Under This Law.* New York: Ronald Press, 1938.

Peritz, Rudolph. *Competition Policy in America: History, Rhetoric, Law.* Oxford: Oxford University Press, 1996.

Perrow, Charles. *Organizing America: Wealth, Power, and the Origins of Corporate Capitalism.* Princeton, NJ: Princeton University Press, 2002.

Peterson, Merrill D. *Thomas Jefferson and the New Nation: A Biography.* New York: Oxford University Press, 1970.

Pettit, Philip. *Republicanism: A Theory of Freedom and Government.* Oxford: Oxford University Press, 1999.

Philippon, Thomas. *The Great Reversal: How America Gave Up on Free Markets.* Cambridge, MA: Belknap Press of Harvard University Press, 2019.

Piketty, Thomas. *Capital in the Twenty-First Century.* Cambridge, MA: Belknap Press of Harvard University Press, 2014.

Plumb, John Harold. *Sir Robert Walpole: The Making of a Statesman.* Boston: Houghton Mifflin, 1956.

———. *Sir Robert Walpole: The King's Minister.* London: Penguin, 1960.

Polgar, Paul. *Standard-Bearers of Equality: America's First Abolition Movement.* Chapel Hill: University of North Carolina Press, 2019.

Popper, Karl. *Open Society and Its Enemies: The Spell of Plato.* Princeton, NJ: Princeton University Press, 1971.

———. *Open Society and Its Enemies: The High Tide of Prophecy: Hegel, Marx, and the Aftermath.* Princeton, NJ: Princeton University Press, 1971.

Posner, Richard. *Antitrust Law.* Chicago: University of Chicago Press, 1976.

———. *Economic Analysis of Law.* 3rd ed. Boston: Little, Brown, 1986.

Postel, Charles. *The Populist Vision.* Oxford: Oxford University Press, 2009.

———. *Equality: An American Dilemma, 1866–1896.* New York: Farrar, Straus and Giroux, 2019.

Quarles, Benjamin. *The Negro in the American Revolution.* Chapel Hill: University of North Carolina Press, 1996.

Rahman, K. Sabeel. *Democracy Against Domination.* Oxford: Oxford University Press, 2017.

Rana, Aziz. *The Two Faces of American Freedom.* Cambridge, MA: Harvard University Press, 2010.

Reich, Robert. *The Work of Nations.* New York: Vintage, 1992.

———. *Supercapitalism.* New York: Knopf, 2007.

Remini, Robert. *The Life of Andrew Jackson.* New York: Harper & Row, 1988.

Robbins, Roy. *Our Landed Heritage: The Public Domain 1776–1970.* Lincoln: University of Nebraska Press, 1976.

Robinson, Joan. *The Economics of Imperfect Competition.* London: Macmillan, 1933.

Rosen, Jeffrey. *Louis D. Brandeis: American Prophet*. New Haven, CT: Yale University Press, 2016.

Rothstein, Richard. *The Color of Law: A Forgotten History of How Our Government Segregated America*. New York: Liveright, 2017.

Saulnier, Raymond. *Constructive Years: The U.S. Economy Under Eisenhower*. Lanham, MD: University Press of America, 1991.

Sawyer, Laura Phillips. *American Fair Trade: Proprietary Capitalism, Corporatism, and the "New Competition," 1890–1940*. Cambridge: Cambridge University Press, 2018.

Saxton, Alexander. *The Rise and Fall of the White Republic: Class Politics and Mass Culture in Nineteenth-Century America*. London: Verso, 1990.

Schlesinger, Arthur, Jr. *The Age of Jackson*. Old Saybrook, CT: Konecky & Konecky, 1971.

———. *The Crisis of the Old Order*. Boston: Houghton Mifflin, 1957.

———. *The Coming of the New Deal*. Boston: Houghton Mifflin, 1959.

———. *The Politics of Upheaval*. Boston: Houghton Mifflin, 1960.

Sensabaugh, George. *Milton in Early America*. Princeton, NJ: Princeton University Press, 1964.

Shelton, Tamara Venit. *A Squatter's Republic: Land and the Politics of Monopoly in California, 1850–1900*. Berkeley: University of California Press, 2013.

Sinha, Manisha. *The Slave's Cause: A History of Abolition*. New Haven, CT: Yale University Press, 2016.

Sitaraman, Ganesh. *The Crisis of the Middle-Class Constitution*. New York: Knopf, 2017.

Slobodian, Quinn. *Globalists: The End of Empire and the Birth of Neoliberalism*. Cambridge, MA: Harvard University Press, 2018.

Smith, Adam. *Theory of Moral Sentiments*. Oxford: Oxford University Press, 1976.

———. *The Wealth of Nations*. New York: Modern Library, 1994.

Sperling, Gene. *Economic Dignity*. New York: Penguin, 2020.

Stiles, T. J. *The First Tycoon: The Epic Life of Cornelius Vanderbilt*. New York: Vintage, 2009.

Stoller, Matt. *Goliath: The 100-Year War Between Monopoly Power and Democracy*. New York: Simon & Schuster, 2019.

Stone, Brad. *The Everything Store: Jeff Bezos and the Age of Amazon*. New York: Little, Brown, 2013.

Strum, Philippa. *Louis D. Brandeis: Justice for the People*. Cambridge, MA: Harvard University Press, 1984.

Taplin, Jonathan. *Move Fast and Break Things: How Facebook, Google, and Amazon Cornered Culture and Undermined Democracy*. New York: Hachette, 2017.

Teachout, Zephyr. *Corruption in America: From Benjamin Franklin's Snuff Box to Citizens United*. Cambridge, MA: Harvard University Press, 2014.

———. *Break 'em Up: Recovering Our Freedom from Big Ag, Big Tech, and Big Money*. New York: St. Martin's Press, 2020.

Temen, Peter. *The Jacksonian Economy*. New York: W. W. Norton, 1969.

Thorelli, Hans. *The Federal Antitrust Policy*. Baltimore: Johns Hopkins University Press, 1955.

Tocqueville, Alexis de. *Democracy in America*. 2 vols. New York: Knopf, 1994.

Tooze, Adam. *Crashed: How a Decade of Financial Crises Changed the World*. New York: Viking, 2018.

Treat, Payson Jackson. *The National Land System 1785–1820*. New York: E. B. Treat, 1910.

Trevelyan, George Macaulay. *The Life of John Bright*. Boston: Houghton Mifflin, 1913.

Tugwell, Rexford. *The Democratic Roosevelt*. Garden City, NY: Doubleday, 1957.

Twain, Mark, and Dudley Warner. *The Gilded Age*. New York: Modern Library, 2006.

Urofsky, Melvin. *Louis D. Brandeis: A Life*. New York: Pantheon, 2009.

Van Buren, Martin. *Inquiry into the Origin and Course of Political Parties in the United States* (1867). New York: August M. Kelly, 1967.

Viscelli, Steve. *The Big Rig: Trucking and the Decline of the American Dream*. Berkeley: University of California Press, 2016.

Waldman, Steven. *Founding Faith: Providence, Politics, and the Birth of Religious Freedom in America*. New York: Random House, 2008.

Wall, Joseph Frazier. *Andrew Carnegie*. New York: Oxford University Press, 1970.

Walras, Leon. *Elements of Pure Economics: Or the Theory of Social Wealth* (1877). Abingdon, Oxfordshire: Routledge, 2003.

Walton, Sam. *Made in America*. New York: Bantam Books, 1992.

Wells, Wyatt. *Antitrust and the Formation of the Postwar World*. New York: Columbia University Press, 2002.

Werth, Barry. *Banquet at Delmonico's*. New York: Random House, 2009.

Weyl, Walter. *The New Democracy* (1912). New York: Harper & Row, 1964.

White, Richard. *The Middle Ground: Indians, Empires, and Republics in the Great Lakes Region, 1650–1815*. Cambridge: Cambridge University Press, 1991.

———. *Railroaded: The Transcontinentals and the Making of Modern America*. New York: W. W. Norton, 2011.

———. *The Republic for Which It Stands*. Oxford: Oxford University Press, 2017.

Whitman, Walt. *Specimen Days and Collect* (1882). Brooklyn, NY: Melville House, 2015.

Wilentz, Sean. *The Rise of American Democracy: Jefferson to Lincoln*. New York: W. W. Norton, 2005.

Williams, Juan. *Thurgood Marshall, American Revolutionary*. New York: Crown, 1998.

Wilson, Woodrow. *The New Freedom: A Call for the Emancipation of the Generous Energies of a People*. New York: Doubleday, 1913.

Wood, Gordon. *The Creation of the American Republic 1776–1787*. Chapel Hill: University of North Carolina Press, 1969.

———. *The Radicalism of the American Revolution*. New York: Vintage Books, 1991.

———. *Empire of Liberty: A History of the Early Republic, 1789–1815*. Oxford: Oxford University Press, 2009.

Woodward, C. Vann. *Origins of the New South 1877–1913*. Baton Rouge: Louisiana State University Press, 1951.

Wu, Tim. *The Curse of Bigness: Antitrust in the New Gilded Age*. New York: Columbia Global Reports, 2018.

X, Malcolm. *Malcolm X Speaks: Selected Speeches and Statements*. New York: Grove, 1994.

Zuboff, Shoshana. *The Age of Surveillance Capitalism: The Fight for a Human Future at the New Frontier of Power*. New York: PublicAffairs, 2019.

NOTES

INTRODUCTION

1. Jane E. Brody, "Half of Us Face Obesity, Dire Projections Show," *New York Times*, February 10, 2020.
2. Karen Weise, "Prime Power: How Amazon Squeezes the Businesses Behind Its Store," *New York Times*, December 19, 2019.
3. Two recent notable exceptions are K. Sabeel Rahman's *Democracy Against Domination* (Oxford: Oxford University Press, 2017), and Tim Wu's *The Curse of Bigness: Antitrust in the New Gilded Age* (New York: Columbia Global Reports, 2018).
4. Lepore covers the subject of "antitrust" law but once in her more-than-700-page book, and then only in passing, yet writes in great depth about the contemporary professional race-baiter Alex Jones. Jill Lepore, *These Truths* (New York: W. W. Norton, 2018).
5. One recent exception to this is James Huston's *Securing the Fruits of Labor*. Huston provides an excellent recounting of the importance of what he calls the "labor theory of property" in the thinking of early Americans, an issue I examine in depth in chapter three. Huston also details American fears of aristocratic ownership structures. But other than a passing reference to the Sherman Antitrust Act, he spends little time looking at how Americans distributed power and wealth. James Huston, *Securing the Fruits of Labor: The American Concept of Wealth Distribution, 1765–1900* (Baton Rouge: Louisiana State University Press), 1998.
6. Leslie Harris, "I Helped Fact-Check the 1619 Project. The Times Ignored Me," *Politico*, March 6, 2020.
7. W. E. B. Du Bois, *Black Reconstruction* (New York: Atheneum, 1992), 25.
8. Ibid., 648.
9. Robert Reich, "The Political Roots of Widening Inequality," *American Prospect*, April 28, 2015.
10. Ibram X. Kendi, *Stamped from the Beginning* (New York: Bold Type Books, 2016), 508.

CHAPTER ONE

1. Zach Matthews, "A Bird in the Bush," *Arkansas Life*, December 11, 2013.
2. Sam Walton, *Made in America* (New York: Bantam Books, 1992), 40.
3. Ibid., 31–32.
4. Ibid., 66, 237.
5. "1940s: A New Generation," Timeline, Walmart Digital Museum, accessed April 5, 2020.

https://www.walmartmuseum.com/content/walmartmuseum/en_us/timeline/decades/1940 .html.

6. The Wal-Mart Timeline, Wal*MartFacts.com, July 10, 2006, Internet Archive, accessed April 5, 2020. https://web.archive.org/web/20060719071543/http://www.walmartfacts.com /content/default.aspx?id=3.

7. The writer William Whyte coined the term "Organization Man" in his 1956 book of the same name. For a smart take on how the financial and corporate culture has changed, see Nicholas Lemann's *Transaction Man: The Rise of the Deal and the Decline of the American Dream* (New York: Farrar, Straus and Giroux, 2019).

8. For a good example of how working people organized an industry in which power was not centralized, see Steve Viscelli, *The Big Rig: Trucking and the Decline of the American Dream* (Berkeley: University of California Press, 2016).

9. The resulting contrast in land ownership between the United States and Britain is striking. For details, see James Huston, *The British Gentry, The Southern Planter, and the Northern Family Farmer: Agriculture and Sectional Antagonism in North America* (Baton Rouge: Louisiana State University Press, 2015).

10. There are 4,756 stores, each of which is at least 30 times bigger (at least 130,000 square feet on average). Liam O'Connell, "Total Number of Walmart U.S. Stores in the United States from 2012 to 2020, by Type," *Statista*, April 3, 2020, accessed April 5, 2020.

11. Stacy Mitchell, "Walmart's Monopolization of Local Grocery Markets," Institute for Local Self-Reliance, June 2019.

12. Paul Wilenius, "Enemies Within: Thatcher and the Unions," BBC News, March 5, 2004.

13. Howard Metzenbaum, "Is William Baxter Anti-Antitrust?," *New York Times*, October 18, 1981.

14. Howard Metzenbaum and Herman Schwartz, "Merger Madness," *New York Times*, August 5, 1981.

15. Jack Welch, *Straight from the Gut* (New York: Warner Books, 2001), Appendix A.

16. José Azar, Ioana Marinescu, and Marshall I. Steinbaum, "Labor Market Concentration," Working Paper 24147, National Bureau of Economic Research, Cambridge, December 2017, revised February 2019. http://www.nber.org/papers/w24147.

17. Dwight D. Eisenhower, Farewell Address, January 17, 1961, Public Papers of the Presidents of the United States, Volume 7, 1960–61, p. 1038, Federal Register, Washington, DC, 1961.

18. William McClenahan and William Becker, *Eisenhower and the Cold War Economy* (Baltimore: Johns Hopkins University Press, 2011). See also Raymond Saulnier, *Constructive Years: The U.S. Economy Under Eisenhower* (Lanham, MD: University Press of America, 1991), 163–166.

19. John Mintz, "How a Dinner Led to a Feeding Frenzy," *Washington Post*, July 4, 1997; "Land of the Giants," *The Economist*, June 12, 1997; "Merger Timeout," *Washington Post*, March 25, 1998.

20. The only real exception to this thrust was Robert Pitofsky, who in 1995 was appointed by President Clinton to head the FTC and who served until May 2001. He paid especially close attention to mergers that affected the news media, in 2000 telling the *Washington Post*, "If somebody monopolizes the cosmetics fields, they're going to take money out of consumers' pockets, but the implications for democratic values are zero. On the other hand, if they monopolize books, you're talking about implications that go way beyond what the wholesale price of the books might be." Alec Klein, "A Hard Look at Media Mergers," *Washington Post*, November 29, 2000. Pitofsky in 1979 published one of the last defenses of traditional antitrust philosophy before the Reagan administration's radical changes in the early 1980s. Robert Pitofsky, "Political Content of Antitrust," *University of Pennsylvania Law Review* 1051 (1979): 127.

21. Dan Roberts, "Wall Street Deregulation Pushed by Clinton Advisers, Documents Reveal," *The Guardian*, April 19, 2014.

22. James MacDonald, "Mergers and Competition in Seeds and Agricultural Chemical Markets," *Amber Waves Magazine*, U.S. Department of Agriculture, April 3, 2017.

23. "2000 Commodities Act Paved Way for Problems," *All Things Considered*, National Public Radio, March 20, 2009.

24. Brian Cheffins, *The Public Company Transformed* (Oxford: Oxford University Press, 2018); Sarah Anderson, "The Failure of Bill Clinton's CEO Pay Reform," *Politico*, August 31, 2016; Jena McGregor, "This Tax Loophole Led to Massive CEO Pay Packages," *Washington Post*, November 22, 2017. See also Lemann, *Transaction Man: The Rise of the Deal and the Decline of the American Dream*.

25. From the Civil War until the election of President Woodrow Wilson in 1912, the U.S. tariff system served as a prime bulwark of America's monopolists, protecting them from foreign competition. The Underwood Tariff of 1913 began the process of eliminating this practice.

26. Beth Baltzan, "The Old-School Answer to Global Trade," *Washington Monthly*, April 2019.

27. David Frum captured the idea well in a 2010 interview on *Nightline*, saying, "Republicans originally thought that Fox worked for us, and now we are discovering we work for Fox." Media Matters Staff, *Media Matters*, March 23, 2010.

28. Daniel Yergin and Joseph Stanislaw, The Commanding Heights: *The Battle Between Government and the Marketplace That Is Remaking the Modern World* (New York: Simon & Schuster, 1998).

29. Simon Johnson, "The Quiet Coup," *The Atlantic*, May 2009.

30. Laura Kusisto, "Many Who Lost Homes to Foreclosure in Last Decade Won't Return—NAR," *Wall Street Journal*, April 20, 2015; Alana Semuels, "The Never-Ending Foreclosure," *The Atlantic*, December 1, 2017.

31. Charles Fishman, *The Wal-Mart Effect* (New York: Penguin, 2006), 2, 79, 93.

32. For a more extensive discussion on the combination of concentrated private power, see chapter eight of my book *Cornered*: Barry C. Lynn, *Cornered: The New Monopoly Capitalism and the Economics of Destruction* (Hoboken, NJ: Wiley, 2010).

33. The most complete explanation of this system is in Christopher Leonard, *The Meat Racket: The Secret Takeover of America's Food Business* (New York: Simon & Schuster, 2014). Another good source is Lina Khan, "Obama's Game of Chicken," *Washington Monthly*, November 2012.

34. Barry Lynn, "Killing the Competition," *Harper's Magazine*, February 2012.

CHAPTER TWO

1. Mike Konczal, "Socialize Uber: It's Easier Than You Think," *The Nation*, December 10, 2014; Heather Somerville, "California Regulator Proposes Regulating Uber Like Tour Buses, Limos," Reuters, March 19, 2018.

2. For a useful discussion of the origins and potential political uses of the term "technology," read Leo Marx's essay, "Technology: The Emergence of a Hazardous Concept," in *Technology and Culture* 51, no. 3 (2010): 561–577.

3. Joshua Franklin, "Uber Unveils IPO with Warning It May Never Make a Profit," Reuters, April 11, 2019. For a more detailed discussion of such predatory pricing strategies, see Shaoul Sussman, "Prime Predator: Amazon and the Rational of Below Average Variable Cost Pricing Strategies Among Negative-Cash Flow Firms," *Journal of Antitrust Enforcement* 7, no. 2 (July 2019): 203–219.

4. Adam Tanner, "Different Customers, Different Prices, Thanks to Big Data," *Forbes*, May 26, 2014; Ryan Cooper, "How Uber Could Become a Nightmarish Monopoly," *The Week*, February 9, 2017; Eric Newcomer, "Uber Starts Charging What It Thinks You're Willing to Pay," *Bloomberg*, May 19, 2017; Charlie Osborne, "Uber Uses Artificial Intelligence to Figure Out Your Personal Price Hike," ZDNet, May 22, 2017; Jordi McKenzie, "The Economics Behind Uber's New Pricing Model," *The Conversation*, May 24, 2017; Patrick J. Kehoe, Brad Larsen, and Elena Pastorino, "Dynamic Competition in the Era of Big Data," Stanford University and the Federal Reserve Bank of Minneapolis, December 2017; Oren Bar-Gill, "Algorithmic Price Discrimination When Demand Is a Function of Both Preferences and (Mis)Perceptions," *University of Chicago Law Review*, vol. 86, May 2018; Brian Wallheimer, "Are You

Ready for Personalized Pricing?" *Chicago Booth Review*, February 26, 2018; Nicole Martin, "Uber Charges More If They Think You Are Willing to Pay More," *Forbes*, March 30, 2019.

5. Americans have long accepted the idea that certain providers of services can discriminate among different classes of people or goods, such as when a theater charges senior citizens less money for a seat or a railroad charges shippers of stone less per pound than shippers of fresh fruit.

6. The fact that Uber drivers are classified as contractors and not employees makes it easier for Uber to engage in such extreme manipulation of their work and income. The state of California in 2019 passed a law that categorizes Uber drivers—and other people whose work is managed by online platforms—as employees (Kate Conger and Noam Scheiber, "California Bill Makes App-Based Companies Treat Workers as Employees," *New York Times*, September 11, 2019). Uber has made clear that this would have a huge effect. In its filing for a public offering, the corporation told prospective investors that having to classify drivers as employees would cause it to "incur significant additional expenses" and "require us to fundamentally change our business model, and consequently have an adverse effect on our business and financial condition." But Uber and other affected corporations have launched a number of practical and legal challenges to the law (Aarian Marshall, "Now the Courts Will Decide Whether Uber Drivers Are Employees," *Wired*, January 3, 2020). And the Trump administration has sided strongly with the corporations (Noam Scheiber, "Labor Dept. Says Workers at a Gig Company Are Contractors," *New York Times*, April 29, 2019).

7. Newcomer, "Uber Starts Charging What It Thinks You're Willing to Pay."

8. Ruth Reader, "Uber Wants to Know When You're Drunk," *Fast Company*, June 11, 2018; Sara Jeong, "Uber Knows Too Much About You," *Motherboard*, May 27, 2016; Noam Scheiber, "How Uber Uses Psychological Tricks to Push Its Drivers' Buttons," *New York Times*, April 22, 2017; Sarah Mason, "High Score, Low Pay: Why the Gig Economy Loves Gamification," *The Guardian*, November 20, 2018.

9. Mike Isaac, "How Uber Deceives the Authorities Worldwide," *New York Times*, March 3, 2017.

10. "Personalized Pricing in the Digital Era—Note by the European Union," presented at a joint meeting of the Competition Committee and the Committee on Consumer Policy of the OECD, November 28, 2018, p. 12.

11. The issues of taxation and representation were largely secondary within a "much more basic constitutional struggle." Bernard Bailyn, *The Ideological Origins of the American Revolution* (Cambridge, MA: Harvard University Press, 1967), 162.

12. For a good recent summary, see Thomas M. Hanna, "The Public Ownership Solution," *Jacobin*, December 10, 2018.

13. Airlines have begun to experiment with some forms of first-degree price discrimination in the sale of seats and other products that passengers purchase with miles. Arthur Pigou coined the term "first degree" price discrimination in 1920. Arthur Pigou, *The Economics of Welfare* (London: Macmillan, 1920).

14. Darrell Proctor, "Leap, Google Nest Using Automation for Demand Response," *Power*, August 20, 2019.

15. Legal and economic scholars who work for these corporations have come up with a concept to hide what is really happening: the idea that markets can have two "sides" or even multiple "sides." For more information on the concept, please see the brief of the Open Markets Institute in *Ohio v. American Express*, filed with the Supreme Court, December 14, 2017. See also Barry Lynn, "The Amex Ruling Cements the Domination of Big Companies," *Financial Times*, June 27, 2018; and Victoria Graham, "Goldman, NCAA Test Limits of AmEx Two-Sided Antitrust Defense," *Bloomberg Law*, February 26, 2020.

16. Rachel Siegel and Joanna Slater, "International Pushback Disrupts Amazon's Momentum to Expand Its Empire Worldwide," *Washington Post*, May 10, 2019; Emma Thomasson and Matthias Inverardi, "Amazon's Treatment of Sellers Comes Under Scrutiny in Germany," Reuters, November 29, 2018.

17. Lina Khan, "Amazon's Antitrust Paradox," *Yale Law Review*, vol. 126, January 2017.

18. Dan O'Shea, "Amazon Exclusives Brands Now Outnumber Its Private Labels," *Retail Dive*, February 19, 2019.

19. Tara Johnson, "Amazon's Private Label Brands—The Complete List," *CPC Strategy*, July 5, 2017; Jason Del Rey, "Surprise! Amazon Now Sells More Than 70 of Its Own Private Label Brands," *Vox*, April 7, 2018. A good source for the latest figure is the TJI Amazon Brand Database. Available online at https://this.just.in/amazon-brand-database/.

20. Alison Griswold, "Amazon Is Becoming a Toymaker," *Quartz*, December 11, 2018.

21. Jay Greene, "Aggressive Amazon Tactic Pushes You to Consider Its Own Brand Before You Click 'Buy,'" *Washington Post*, August 28, 2019.

22. Jeffrey P. Bezos, "2018 Letter to Shareholders," April 11, 2019, Securities and Exchange Commission, Exhibit 99.1.

23. Erica Sweeney, "73% of Online Shoppers Click on Amazon Product Ads While Browsing, Study Finds," *Marketing Dive*, March 20, 2019.

24. Stacy Mitchell and Olivia LaVecchia, "Amazon's Next Frontier: Your City's Purchasing," Institute for Local Self-Reliance, July 10, 2018.

25. Jon Brodkin, "Amazon Cloud Has 1 Million Users and Is Near $10 Billion in Annual Sales," *Ars Technica*, April 7, 2016.

26. Spencer Soper, "Bezos Disputes Amazon's Market Power, but His Merchants Feel the Pinch," Bloomberg, April 17, 2019.

27. Laura Stevens, "Amazon Snips Prices on Other Sellers' Items Ahead of Holiday Onslaught," *Wall Street Journal*, November 5, 2017.

28. Brad Stone, *The Everything Store: Jeff Bezos and the Age of Amazon* (New York: Little, Brown, 2013), 243. On Bloomsbury, see Doreen Carvajal, "Small Publishers Feel Power of Amazon's 'Buy' Button," *New York Times*, June 16, 2008.

29. Josh Dzieza, "Prime and Punishment: Dirty Dealing in the $175 Billion Amazon Marketplace," *The Verge*, December 19, 2018.

30. James Hercher, "Pivotal Forecasts Amazon Ad Revenue to Reach $38 Billion," *Ad Exchanger*, January 7, 2019.

31. Soper, "Bezos Disputes Amazon's Market Power."

32. Shaoul Sussman, "How Amazon Controls Its Marketplace," *The American Prospect*, July 26, 2019.

33. "About three-quarters of the time, Amazon placed its own products and those of companies that pay for its [FBA] services in [the buy-box] position even when there were substantially cheaper offers available from others." Julia Angwin and Surya Mattu, "Amazon Says It Puts Customers First. But Its Pricing Algorithm Doesn't," *ProPublica*, September 20, 2016.

34. "The two San Francisco companies have already lost a combined $13 billion. And with no clear road to profits ahead, no one else has much of an incentive to mount a challenge using the same model relying on people driving their own cars to pick up passengers that summon them on a smartphone app, said Susan Shaheen, co-director of the Transportation Sustainability Research Center at the University of California, Berkeley." Tom Krisher, "Uber, Lyft Losses Keep Competitors at Bay," *Business Insider*, May 11, 2019. See also Noel Randewich, "Lyft Hits Record Low as Uber Slumps in Wall Street Debut," Reuters, May 10, 2019.

35. Jillian D'Onfro, "With Increasing 'Overlap' Between Self-Driving Car Efforts, An Alphabet Exec Has Stepped Down from Uber's Board," *Business Insider*, August 29, 2016.

36. Maya Kosoff, "Uber Just Bought Part of Microsoft's Bing's Mapping Technology, Including 100 Employees," *Business Insider*, June 29, 2015; Aleks Buczkowski, "Uber Hires Former Google's Head of Search to Lead Its Maps Division," *Geo*, January 21, 2017.

37. Jordan Novet, "Uber Paid Google $58 Million over Three Years for Map Services," CNBC, April 11, 2019.

38. Natasha Frost, "Uber's Biggest Investors Include SoftBank, Google, and the Saudi Arabian Government," *Quartz*, April 11, 2019.

39. Ari Levy, "Google Parent Company Alphabet Has More Than Doubled Its Money on Lyft to $1 Billion in Just 17 Months," CNBC, March 29, 2019.

40. Novet, "Uber Paid Google $58 Million."

41. Ben Elgin, "Google Buys Android for Its Mobile Arsenal," *Bloomberg BusinessWeek*, August 17, 2005.

42. Mark Bergen, "Nobody Wants to Let Google Win the War for Maps All Over Again," Bloomberg, February 21, 2018.

43. Sean O'Kane, "Ford and Volkswagen Form Global Alliance, Will Start by Building Trucks and Vans," *The Verge*, January 15, 2019.

44. Bertel Schmitt, "Toyota's Tri-Ad Division Wants Open Source Maps to Guide the Self-Driving Cars of Tomorrow," *The Drive*, January 31, 2019.

45. "Softbank's Monopoly Manufacturing Machine," *The Corner*, Open Markets Institute, June 28, 2018.

46. "Paul Lienert and Sanjana Shivdas, "SoftBank Joins GM in Self-Driving Car Race; GM Shares Soar," Reuters, May 30, 2018. See also Naomi Tajitsu and Sam Nussey, "Toyota, Soft-Bank in First-Ever Alliance, Target Self-Driving Car Services," Reuters, October 3, 2018.

47. As a *Wired* reporter explained it, "Most venture capitalists avoid backing any company that could compete with existing investments. But SoftBank is able to sit at the center of this increasingly tangled web because its $93 billion Vision Fund, an unprecedented pile of cash, gives it the power to do things venture investors have typically avoided for fear of angering their portfolio companies. SoftBank has flipped that dynamic on its head." Erin Griffith, "SoftBank Flips the Venture-Capital Script Again with GM Deal," *Wired*, May 31, 2018.

48. Sara Ashley O'Brien, "Apple Buys 11 Map Startups—but Still Trails Google," *CNN Business*, September 28, 2015; Eric Johnsa, "Apple Faces a Catch-22 in Its Maps and Cloud Battle with Google," *Real Money*, December 2, 2016.

49. Lisa Marie Segarra, "Google to Pay Apple $12 Billion to Remain Safari's Default Search Engine in 2019: Report," *Fortune*, September 29, 2018.

50. John Rosevear, "Waymo to General Motors: Catch Us If You Can," *Motley Fool*, May 31, 2018.

51. Keiichi Furukawa and Natsuki Yamamoto, "Nissan-Renault Alliance to Join Google on Self-Driving Cars," *Nikkei Asian Review*, February 5, 2019.

52. Amanda Coletta, "Quayside, Toronto's Google-Linked Smart City, Draws Opposition over Privacy, Costs," *Washington Post*, May 7, 2019.

53. "Canada Group Sues Government over Google Sidewalk Labs," BBC News, April 16, 2019.

54. Nicholas Thompson and Fred Vogelstein, "Inside the Two Years That Shook Facebook—and the World," *Wired*, February 12, 2018.

55. J. Clement, "Advertising Revenue of Google from 2001 to 2019," *Statista*, February 5, 2020; Robert Williams, "Facebook's 2018 Ad Revenue Surges 38% to $55 Billion Amid Stories Ad Growth," *Mobile Marketer*, January 31, 2019; Jeanine Poggi, "Google-Facebook Duopoly Set to Lose Some of Its Share of Ad Spend," *Ad Age*, February 20, 2019.

56. Elizabeth Grieco, "U.S. Newsroom Employment Has Dropped by a Quarter Since 2008, with Greatest Decline at Newspapers," Pew Research Center, July 9, 2019; Alex Williams, "Employment Picture Darkens for Journalists at Digital Outlets," *Columbia Journalism Review*, September 27, 2016.

57. Nicholas Thompson and Fred Vogelstein, "Fifteen Months of Fresh Hell Inside Facebook," *Wired*, May 2019, emphasis added.

58. Woodrow Wilson, *The New Freedom: A Call for the Emancipation of the Generous Energies of a People* (New York: Doubleday, 1913), 259.

59. Colleen Wright, "Uber Says Proposed Freeze on Licenses in New York City Would Limit Competition," *New York Times*, June 30, 2015; Dieter Bohn, "Uber Trolls New York City Mayor in Its App," *The Verge*, July 16, 2015; Carl Campanile, "Uber Blasts De Blasio Again—Don't Strand New York!," *New York Post*, July 20, 2015; Matt Flegenheimer, "De Blasio Administration Dropping Plan for Uber Cap, for Now," *New York Times*, July 22, 2015.

60. Kenneth Vogel, "Google Critic Ousted from Think Tank Funded by the Tech Giant," *New York Times*, August 30, 2017; Jack Nicas and Matthew Rosenberg, "A Look Inside the Tactics of Definers, Facebook's Attack Dog," *New York Times*, November 15, 2018.

61. Caroline O'Donovan and Ken Bensinger, "The Cost of Next-Day Delivery," *BuzzFeed*, August 31, 2019.

CHAPTER THREE

1. Marc Kaufman, "Jefferson Changed 'Subjects' to 'Citizens' in Declaration of Independence," *Washington Post*, July 3, 2010.
2. Or as Madison said in 1794: "the censorial power is in the people over the Government, not in the Government over the people." Akhil Reed Amar, *America's Constitution: A Biography* (New York: Random House, 2005), 103.
3. In the words of Drew McCoy, "They had to define, and then attempt to secure, a form of economy and society that would be capable of sustaining the virtuous character of a republican citizenry." Drew McCoy, *The Elusive Republic* (Chapel Hill: University of North Carolina Press, 1980), 7.
4. Edmund Morgan, *American Slavery, American Freedom: The Ordeal of Colonial Virginia* (New York: W. W. Norton, 1975).
5. Frederick Douglass, *Selected Speeches and Writings*, edited by Philip Foner and Yuval Taylor (Chicago: Chicago Review Press, 1999), 196.
6. Amar, *America's Constitution*, 80. Importantly, this very much included free blacks, who led much of the fight against slavery; see Leslie Harris, *In the Shadow of Slavery: African Americans in New York City, 1626–1863* (Chicago: University of Chicago Press, 2003), 49. See also *The American Revolution: Explorations in the History of American Radicalism*, edited by Alfred Young (Dekalb: Northern Illinois University Press, 1976); and Benjamin Quarles, *The Negro in the American Revolution* (Chapel Hill: University of North Carolina Press, 1996).
7. "Address for the Promotion of Colored Enlistments," quoted in Du Bois, *Black Reconstruction*, 102.
8. Bailyn, *The Ideological Origins of the American Revolution*, 34.
9. Fritz Machlup, *The Political Economy of Monopoly: Business, Labor, and Government Policies* (Baltimore: Johns Hopkins University Press, 1952), 185.
10. An excellent introduction to how the founding generation in the United States thought about corruption, and its connections to corporate structures, is Zephyr Teachout, *Corruption in America: From Benjamin Franklin's Snuff Box to Citizens United* (Cambridge, MA: Harvard University Press, 2014).
11. Barbara Lewalski, *The Life of John Milton* (Oxford: Blackwell, 2000), 211.
12. Gary Nash, *The Unknown American Revolution* (New York: Viking, 2005), 236.
13. Ralph Ketcham, *James Madison: A Biography* (Newtown, CT: American Political Biography Press, 1971), 38–39.
14. Ibid., 39.
15. John Keane, *Tom Paine: A Political Life* (New York: Grove, 1995), 47.
16. Amar, *America's Constitution*, 17.
17. Ibid., 7.
18. John Milton, "The Ready and Easy Way to Establish a Free Commonwealth," in *John Milton Prose*, edited by David Loewenstein (West Sussex: Wiley Blackwell, 2013).
19. Gordon Wood, *The Radicalism of the American Revolution* (New York: Vintage Books, 1991), 179.
20. Ibid., 53.
21. John Adams, "Letter to John Taylor, April 15, 1814," quoted in Luke Mayville, *John Adams and the Fear of American Oligarchy* (Princeton, NJ: Princeton University Press, 2016), 87–88.
22. Ibid., 45.
23. John Adams in 1776, quoted in Nash, *The Unknown American Revolution*, 202.
24. Ketcham, *James Madison*, 152.
25. Wood, *The Radicalism of the American Revolution*, 55.
26. Nash, *The Unknown American Revolution*, 246.
27. Daniel Webster, "First Settlement of New England: A Discourse Delivered at Plymouth, on

the 22nd of December, 1820," in *The Great Speeches and Orations of Daniel Webster* (Boston: Little, Brown, 1891), 45.

28. C. Ray Keim, "Primogeniture and Entail in Colonial Virginia," *William and Mary Quarterly* 25, no. 4 (October 1968): 545–586.

29. Thomas Jefferson, "Thomas Jefferson to John Adams," October 28, 1813, *The Thomas Jefferson Papers at the Library of Congress*, Series 1. Available online at http://hdl.loc.gov/loc.mss/mtj .mtjbib021548.

30. Nash, *The Unknown American Revolution*, 389.

31. Thomas Jefferson, "Thomas Jefferson to James Madison, 28 Oct. 1785," in *The Founders Constitution*, edited by Philip Kurland and Ralph Lerner, 1986, vol. 1, Chapter 15, Document 32. Available online at http://press-pubs.uchicago.edu/founders/documents/v1ch15s32.html.

32. Amar, *America's Constitution*, 408.

33. Bailyn, *The Ideological Origins of the American Revolution*, 373–374.

34. David Hounshell, *From the American System to Mass Production, 1800–1932* (Baltimore: Johns Hopkins University Press, 1984). Drew McCoy writes that "it was only the 'Great Establishments of Manufactures that had no place in republican America—establishments that employed poverty stricken, landless laborers." McCoy, *The Elusive Republic*, 65.

35. Annette Gordon-Reed and Peter Onuf, *Most Blessed of the Patriarchs: Thomas Jefferson and the Empire of the Imagination* (New York: W. W. Norton, 2016), 81.

36. Nash, *The Unknown American Revolution*, 284. In Maryland in 1776, "people in five counties who did not meet the property qualifications thronged the polls, threw out the election judges, and insisted that anyone who bore arms was entitled to vote."

37. McCoy, *The Elusive Republic*, 65.

38. B. Zorina Kahn, *The Democratization of Invention: Patents and Copyrights in American Economic Development, 1790–1920* (Cambridge: Cambridge University Press, 2005); Lewis Hyde, *Common Air: Revolution, Art, and Ownership* (New York: Farrar, Straus and Giroux, 2010), 89–91.

39. "Every man has a property in his own person. This nobody has any right to but himself." John Locke, *Second Treatise of Government* (Indianapolis: Bobbs-Merrill, 1952), Chapter 5, Section 27, 17.

40. James Madison, "Property," published originally in the *National Gazette*, March 29, 1792, in *The Selected Writings of James Madison*, edited by Ralph Ketcham (Indianapolis: Hackett, 2006), 222. In addition to Locke, Madison could also have adopted this from Smith, who in *The Wealth of Nations* wrote, "The property which every man has in his own labour, so it is the original foundation of all other property, so it is the most sacred and inviolable. The patrimony of a poor man lies in the strength and dexterity of his hands, and to hinder him from employing this strength and dexterity in what manner he thinks proper, without injury to his neighbor, is a plain violation of this most sacred property. It is a manifest encroachment upon the just liberty both of the workman, and of those who might be disposed to employ him." Adam Smith, *The Wealth of Nations* (New York: Modern Library, 1994), 140.

41. Ketcham, *James Madison*, 330.

42. James Madison, "Debates in the Federal Convention," The Avalon Project, Yale Law School, August 7, 1787. Available online at http://avalon.law.yale.edu/18th_century/debates_807.asp.

43. Ketcham, *James Madison*, 220. Here again Madison echoed the more radical voices of the English Revolution, especially Milton, who in 1650 wrote that "meerly by the liberty and right of free born Men, to be govern'd as seems to them best," the people must be allowed to freely choose their own king. John Milton, "The Tenure of Kings and Magistrates," in *John Milton Prose*, 252.

44. Ketcham, *James Madison*, 221.

45. "The Report of a Constitution or Form of Government for the Commonwealth of Massachusetts, 28–31 October 1779," *Founders Online*, National Archives, https://founders.archives .gov/documents/Adams/06-08-02-0161-0002. (Original source: *The Adams Papers*, Papers of John Adams, vol. 8, *March 1779 – February 1780*, ed. Gregg L. Lint, Robert J. Taylor, Richard

Alan Reyerson, Celeste Walker, and Joanna M. Revelas [Cambridge, MA: Harvard University Press, 1989], 236–271.)

46. Catherine Drinker Bowen, *The Lion and the Throne: The Life and Times of Sir Edward Coke* (Boston: Little Brown, 1956), 313.

47. Ibid., 164.

48. Ibid., 420, 462.

49. David Hume, *Of the Rise and Progress of the Arts and Sciences, Essays: Moral, Political, and Literary* (Indianapolis: Liberty Fund, 1987), 127.

50. Adams in a letter the day after the Tea Party wrote, "This is the grandest, Event, which has ever yet happened Since, the Controversy, with Britain, opened!" He added, "The Sublimity of it, charms me!" John Adams, "Letter to James Warren, Dec. 17, 1773," in *John Adams: Revolutionary Writings 1755–1775* (New York: Library of America, 2011), 288.

51. Bowen, *The Lion and the Throne*, 513–514.

52. Wood, *The Radicalism of the American Revolution*, 191.

53. Bailyn, *The Ideological Origins of the American Revolution*, 160.

54. Barbara Lewalski, *The Life of John Milton*, 285. (In the pamphlet, titled "The Fourth Paper Presented by Major Butler," Williams also called for the Jews of Britain to be granted full freedom. Andrew Crome, *Christian Zionism and English National Identity, 1600–1850* [Manchester: Macmillan, 2018], 89.) Milton in 1660 expressed a similar vision of democratic community as centering on the liberty of reason. "The happiness of a nation must needs be firmest and certainest," Milton wrote, "in a full and free Councel of thir own electing, where no single person, but reason only swaies." John Milton, "The Ready and Easy Way," 434.

55. Ketcham, *James Madison*, 73.

56. Madison, "Property."

57. McCoy, *The Elusive Republic*, 7.

58. The number of Baptist churches rose from 7 to 54 in Virginia between 1769 and 1774 (Wood, *The Radicalism of the American Revolution*, 144). Madison himself in 1774 fought to get six Baptist preachers released from Culpeper county jail (Ketcham, *James Madison*, 57).

CHAPTER FOUR

1. Original quote from 1795, in Peter Onuf, *Statehood and Union: A History of the Northwest Ordinance* (Bloomington: Indiana University Press, 1987), 22.

2. A "system of land surveys which, perfected by practice and experience, [would later be] adopted by nearly every" country in the world. Roy Robbins, *Our Landed Heritage: The Public Domain 1776–1970* (Lincoln: University of Nebraska Press, 1976), 8.

3. Richard White, *The Middle Ground: Indians, Empires, and Republics in the Great Lakes Region, 1650–1815* (Cambridge: Cambridge University Press, 1991), 469.

4. Jerry Ostler, "'Just and Lawful War' as Genocidal War in the (United States) Northwest Ordinance and Northwest Territory, 1787–1832," *Journal of Genocide Research* 18, no. 1 (2016).

5. White, *Middle Ground*, 474. Jefferson, for instance, as president, held that the Indians would simply be subsumed into white society through property ownership and marriage. In a December 1808 letter to the Miami, Potawatomie, Delaware, and Chippewa, he wrote, "When once you have property, you will want laws and magistrates to protect your property and persons, and to punish those among you who commit crimes. You will find that our laws are good for this purpose. You will wish to live under them; you will unite yourselves with us, join in our great councils, and form one people with us, and we shall all be Americans. You will mix with us by marriage. Your blood will run in our veins and will spread with us over this great island." (Gary Nash, "The Hidden History of Mestizo America," *Journal of American History* 2, no. 3 [December 1995]); Aziz Rana, *The Two Faces of American Freedom* (Cambridge, MA: Harvard University Press, 2010), 3.

6. Thomas Hart Benton, *Thirty Years View: Or a History of the Workings of the American Government, from 1820 to 1850* (New York: D. Appleton, 1854), 104. (Reprinted New York: Greenwood Press, 1968.)

7. Tamara Venit Shelton, *A Squatter's Republic: Land and the Politics of Monopoly in California, 1850–1900* (Berkeley: University of California Press, 2013).

8. Claude Oubre, *40 Acres and a Mule* (Baton Rouge: Louisiana State University Press, 2012). About 1,000 black families did end up with deeds.

9. On the Preemption Act of 1830, see Robbins, *Our Landed Heritage*, 50; on the Preemption Act of 1841, see ibid., 89; on the Homestead Act of 1862, see ibid., 206; on the Southern Homestead Act, see Oubre, *40 Acres and a Mule*; on the Timber Culture Act of 1872, see Robbins, *Our Landed Heritage*, 218; on the Desert Land Act of 1877, see ibid., 249; on the Reclamation Act of 1902, see Richard Wahl, "Redividing the Waters: The Reclamation Act of 1902," *National Resources & Environment* 10, no. 1 (Summer 1995): 31–38.

10. As Roy Robbins explained, "Congress intended that the domain not fall into the hands of those who already had enough land" (Robbins, *Our Landed Heritage*, 89).

11. Ibid., 207. At the same time, to ensure public control of the overall process of settlement, the Act also broke the railroad's landholdings into carefully isolated portions. By 1871, citizens put an end to railroad land grants entirely and began to claw back what they had given away, and by 1884 they had moved to take back lands the railroads had not used or sold off (ibid., 277–278).

12. Paul S. Taylor, "The 160-Acre Water Limitation and the Water Resources Commission," *Western Political Quarterly* 3, no. 3 (September 1950): 435–450.

13. Robbins, *Our Landed Heritage*, 273.

14. And so the goal remained 150 years later, when in the middle of the Great Depression, agriculture secretary Henry Wallace wrote, "I know of no better means of reconstructing our agriculture on a thoroughly sound and permanently desirable basis than to make as its foundation the family-size, owner-operated farm" (Arthur Schlesinger Jr., *The Coming of the New Deal*, vol. 2 of *The Age of Roosevelt* [Boston: Houghton Mifflin, 1959], 380).

15. Don Fehrenbacher, *The Dred Scott Case* (Oxford: Oxford University Press, 1978), 83.

16. Onuf, *Statehood and Union*, xvii.

17. Ibid., 133.

18. Ketcham, *James Madison*, 301.

19. The most well-known proponent is Robert Nozick, in *Anarchy, State, and Utopia* (New York: Basic Books, 1974), 25–27. The term was originally used in a negative sense by the German socialist Ferdinand Lassalle in 1862.

20. Philip Pettit, *Republicanism: A Theory of Freedom and Government* (Oxford: Oxford University Press, 1999), 25.

21. Du Bois, *Black Reconstruction*, 8.

22. Onuf writes that in the Ordinance, Americans structured the market to promote "compact" townships. Their goal was to create "larger, denser, more productive settlements" (Onuf, *Statehood and Union*, 29–31). Robbins writes that until the Revolution, America had been developed under two very different systems of land use. In New England, under the township system, entire communities would first form and then pioneer a new town together. In the "proprietary colonies" of the South, by contrast, there was little to no planning, and individuals tended to squat in isolated homesteads and sparsely populated communities. "By time of independence, even southerners recognized that experience attested to the fact that the nature of society was to a very great extent determined by land policy" (Robbins, *Our Landed Heritage*, 7).

23. Original text of the Ordinance, cited in Onuf, *Statehood and Union*, 24.

24. Onuf writes that the authors of the Ordinance aimed to establish "a national market for western lands" in which it was Congress that regulated supply of land. The authors believed that it was surveying itself—the careful demarcation of the parcels of property themselves—that made "a true market situation" characterized by "open competitive bidding" possible (Onuf, *Statehood and Union*, 15, 35, 42).

25. Ibid., 60.

26. Richard John, *Spreading the News: The American Postal System from Franklin to Morse* (Cambridge, MA: Harvard University Press, 1998).

27. Manessah Cutler, a land company promoter, quoted in Onuf, *Statehood and Union*, 38.

28. Ketcham's words, in *James Madison*, 301.

29. James Madison, "Who Are the Best Keepers of the Peoples Liberties," *National Gazette*, December 20, 1792, emphasis added. Available online at *Founders Online*, National Archives, https://founders.archives.gov/documents/Madison/01-14-02-0384. (Original source: *The Papers of James Madison*, vol. 14, *6 April 1791–16 March 1793*, ed. Robert A. Rutland and Thomas A. Mason [Charlottesville: University Press of Virginia, 1983], 426–427.)

30. James Madison, "Republican Distribution of Citizens," March 5, 1792, in *The Writings of James Madison*, edited by Gaillard Hunt (New York: G. P. Putnam's Sons, 1900). Available online at https://oll.libertyfund.org/titles/madison-the-writings-vol-6-1790-1802.

31. Gabor Boritt, *Lincoln and the Economics of the American Dream* (Urbana: University of Illinois Press, 1978), 275.

32. Walt Whitman, *Speciman Days and Collect* (Brooklyn, NY: Melville House, 2015), 255.

33. John Rae, *Life of Adam Smith* (New York: Macmillan, 1895).

34. Thomas Jefferson, "Letter to Thomas Mann Randolph Jr.," *Founders Online*, National Archives, May 30, 1790, https://founders.archives.gov/documents/Jefferson/01-16-02-0264. (Original source: *The Papers of Thomas Jefferson*, vol. 16, *30 November 1789–4 July 1790*, ed. Julian P. Boyd [Princeton, NJ: Princeton University Press, 1961], 448–450.)

35. In Britain, regulation of local markets for foods and other goods traces at least as far back as 1086, when William the Conqueror ordered the survey of all Britain's lands and towns and institutions, for what came to be known as the Domesday Book. George Williams, "Early Markets and the Market Cross," in *Economic Action in Theory and Practice: Anthropological Investigations* (*Research in Economic Anthropology, Vol. 30*), edited by D. Wood (Bingley, UK: Emerald Group Publishing Limited, 2010), 257–274.

36. William Novak, *The People's Welfare* (Chapel Hill: University of North Carolina Press, 1996), 95, 96.

37. That evening handbills signed "Joyce Junior" were nailed up about town, in 1776 or 1777 (Nash, *The Unknown American Revolution*, 237).

38. Ibid., 311.

39. Adam Smith, in *The Wealth of Nations*, wrote that such a monopoly results in a variety of harms, including that "all the other subjects of the state are taxed very absurdly in two different ways; first, by the high price of goods, which, in the case of a free trade, they could buy much cheaper; and, *secondly, by their total exclusion from a branch of business, which it might be both convenient and profitable for many of them to carry on* [emphasis added]." Adam Smith, *The Wealth of Nations* (New York: Modern Library, 1994), 814. The idea that monopolies infringe on the liberty of individuals to engage in certain lines of business or work later played a major role in the concept of "industrial liberty" as defined by Senator John Sherman in his speech defending the antitrust law that bears his name ("Trusts, Speech of Hon. John Sherman of Ohio, Delivered in the Senate of the United States," Friday, March 21, 1890, available through the HathiTrust Digital Library, University of Wisconsin, Madison), and later used by Louis Brandeis (see, for instance, "The Regulation of Competition versus the Regulation of Monopoly," An Address to the Economic Club of New York, November 1, 1912). James Huston traces this "free labor ideology" to what he calls the "doctrine of calling," and writes that "This mastery of contribution—of production, of manufacture, of skill" enabled individual men and women to develop "pride" being able to take productive part in society. Huston, *The British Gentry*, 11.

40. Smith famously concluded this section with the observation that "without the assistance and co-operation of many thousands, the very meanest person in a civilised country could not be provided, even according to what we very falsely imagine the easy and simple manner in which he is commonly accommodated." Smith, *The Wealth of Nations*, 13.

41. "The wise and virtuous man is at all times willing that his own private interest should be sacrificed to the public interest of his own particular order or society. He is at all times willing, too,

that the interest of this order or society should be sacrificed to the greater interest of the state or sovereignty, of which it is only a subordinate part. He should, therefore, be equally willing that all those inferior interests should be sacrificed to the greater interest of the universe, to the interest of that great society of all sensible and intelligent beings, of which God himself is the immediate administrator and director." Adam Smith, *The Theory of Moral Sentiments* (Oxford: Oxford University Press, 1976), C. III.

42. Edmund Burke, "Speech on Fox's East India Bill, December 1, 1783," in *The Speeches of the Right Hon. Edmund Burke* (Dublin: James Duffy, 1862).

43. Smith, *Wealth of Nations*, 812.

44. Wood, *The Radicalism of the American Revolution*, 321.

45. "The right of incorporation as practiced in early America was a special gift (accompanied by special privileges) bestowed by the polity upon select associations as quid pro quo for the performance of special duties and obligations" (Novak, *The People's Welfare*, 105). With these regulations in place, Americans sped up the creation of new corporations, to 114, between 1791 and 1795 (Wood, *The Radicalism of the American Revolution*, 321).

46. Samuel Blodget, *Economica: A Statistical Manual for the United States of America* (City of Washington: Printed for the author, 1806), in Wood, *The Radicalism of the American Revolution*, 321.

47. Wood, *The Radicalism of the American Revolution*, 321.

48. Eric Hilt, "Early American Corporations and the State," in *Corporations and American Democracy*, edited by Naomi Lamoreaux and William Novak (Cambridge, MA: Harvard University Press, 2017).

49. Novak, *The People's Welfare*, 294, note 111. For religious establishments in the 1780s, see also George Heberton Evans Jr., *Business Incorporations in the United States 1800–1943* (New York: National Bureau of Economic Research, 1948).

50. Forrest McDonald, *Alexander Hamilton: A Biography* (New York: W. W. Norton, 1982), 4.

51. Ibid., 215.

52. "The result would be a regional and class concentration of power Madison could only view with alarm" (Ketcham, *James Madison: A Biography*, 313).

53. Nash, *The Unknown American Revolution*, 395.

54. Hamilton's financial system *was* modeled in part on Walpole's corrupt manipulation of the House of Commons (using Crown patronage). John Harold Plumb, *Sir Robert Walpole: The King's Minister* (London: Penguin Press, 1960).

55. Ketcham, *James Madison*, 322.

56. Ibid., 314.

57. Bray Hammond, *Banks and Politics in America: From the Revolution to the Civil War* (Princeton, NJ: Princeton University Press, 1967), 144–145.

58. Sean Wilentz, *The Rise of American Democracy: Jefferson to Lincoln* (New York: W. W. Norton, 2005), 396. See also Sharon Ann Murphy, *Other People's Money: How Banking Worked in the Early American Republic* (Baltimore: Johns Hopkins University Press, 2017); Peter Temen, *The Jacksonian Economy* (New York: W. W. Norton, 1969); and Hammond, *Banks and Politics in America*.

59. Martin Van Buren, *Inquiry into the Origin and Course of Political Parties in the United States* (New York: August M. Kelly, 1967), 166.

60. Ketcham, *James Madison*, 297.

61. Keane, *Tom Paine*, 90.

62. "By the late 1780s many of the younger revolutionary leaders like James Madison were willing to confront the reality of interests in America with a very cold eye" (Wood, *The Radicalism of the American Revolution*, 252).

63. David Hume, "Of the Independency of Parliament," 1742, in *David Hume: Political Writings*, edited by Stuart Warner and Donald Livingston (Indianapolis: Hackett, 1994), 113.

64. Makan Delrahim, "Remarks for the Antitrust New Frontiers Conference," Tel Aviv, June 11, 2019. We also see such thinking among progressives; Ralph Nader in a 1976 book called *Taming the Giant Corporation* notes on the very first page that "The Constitution of the

United States does not explicitly mention the business corporation" (Ralph Nader, Mark Green, and Joel Seligman, *Taming the Giant Corporation: How the Largest Corporations Control Our Lives* [New York: W. W. Norton, 1977], 15).

65. James Madison, "Federalist 10," in Alexander Hamilton, John Jay, and James Hamilton, *The Federalist: A Commentary on the Constitution of the United States*, edited by Robert Scigliano (New York: Modern Library, 2001).

66. James Madison, "Letter to Thomas Jefferson," October 17, 1788, *The James Madison Letters*, vol. 1, *1769–1793* (New York: Townsend Mac Coun, 1884), 427.

67. E. A. J. Johnson, *The Foundations of American Economic Freedom: Government and Enterprise in the Age of Washington* (Minneapolis: University of Minnesota Press, 1973), 188.

68. Jefferson in 1816: "In so complicated a science as political economy, no one axiom can be laid down as wise and expedient for all times and circumstances, and for their contraries" (McCoy, *The Elusive Republic*, 7).

69. Madison, "Federalist 51," *The Federalist*, Scigliano, emphasis added.

70. Hounshell, *From the American System to Mass Production*, 25–26.

71. Alexis de Tocqueville, *Democracy in America* (New York: Alfred A. Knopf, 1945), vol. 2, 156–157.

72. Wood, *The Radicalism of the American Revolution*, 308.

73. Ibid., 328.

74. Ibid., 7.

75. Sven Beckert, *Empire of Cotton: A Global History* (New York: Knopf, 2014).

76. "The breadth of its devastation cannot be overstated" (Leigh Merritt, *Masterless Men: Poor Whites and Slavery in the Antebellum South* [Cambridge: Cambridge University Press, 2017], 4).

77. Du Bois, *Black Reconstruction*, 49–50.

78. Rod Soodalter, "These Pimps of Piracy," *New York Archives Magazine* 9, no. 1 (Summer 2009).

79. *Charles Sumner, His Complete Works* (Boston: Lee and Shepard, 1900), 43.

80. Abraham Lincoln, "Address at Sanitary Fair in Baltimore," April 18, 1864, in *The Writings of Abraham Lincoln, 1863–1865* (New York: G. P. Putnam's Sons, 1923), 121.

81. Jefferson in his 1784 draft of the Ordinance proposed excluding slavery from all western lands after 1800, a plan that failed due to absence of one delegate. Rufus King of Massachusetts resurrected the idea, and Jefferson's language, in 1785. King's language was then retained almost verbatim in the final version approved by Congress in July 1787 (Onuf, *Statehood and Union*, 110–111).

82. Amar, *America's Constitution*, 260 and 264–266.

83. The numbers added up. The 1820 census showed that over the previous two decades the population of Ohio grew by 200,000 more than Kentucky's (Onuf, *Statehood and Union*, 127).

84. Du Bois, *Black Reconstruction*, 18.

85. Celebration of the 47th Anniversary of the First Settlement of the State of Ohio, by Native Citizens, 1835 (Onuf, *Statehood and Union*, 138). As Onuf would conclude, "Here, in short, was a republican landscape, beautiful in its diversity and its busy pursuits, as well as for its ennobling effects on an enterprising citizenry" (ibid., 146).

86. In the years leading up to the Civil War, a main subject of debate was the validity of the Ordinance's prohibition on slavery. We see this in Justice Roger Taney's contortionist efforts, in his notorious *Dred Scott* decision of 1857, to prise apart the Ordinance, with what one historian characterized as a "phantasmal history of the United States" (Fehrenbacher, *The Dred Scott Case*, 372). We see this also in Lincoln's strong defense of the validity of the prohibition in the Ordinance, in his debates with Stephen Douglas (Harry Jaffa, *Crisis of the House Divided: An Interpretation of the Issues in the Lincoln-Douglas Debates* [Chicago: University of Chicago Press, 1959], 295).

87. Du Bois, *Black Reconstruction*, 266.

88. Onuf, *Statehood and Union*, 33.

89. Merritt, *Masterless Men*, 6.

90. Walt Whitman, "Democratic Vistas," in *Specimen Days and Collect* (Brooklyn, NY: Melville House, 2014), 252.

91. On the goal of full economic independence, Douglass wrote: "My politics in regard to the negro is simply this . . . Give him fair play and let him alone, but be sure you give him fair play [as] a man before the law. . . . If you see a negro wanted to purchase land, let him alone; let him purchase it. If you see him on the way to school, let him go; don't say he shall not go into the same school with other people. . . . If you see him on his way to the workshop, let him alone; let him work; don't say you will not work with him" (David Blight, *Frederick Douglass, Prophet of Freedom* [New York: Simon & Schuster, 2018], 563). On having the same voting power as white citizens: ibid., 264. On sharing the principles of the Declaration: "I have said that the Declaration of Independence is the ring-bolt to the chain of your nation's destiny; so, indeed, I regard it. The principles contained in that instrument are saving principles. Stand by those principles, be true to them on all occasions, in all places, against all foes, and at whatever cost" (Douglass, "The Meaning of July Fourth, for the Negro," July 5, 1852, *Selected Speeches and Writings*, 188).

92. Blight, *Frederick Douglass*, 304. A fan of Lord Byron, Douglass often quoted *Childe Harold's Pilgrimage*: "Who would be free, themselves must strike the blow." Blight, *Frederick Douglass*, 287.

93. Ibid., 395.

94. Ibid., 637.

95. Martin Luther King Jr., *Where Do We Go From Here: Chaos or Community* (Boston: Beacon Press, 1968), 84.

96. Du Bois, *Black Reconstruction*, 30.

CHAPTER FIVE

1. Theodore Roosevelt, "The New Nationalism," August 31, 1910. Available online at the Obama White House Archives, https://obamawhitehouse.archives.gov/blog/2011/12/06/archives-president-teddy-roosevelts-new-nationalism-speech.

2. Robert La Follette, *Robert La Follette's Autobiography: A Personal Narrative of Political Experiences* (Madison: University of Wisconsin Press, 1960), 295.

3. Walter Lippmann, *Drift & Mastery: An Attempt to Diagnose the Current Disease* (New York: Mitchell Kennerley, 1914; reprint Madison: University of Wisconsin Press, 1987), 87.

4. Ibid., 41.

5. Charles Forcey, *The Crossroads of Liberalism: Croly, Weyl, Lippmann, and the Progressive Era* (Oxford: Oxford University Press, 1961), 33.

6. Herbert Croly, *The Promise of American Life* (New York: Macmillan, 1909; reprint Cambridge, MA: Harvard University Press, 1965), 192–193.

7. "Croly did not so much influence Roosevelt as read into his career an intellectual coherence which Roosevelt then adopted as his own view of things." Christopher Lasch, "Herbert Croly's America," *New York Review of Books*, July 1, 1965.

8. Hans Thorelli, *The Federal Antitrust Policy* (Baltimore: Johns Hopkins University Press, 1955), 425.

9. La Follette, *Robert La Follette's Autobiography*, 290.

10. Ibid., 292, emphasis in original.

11. Ibid., 296.

12. Ronald Pestritto, *Woodrow Wilson and the Roots of Modern Liberalism* (Lanham, MD: Rowman & Littlefield, 2005), 209.

13. Thomas Frank's *The People, NO: A Brief History of Antipopulism* (New York: Metropolitan Books, 2020) and Charles Postel's *The Populist Vision* (Oxford: Oxford University Press, 2009) provide excellent histories of the movement and of efforts to crush it.

14. Du Bois, *Black Reconstruction*, 330–333, 340.

15. Wilson, *The New Freedom*, 57.

16. Ibid., 49–50.

17. The author Jack London in 1908 published a novel titled *The Iron Heel*, about the overthrow of the U.S. government by an oligarchy, and the imposition of political tyranny.

18. Guy Gugliotta, "New Estimate Raises Civil War Death Toll," *New York Times*, April 2, 2012.

19. One excellent exception to the confusion over the U.S. political economy of the late nineteenth century is Richard White, *The Republic for Which It Stands* (Oxford: Oxford University Press, 2017).

20. Maury Klein, *The Life and Legend of Jay Gould* (Baltimore: Johns Hopkins University Press, 1986). See also Ron Chernow, *Grant* (New York: Penguin, 2017), 673, 748.

21. Mark Twain and Dudley Warner, *The Gilded Age* (New York: Modern Library, 2006). On "The Revised Catechism," see Justin Kaplan, *Mr. Clemens and Mark Twain: A Biography* (New York: Simon & Schuster, 1966). On Jay Gould, see Mark Twain, *Mark Twain in Eruption: Hitherto Unpublished Pages About Men and Events* (New York: Harper, 1940).

22. For origins of the term, see Richard John, "Robber Barons Redux: Antimonopoly Reconsidered," *Enterprise & Society* 13, no. 1 (2012): 1–38.

23. Naomi Lamoreaux, *The Great Merger Movement in American Business* (Cambridge: Cambridge University Press, 1985), 1.

24. Thorelli, *The Federal Antitrust Policy*, 94. Thorelli added that Standard Oil's "relations with the railroads provide an excellent example of the monopoly-fostering effect of freight discrimination" (ibid., 91).

25. The text reads: "That messages received from any individual, company, or corporation, or from any telegraph lines connecting with this line at either of its termini, shall be impartially transmitted in the order of their reception, excepting that the dispatches of the government shall have priority." *Statutes at Large, Treaties and Proclamations of the United States of America, from December 5, 1859, to March 8, 1863*, vol. 12 (Boston: Little, Brown, 1863), 42.

26. Saule Omarova, "The Merchants of Wall Street: Banking, Commerce, and Commodities," *Minnesota Law Review* 98 (2013).

27. Arthur T. Hadley, *Railroad Transportation—Its History and Its Laws* (New York: G. P. Putnam's Sons, 1885).

28. Ibid., 21.

29. Ibid., 121.

30. Ibid., 120.

31. An 1886 report by Senator Cullum's committee detailed "an elaborate system of secret special rates, rebates, drawbacks, and concessions, to foster monopoly, to enrich favored shippers, and to prevent free competition in many lines of trade in which the item of transportation is an important factor." The report went on to characterize the resulting "unjust discrimination between persons, places, commodities" as the "paramount evil" posed by the railroad monopolies, and held that, in the words of Hans Thorelli, the railroad "discriminations were a source of grave danger to the very existence of competitive enterprise in other industries." In the event, the act required that all charges be "reasonable and just"; banned discriminations between localities, classes of freight, and connecting lines; said that short hauls could not cost more than long hauls; required railroads to print and post all rates; and required that railroads give at least ten days' notice before any change in rate (Thorelli, *The Federal Antitrust Policy*, 90, 153, 154).

32. The vote to approve the ICA was 219–41 in the House and 43-15 in the Senate. Scott James, *Presidents, Parties, and the State* (Cambridge: Cambridge University Press, 2000), 117. See also David K. Zucker, "The Origin and Development of the Interstate Commerce Commission and Its Impact on the Origination of Independent Regulatory Commissions in the American Legal System: A Historical Perspective," Master's thesis, 2016, Harvard Extension School.

33. Louis Brandeis, *Other People's Money and How the Bankers Use It* (Boston: Bedford Books of St. Martin's Press, 1995), 92, 132.

34. Sherman, "Trusts," 15.

35. Ibid., 8.

36. Ibid., 6.

37. Thorelli, *The Federal Antitrust Policy*, 214.

38. Lamoreaux, *The Great Merger Movement in American Business*, 3. See also Lynn, *Cornered*, 162, 163.

39. Thorelli, *The Federal Antitrust Policy*, 306.

40. Ibid., 308.

41. Brandeis, *Other People's Money and How the Bankers Use It*, 2.

42. Ibid., 16. For a nuanced view of Morgan's role in building AT&T, see Richard John, *Network Nation: Inventing American Telecommunications* (Cambridge, MA: Harvard University Press, 2010), 312.

43. La Follette, *Robert La Follette's Autobiography*, 290. As detailed in a report of the congressional subcommittee in 1912, "The acts of this inner group . . . strike at the very vitals of potential competition in every industry that is under their protection, a condition which if permitted to continue, will render impossible all attempts to restore normal competitive conditions in the industrial world" (Brandeis, *Other People's Money and How the Bankers Use It*, 49).

44. Moody is quoted in Brandeis, *Other People's Money and How the Bankers Use It*, 17. The Morgan and Rockefeller groups even invested jointly in certain ventures, such as the New Haven system railroad (ibid., 141).

45. Ibid., 49.

46. Ibid., 50.

47. Ibid., 56.

48. Ibid., 139.

49. Gerald Berk, *Louis D. Brandeis and the Making of Regulated Competition, 1900–1932* (Cambridge: Cambridge University Press, 2009), 1.

50. John, *Network Nation*.

51. Berk, *Louis D. Brandeis and the Making of Regulated Competition, 1900–1932*, 44. In a 1921 letter to Harold Laski, Brandeis wrote that the challenge was to develop "vision, wisdom and ingenuity enough to adjust our institutions to the wee size of man and thus render possible his growth and development" (Arthur Schlesinger Jr., *The Politics of Upheaval*, vol. 3 of *The Age of Roosevelt* [Boston: Houghton Mifflin, 1960], 220).

52. In 1910 Congress had reinforced these rules with the Mann-Elkins Act, which banned many forms of vertical integration. One of the main advances of the Wilson administration was to begin to develop ways to use antitrust laws to achieve these ends, rather than the sorts of top-down regulatory approaches we see in the Interstate Commerce Commission and the Public Utility Commissions.

53. Berk, *Louis D. Brandeis and the Making of Regulated Competition, 1900–1932*, 61–62.

54. A 1961 study of 107 judgments estimated that this policy had resulted in the compulsory licensing of 40,000 to 50,000 patents between 1941 and 1959. In all, the policy forced the sharing of perhaps more than 100,000 technological "source codes." Generally, the licenses were free to any U.S. corporation, but the patent holder was allowed to charge foreign firms small fees. See Barry Lynn, "Estates of Mind," *Washington Monthly* (July/August 2013).

55. One of the key innovations during the Wilson administration, in order to buttress the 160-acre American farm, was the regulation of agricultural markets both to prevent consolidation and to stabilize market prices. Actions included the Cotton Futures Acts of 1914 and 1916, the Grain Standards Act of 1916, the Wheat Price Guarantee Act of 1919, the Futures Trading Act of 1921, and the Grain Futures Act of 1922. It also included preparing the ground for the passage of the Packers and Stockyards Act in 1922, which gave the Department of Agriculture immense rulemaking authority over farm markets.

56. Wilson, *The New Freedom*, 132.

57. Croly, *The Promise of American Life*, 188.

58. As Brandeis put it later, in a dissent to a 1932 Supreme Court case, "There must be power in the states and the nation to remold, through experimentation, our economic practices and institutions to meet changing social and economic needs ... To stay experimentation in things social and economic is a grave responsibility. Denial of the right to experiment may be fraught with serious consequences to the nation." New State Ice Co. v. Liebmann, 285 U.S. 262 (1932).

59. Woodrow Wilson, "Letter to Majority Leader Underwood of the House of Representatives," October 17, 1914, in "Antitrust Legislation," *Public Service Regulation and Federal Trade Reporter*, November 1, 1914, p. 1.

60. Regarding Sherman, see Thorelli, *The Federal Antitrust Policy*, 180.

61. Ibid., 450, 451. See also Rudolph Peritz, *Competition Policy in America: History, Rhetoric, Law* (Oxford: Oxford University Press, 1996), 33. See also Daniel Ernst, *Lawyers Against Labor: From Individual Rights to Corporate Liberalism* (Urbana: University of Illinois Press, 1995), 175; Edward Berman, *Labor and the Sherman Act* (New York: Harper & Brothers, 1930).

62. Samuel Gompers, *Seventy Years of Life and Labor: An Autobiography* (New York: E. P. Dutton, 1925).

63. One pathway was an 1833 book by Thomas Hamilton, an aristocratic former soldier who was generally appalled by American ways. Hamilton's coverage of the "workies" movement in New York was especially influential. Thomas Hamilton, *Men and Manners in America* (Edinburgh: William Blackwood, 1833; reprint New York: Augustus Kelley, 1968), 306. See also Lewis S. Feuer, "The North American Origin of Marx's Socialism," *Western Political Quarterly* 16, no. 1 (1963): 53–67, accessed February 29, 2020, doi:10.2307/445958.

64. Arthur Schlesinger Jr., *The Age of Jackson* (Old Saybrook, CT: Konecky & Konecky, 1971), 193. And, further, that the per-day wages should remain the same, meaning employees earned far more per hour worked (ibid., 265).

65. *Commonwealth v. Hunt*, 1842 (Schlesinger, *The Age of Jackson*, 340).

66. Thorelli, *The Federal Antitrust Policy*, 147–148.

67. Kendrick Clements, *The Presidency of Woodrow Wilson* (Lawrence: University Press of Kansas, 1992), 145.

68. John R. Brake, "A Perspective on Federal Involvement in Agricultural Credit Programs," *South Dakota Law Review* 19 (1975).

69. Berk, *Louis D. Brandeis and the Making of Regulated Competition, 1900–1932*, 60. See also Laura Phillips Sawyer, *American Fair Trade: Proprietary Capitalism, Corporatism, and the "New Competition," 1890–1940* (Cambridge: Cambridge University Press, 2018), 194–195.

70. David Levering Lewis, *W. E. B. Du Bois, Biography of a Race, 1868–1919* (New York: Henry Holt, 1993), 424.

71. Ibid.

72. Ibid., 324. Roosevelt, after winning the 1904 election, "immediately began to distance himself from his many African American admirers" (ibid., 331).

73. Ibid., 404.

74. On "backward race," see ibid., 331. On "altogether inferior," see Edmund Morris, *Theodore Rex* (New York: Random House, 2001), 53.

75. Levering Lewis, *W. E. B. Du Bois, Biography of a Race, 1868–1919*, 331.

76. Ibid., 510; Thomas Gossett, *Race: The History of an Idea in America* (Dallas: Southern Methodist University Press, 1963), 279.

77. Dick Lehr, "The Racist Legacy of Woodrow Wilson," *The Atlantic*, November 27, 2015.

78. Charles Postel, *Equality: An American Dilemma, 1866–1896* (New York: Farrar, Straus and Giroux, 2019); Omar H. Ali, *In the Lion's Mouth: Black Populism in the New South, 1880–1900* (Jackson: University Press of Mississippi, 2010); Timothy Thomas Fortune, *Black and White: Land, Labor, and Politics in the South* (originally published 1884) (Chicago: Johnson Publishing, 1970).

79. Martin Luther King Jr., "Our God Is Marching On," Speech in Montgomery, Alabama, March 25, 1965. Available online at the Martin Luther King Jr. Research and Education Institute, Stanford University.

80. The suffering of poor whites, before and after the Civil War, has been well documented. See Merritt, *Masterless Men*, 327; and Stephen V. Ash, "Poor Whites in the Occupied South, 1861–1865," *Journal of Southern History* 57, no. 1 (February 1991): 39–62. That middle-class and poor white men in both the South and the North planned to organize a new political economy just for themselves was amply evident by July 4, 1875, when Frederick Douglass, in a speech in Washington, asked ruefully, "If war among the whites brought peace and liberty to the blacks, what will peace among the whites bring?" (Blight, *Frederick Douglass, Prophet of Freedom*, 557).

81. As David Levering Lewis wrote in his biography of Du Bois, after Wilson took power in 1913, "The reality in the United States, however, was first the gradual and then the accelerated expulsion and exclusion of African-Americans from the unions" (Levering Lewis, *W. E. B. Du Bois, Biography of a Race, 1868–1919*, 419). As Du Bois himself put it in 1912, "So long as labor fights for humanity, its mission is divine; but when it fights for a clique of Americans, Irish or German monopolists who have cornered or are trying to corner the market in a certain type of service . . . while other competent workmen starve, they deserve themselves the starvation which they plan for their darker and poorer fellows." See Paul Moreno, *Black Americans and Organized Labor: A New History* (Baton Rouge: Louisiana State University Press, 2006), 92.

82. Daniel Okrent, *The Guarded Gate: Bigotry, Eugenics, and the Law That Kept Two Generations of Jews, Italians, and Other European Immigrants out of America* (New York: Scribner, 2019), 208–209.

83. W. E. B. Du Bois, "Awake America," *The Crisis* 14, no. 5 (September 1917). Available online through the Blackbird Archive, vol. 16, no. 2 (Fall 2017).

84. Pete Daniel, *Dispossession: Discrimination Against African American Farmers in the Age of Civil Rights* (Chapel Hill: University of North Carolina Press, 2014).

85. As Richard Rothstein wrote in *Color of Law*, "Racial segregation in housing was not merely a project of southerners in the former slaveholding Confederacy. It was a nationwide project of the federal government in the twentieth century, designed and implemented by its most liberal leaders." Richard Rothstein, *The Color of Law: A Forgotten History of How Our Government Segregated America* (New York: Liveright, 2017), xii. See also Ira Katznelson, *When Affirmative Action Was White* (New York: W. W. Norton, 2005); and Alexis Madrigal, "The Racist Housing Policy That Made Your Neighborhood," *The Atlantic*, May 22, 2014.

86. Nikole Hannah Jones, "America Wasn't a Democracy, Until Black Americans Made It One," *New York Times*, August 16, 2019.

CHAPTER SIX

1. A. L. A. Schechter Poultry Corp. v. United States.

2. Arthur Schlesinger, *The Politics of Upheaval*, vol. 3 of *The Age of Roosevelt* (Boston: Houghton Mifflin, 1960), 280.

3. Schlesinger, *The Coming of the New Deal*, 331.

4. Ibid., 333.

5. Rexford Tugwell, *The Democratic Roosevelt* (Garden City, NY: Doubleday, 1957), 220, 546. From Tugwell's point of view, one person more than any other was responsible for this revolution. In his recollections a generation later, Tugwell wrote of his colleagues in the Roosevelt administration that "they were infected with the malevolence of old justice Brandeis. The old justice had a gentle manner, too, but no harder character ever played a part in the nation's public life" (545).

6. Schlesinger, *The Politics of Upheaval*, 391.

7. Robert Dallek, *Franklin D. Roosevelt: A Political Life* (New York: Viking, 2017), 18, 19.

8. Roosevelt was concerned about British dominance of the radio business. Roosevelt also turned over the Navy's own radio patents to the new subsidiary and helped to convince Brit-

ain's Marconi to sell control of its American radio unit to General Electric. Barry C. Lynn, *End of the Line: The Rise and Coming Fall of the Global Corporation* (New York: Doubleday, 2005), 73, note 267.

9. Michael A. Janson and Christopher S. Yoo, "The Wires Go to War: The U.S. Experiment with Government Ownership of the Telephone System During World War I," *Faculty Scholarship*, Paper 467, April 1, 2013.

10. Address of Governor Franklin D. Roosevelt, Municipal Auditorium, Portland, Oregon, September 21, 1932. Available online at http://www.fdrlibrary.marist.edu/_resources/images/msf/msf00530.

11. Frank Freidel, *Franklin D. Roosevelt: A Rendezvous with Destiny* (New York: Little, Brown, 1990), 24.

12. On Hoover's bank bailout, see James Stuart Olson, *Saving Capitalism: The Reconstruction Finance Corporation and the New Deal* (Princeton, NJ: Princeton University Press, 1988), 74.

13. As Olson describes the event, "Roosevelt continued to insist until finally Jones caved in" (ibid.). Roosevelt also made clear, Olson reports, that "government ownership or forced consolidation was just not in the cards" (ibid., 119). The administration did insist on salary reductions for executives and cancelled dividends (ibid., 126, 163). By 1935, the RFC had invested more than $1.3 billion in stock and capital notes in more than 6,800 banks, or almost half the total number of banks in the United States (ibid., 81).

14. By 1935, the RFC had made more than 40,000 loans to American businesses. In the first two years of the New Deal, the RFC was the "largest investor in the economy" (ibid., 60). This made it "the most ubiquitous of New Deal agencies" (ibid., 43–44).

15. The Agricultural Adjustment Administration was established to pay farmers not to plant certain products. It used funds collected in the form of a tax on processors (ibid., 85).

16. Ibid., 204.

17. Schlesinger, *The Coming of the New Deal*, 387. "By late 1937, most antitrusters—including Brandeis, Frankfurter, Corcoran, and Cohen—were beginning to fuse the compensatory spending and antitrust philosophies. Federal spending would increase competition by putting more purchasing power in consumers' pockets and creating new opportunities for entrepreneurial initiative. A combination of spending and antitrust activity would provide new outlets for private investment and help break the monopolies' stranglehold on the economy" (Olson, *Saving Capitalism*, 192). See also Ellis Hawley, *The New Deal and the Problem of Monopoly: A Study in Economic Ambivalence* (Princeton, NJ: Princeton University Press, 1966), 299–300.

18. Tugwell, *The Democratic Roosevelt*, 220.

19. Schlesinger, *The Politics of Upheaval*, 290.

20. Franklin Roosevelt, Campaign Address, Chicago, October 14, 1936.

21. Sawyer, *American Fair Trade*, provides an especially good description, 99–105.

22. Smith, *Work of Nations*, 63.

23. Regarding Sherman, see Thorelli, *The Federal Antitrust Policy*, 166.

24. Sherman, "Trusts," 15.

25. One of the first recorded discussions of resale price maintenance was in 1852, in a U.K. commission on book pricing, which included Charles Dickens as a member. In the United States drug companies were using the practice by 1875. The first U.S. legal case on the issue took place in 1885 and involved a thread company. Andrew N. Kleit, "Efficiencies Without Economists: The Early Years of Resale Price Maintenance," *Southern Economic Journal* 59, no. 4 (April 1993): 597–619. Thorelli writes that he could find "no instances" of RPM held illegal before 1890 (Thorelli, *The Federal Antitrust Policy*, 48, 49). Indeed, in the most well-known case before *Dr. Miles*, the New York Supreme Court specifically held that "It is . . . lawful for the manufacturers individually to agree with their customers that those customers shall sell the particular goods manufactured by the vendor for a certain price" (*John D. Park & Sons Co. v. National Wholesale Druggists Association et al.*, 50 N.Y. 1064, in Thorelli, *The Federal Antitrust Policy*, 267).

26. Sawyer, *American Fair Trade*, 141. See also Eleanor M. Fox, "Parallel Imports, The Intraband/

Interbrand Competition Paradigm, and the Hidden Gap Between Intellectual Property Law and Antitrust," *Fordham International Law Journal* 25, no. 4 (2001).

27. Dr. Miles Medical Co. v. John D. Park & Sons Co., 220 U.S. 373 (1911).

28. Wright Patman, *The Robinson–Patman Act: What You Can and Cannot Do Under This Law* (New York: Ronald Press, 1938), 35.

29. Jonathan Bean, *Beyond the Broker State: Federal Policies Toward Small Business, 1936–1961* (Chapel Hill: University of North Carolina Press, 2001), 78. Quote at 83.

30. Robert Bork, *The Antitrust Paradox: A Policy at War with Itself* (New York: The Free Press, 1993), 281.

31. Ibid., 384.

32. "Quantity discounts, promotional discounts, discounts to recognize the purchaser's assumptions of tasks that would otherwise fall on the seller, discounts because of the purchaser's stage in the distribution chain, promotional allowances, advertising allowances—all these and many more are foregone or changed by the law," Bork wrote (ibid., 384).

33. The Roosevelt administration made clear it agreed in the July 1938 "Report to the President on the Economic Conditions of the South" (Washington, DC: National Emergency Council, 1938). "The public utilities in the South are almost completely controlled by outside interests. All the major railroad systems are owned and controlled elsewhere. Most of the great electric holding company systems, whose operating companies furnish the light, heat, and power for southern homes and industries, are directed, managed, and owned by outside interests. Likewise, the transmission and distribution of natural gas, one of the South's great assets, is almost completely in the hands of remote financial institutions." This ownership structure, the report concluded, "makes it possible for residents elsewhere to influence greatly the manner in which the South is developed and to subordinate that development to other interests outside the South."

34. Ernest G. Shinner, *The Forgotten Man* (Chicago: Patterson Publishing, 1933), 110, 149. On Shinner's business of selling meat, see "Champion of Small Business: How E. G. Shinner, Meat Store Wizard, Fights the Big Chains—and Beats Them," *Kiplinger Magazine*, February 1949.

35. As a Federal Reserve history of the act puts it, "Before the act, a Fed member bank was a single corporation operating out of a single building in a narrow range of activities. After the act, a Fed member could be a complex corporation with multiple legal layers operating from multiple locations; these organizations became larger and more complex as decades passed." McFadden Act of 1927, Federal Reserve History, November 22, 2013. Available online at www.federalreservehistory.org/Events/DetailView/11.

36. Louis K. Liggett v. Lee, 288 U.S. 517 (1933).

37. Marc Levinson, *The Great A&P and the Struggle for Small Business in America* (New York: Farrar, Straus and Giroux, 2010). By 1951 every state other than Texas, Missouri, and Vermont had passed such laws. See "Fair Trade Laws, Address by James Mead, Chairman of the Federal Trade Commission Before the New York State Pharmaceutical Association," June 11, 1951.

38. Congressional Record: Proceedings and Debates of the 77th Congress, Second Session, Appendix, Volume 88, Part 9, April 21, 1942, to July 24, 1942, p. A1644.

39. Patman, *The Robinson–Patman Act*, 35.

40. United States v. Von's Grocery Company, 233 F. Supp. 976 (S.D. Cal. 1964).

41. Brian Feldman, "The Real Reason Middle America Should Be Angry," *Washington Monthly*, March 2016.

42. Phillip Longman, "Bloom and Bust: Regional Inequality Is out of Control," *Washington Monthly*, November 2015.

43. Chrysler had two plants in St. Louis, and Ford one big plant. GM built all its Corvettes in St. Louis.

44. In 1980, there were 637 community banks in Missouri, but by 2014 the number had fallen to 262. State of Missouri, "Thirty-Fourth Biennial Report," Division of Finance, July 1, 2012, to June 30, 2014.

45. Feldman, "The Real Reason Middle America Should Be Angry."

46. "McDonnell Douglas F-15 Streak Eagle," National Museum of the United States Air Force. Available online at https://www.nationalmuseum.af.mil/Visit/Museum-Exhibits/Fact-Sheets/Display/Article/197972/mcdonnell-douglas-f-15-streak-eagle/.

47. Walter Lippmann, *The Good Society* (New York: Little, Brown, 1937), 152.

48. Ibid.

49. Regarding Sherman, see Thorelli, *The Federal Antitrust Policy*, 166.

50. Tony Freyer, *Antitrust and Global Capitalism, 1930–2004* (Cambridge: Cambridge University Press, 2009), 247.

51. Ibid., 162. See also John Dower, *Embracing Defeat: Japan in the Wake of World War II* (New York: W. W. Norton, 2000).

52. Lynn, *End of the Line*, 87.

53. Baltzan, "The Old-School Answer to Global Trade."

54. Lynn, *End of the Line*, 61–62.

55. Alfred D. Chandler, *Inventing the Electronic Century* (New York: The Free Press, 2001). AT&T's informal 1952 agreement to license the technologies was later buttressed by an official consent decree with the Eisenhower administration, in 1956.

56. Lynn, "Built to Break: The International System of Bottlenecks in the New Era of Monopoly," *Challenge Magazine* 55, no. 2 (March/April 2012): 87–107.

57. Malcolm X, *Malcolm X Speaks: Selected Speeches and Statements* (New York: Grove Press, 1994), 137.

58. Wilson, *The New Freedom*, 54.

59. Ali, *In the Lion's Mouth*, 114; Postel, *Equality: An American Dilemma*, 308–309; C. Vann Woodward, *Origins of the New South 1877–1913* (Baton Rouge: Louisiana State University Press, 1951), 254–258.

60. Du Bois, *Black Reconstruction*, 633, 703.

61. Brian Feldman, "The Decline of Black Business: And What It Means for American Democracy," *Washington Monthly*, March 2017.

62. In his autobiography, Mason wrote, "Pharmacists represented an economically independent class of black businessmen who might have been thought difficult for the white establishment to control. In many cases, the black-owned pharmacy was itself a nexus in black communities" (ibid.). On Daniel Speed (ibid.) on Selma march, see Taylor Branch, *At Canaan's Edge: America in the King Years 1965–68* (New York: Simon & Schuster, 2006), 144, 149.

63. The suit claimed that the hospitals, which provided more than 75 percent of the city's private hospital beds, discriminated against black physicians. The settlement slowly helped integrate black citizens into the medical profession (Feldman, *Decline of Black Business*).

64. Juan Williams, *Thurgood Marshall, American Revolutionary* (New York: Crown, 1998), 321.

65. Branch, *At Canaan's Edge*, 114.

66. Greenwood was nicknamed Black Wall Street. The riot, which began after black citizens protested the arrest of a teenager for allegedly assaulting a white elevator operator, resulted in the destruction of 1,256 homes and 191 businesses, many burned by gasoline bombs tossed from airplanes. Most reliable estimates put the death toll above 100. Some 10,000 black citizens were left homeless. Tim Madigan, *The Burning: Massacre, Destruction, and the Tulsa Race Riot of 1921* (New York: Thomas Dunne Books, 2001).

67. William Kovacic, "Antitrust in the O'Connor-Rehnquist Era: A View from Inside the Supreme Court," *Antitrust* 20, no. 3 (Summer 2006); William E. Kovacic, "Reagan's Judicial Appointees and Antitrust in the 1990s," *Fordham Law Review* 60, no. 1 (1991); Victor Kramer, "The Road to City of Berkeley: The Antitrust Positions of Justice Thurgood Marshall," *Antitrust Bulletin* 32, no. 335 (1987).

68. *United States v. Topco Associates, Inc.*, argued November 16, 1971, decided March 29, 1972.
69. Du Bois, *Black Reconstruction*, 29.

CHAPTER SEVEN

1. James Reston, "Washington; Kennedy and Bork," *New York Times*, July 5, 1987.
2. Bork did not introduce the concept of "consumer welfare" with publication of *The Antitrust Paradox* in 1978. Mark Green and Ralph Nader, in their 1972 critique of America's antitrust laws, *The Closed Enterprise System*, used the term right at the beginning of that book. "The maximization of consumer welfare [is] our talisman—not the value of small or big enterprise for their own sakes." Indeed, Nader and his allies wrote, it was time for the Federal Trade Commission to abandon its "constituency, the small businessman" and instead focus on "the consumer" (Mark Green, Ralph Nader, and Beverly Moore, *The Closed Enterprise System: Ralph Nader's Study Group Report on Antitrust Enforcement* [New York: Bantam Books, 1972], xviii, 409). But it should also be noted that Bork later claimed to have largely finished *The Antitrust Paradox* in 1969 but then delayed publishing it, due to the illness of his wife and to his work as solicitor general. (George Priest, "Bork's Strategy, Price Fixing, and the Influence of the Chicago School on Modern Antitrust Law," *John M. Olin Center for Studies in Law, Economics, and Public Policy*, Research Paper No. 487, December 11, 2013.)
3. Myers v. United States, 272 U.S. 52, 293, 47 S. Ct. 319, 71 L. Ed. 580 (1927).
4. One of the best histories of this effort is Matt Stoller, *Goliath: The 100-Year War Between Monopoly Power and Democracy* (New York: Simon & Schuster, 2019).
5. In *The Antitrust Paradox*, Bork simply rejects, out of hand, the idea that capitalists will ever sell goods or services below cost in order to drive out rivals, despite an overwhelming body of evidence dating back to the British East India Company. Bork recognizes that it is theoretically possible for corporations to engage in predatory pricing, especially in a case where "the predator has greatly disproportionate reserves or is able to inflict very disproportionate losses" (Bork, *The Antitrust Paradox*, 147). But he then goes on to say that no one had come up with a reasonable theory as to why any corporation would engage in predation. "Unsophisticated theories of predation abound," he writes. And further, that such ideas "foolishly . . . ignore *the constraints the market places* upon firm behavior" (emphasis added, ibid., 144).
6. "Washington News," United Press International, January 12, 1984.
7. Bork, *The Antitrust Paradox*, x.
8. Lippmann, *Drift & Mastery*, 73, 74, 87, 145, 168.
9. Walter Weyl, *The New Democracy* (New York: Macmillan, 1912; reprint New York: Harper & Row, 1964), 250.
10. Ibid., 250.
11. Ibid., 253.
12. Louis Brandeis, "Cutthroat Prices: The Competition That Kills," *Harper's Weekly*, November 15, 1913.
13. Steve Coll, *Deal of the Century: The Breakup of AT&T* (New York: Simon & Schuster, 1988), 29–35, 62.
14. On accusing Baxter of breaking the law, see Charles Babcock, "Baxter Causes Delight and Outrage," *Washington Post*, February 7, 1982. Quotes from Metzenbaum, "Is William Baxter Anti-Antitrust?"
15. Steve Lohr, "Antitrust: Big Business Breathes Easier," *New York Times*, February 15, 1981.
16. Angus Burgin, *The Great Persuasion* (Cambridge, MA: Harvard University Press, 2012); Stoller, *Goliath*, 2019.
17. Christopher Leonard, *Kochland: The Secret History of Koch Industries and Corporate Power in America* (New York: Simon & Schuster, 2019).
18. Green, Nader, and Moore, *The Closed Enterprise System: Enforcement*, xvii, xviii.
19. Sean Wilentz, "General Editors' Introduction," in John Kenneth Galbraith, *The New Industrial State*, 4th ed. (Princeton, NJ: Princeton University Press, 2007).

20. A good example is the following passage from *Economics and the Public Purpose*: "The older socialism allowed of ideology. There could be capitalism with its advantages and disadvantages; there could be public ownership of the means of production with its possibilities and disabilities. There could be a choice between the two. The choice turned on belief—on ideas. Thus it was ideological. The new socialism allows of no acceptable alternatives; it cannot be escaped except at the price of grave discomfort, considerable social disorder and, on occasion, lethal damage to health and well-being. The new socialism is not ideological; it is compelled by circumstance. The compelling circumstance, as the reader will have suspected, is the retarded development of the market system." John Kenneth Galbraith, *Economics and the Public Purpose* (Boston: Houghton Mifflin, 1973), 300–301.

21. Ibid., 234–235.

22. Ibid., 301.

23. Ibid., 299.

24. Ibid., 303.

25. Ibid., 307.

26. Galbraith, Nader wrote, had provided a "useful dichotomy, the American economy could be functionally divided into two economies: the market system and the planning system. In the former, small businessmen and service firms compete among themselves according to the model of the marketplace. But the planning system, by and large the financial, manufacturing and mining sectors, is dominated by our giant corporations" (Nader, Green, and Seligman, *Taming the Giant Corporation*, 27).

27. Interview with Alfred E. Kahn, December 10–11, 1981, final edited transcript, Carter Presidency Project, Charlottesville, Virginia. Kahn was also the mastermind of the "deregulation" of the American airline industry. As Phillip Longman and Lina Khan reported in the *Washington Monthly* in March 2012, in an article titled "Terminal Sickness," not only did deregulation free the airlines to limit the size of seats, it played a huge role in the sharp economic decline of heartland cities like Cincinnati, Minneapolis, Memphis, and St. Louis, relative to cities like New York and Chicago. It also failed to lower prices. See also Paul Dempsey and Andrew Goetz, *Airline Deregulation and Laissez-Faire Mythology* (Westport, CT: Quorum Books, 1992).

28. Stoller, *Goliath*.

29. Robert Reich, *Saving Capitalism: For the Many, Not the Few* (New York: Knopf Doubleday, 2015), 183.

30. Robert Reich, *The Work of Nations* (New York: Vintage, 1992), 140.

31. E. J. Dionne, "Inventing Clintonomics," *Washington Post*, October 15, 1992.

32. Reich, "The Political Roots of Widening Inequality."

33. Jesse Eisinger and Justin Elliott, "These Professors Make More Than a Thousand Bucks an Hour Peddling Megamergers," *ProPublica*, November 16, 2016.

34. 1968 Merger Guidelines, The United States Department of Justice Archives. Available online at https://www.justice.gov/archives/atr/1968-merger-guidelines. Emphasis added.

35. Ibid.

36. 1984 Merger Guidelines, United States Department of Justice Archives. Available online at https://www.justice.gov/archives/atr/1984-merger-guidelines.

37. The Reagan administration Department of Justice published new guidelines in 1982, then revised those in 1984.

38. Bork, *The Antitrust Paradox*, 394.

39. Ibid., 397.

40. Strangely, Bork in *The Antitrust Paradox* defends the practice of resale price maintenance, which as we have seen is one of the most effective tools in preventing price discrimination by powerful intermediaries. Bork characterized the reasoning of Justice Hughes in the *Dr. Miles* case as "mistaken economics" (ibid, 288). Bork's reasoning, however, fits within his larger philosophy. "When a manufacturer wishes to impose resale price maintenance or vertical division of reseller markets, or any other restraint upon the rivalry of resellers, his motive cannot be the

restriction of output and, therefore, can only be the creation of distributive efficiency" (ibid., 289). This contradiction, between defending discrimination and also resale price maintenance, raises the question of whether Bork fully understood the implications of the policies he was promoting.

41. The Clinton administration, during eight years in power, brought only one Robinson-Patman case. William Kovacic, "The Modern Evolution of U.S. Competition Policy Enforcement Norms," *Antitrust Law Journal* 71, no. 2 (2003): 411.

42. Burke, "Speech on Fox's East India Bill."

43. Globalization itself, Reich added, was simply our wish—as consumers—fulfilled. "Intensifying competition for us as consumers and as investors has made the entire economy more productive. In order to be successful, CEOs and financiers have had to move money, machinery, factories, and other assets to where they can be most valuable." Robert Reich, *Supercapitalism: The Transformation of Business, Democracy, and Everyday Life* (New York: Knopf, 2007), 97.

44. For a more complete discussion of how concentration of corporate power can result in the destruction of vital industrial arts and capacities, see my previous book, *Cornered*.

45. John Kwoka's excellent book, *Mergers, Merger Control, and Remedies* (Cambridge, MA: MIT Press, 2014), examines a number of instances in which mergers have resulted in higher prices. A particularly good example of how concentration results in higher prices is the creation of group purchasing organizations, theoretically to assist hospitals in buying supplies, like bedpans or gauze or syringes, as described by Mariah Blake in the article "Dirty Medicine," in the *Washington Monthly*, in July 2010. The antitrust economists Robert Litan and Hal Singer that year released a study in which they estimated that the concentration of power in the GPOs enabled medical device manufacturers to charge Americans $35 billion more than they would be able to in a more competitive market. Margaret Dick Tocknell, "GPOs Driving Up Hospitals' Medical Device Costs, Say Manufacturers," *HealthLeaders Media*, October 10, 2010.

46. As we noted in chapter four, political economists have long understood that the concentration of extreme power over large swaths of the economy and society can result in the destruction of any real sense of "ownership" or "responsibility" over real properties ranging from land to industrial systems.

47. A good short article on the problem is Lynn, "Built to Break: The International System of Bottlenecks in the New Era of Monopoly," *Challenge Magazine*, vol. 55, no. 2, March/April 2012, 87–107.

48. Alessandro Acquisti and Hal Varian, "Conditioning Prices on Purchase History," August 2001 (revised October 2004).

49. Ibid., emphasis added.

CHAPTER EIGHT

1. Kate Conger, "100 Facts for Grand Central Station's 100th Birthday," *Village Voice*, February 1, 2013.

2. Quinn Slobodian, *Globalists: The End of Empire and the Birth of Neoliberalism* (Cambridge, MA: Harvard University Press, 2018), 1.

3. For an excellent description of Zuboff's strengths and weaknesses, see "Capitalism's New Clothes," Evgeny Morozov's review of *Surveillance Capitalism* in the *Baffler*, February 4, 2019. The main problem, he writes, is that Zuboff embraces the analytical methods of the historian Alfred Chandler, who for most of his career never "allowed" any "historical evidence" to "undermine the original causal mechanism behind the analytical model—the one that posits that change is propelled by adaptation and evolution, not by power struggles and revolution."

4. Thomas Jefferson, *Notes on the State of Virginia* (New York: Penguin Books, 1999), Appendix III, 231.

5. One exception was abolition literature, which was routinely suppressed in the southern United States, including for periods of time by the U.S. post office.

6. "Editorial Note: Revisal of the Laws 1776–1786," *Founders Online*, National Archives, ac-

cessed April 11, 2019. See also Steven Waldman, *Founding Faith: Providence, Politics, and the Birth of Religious Freedom in America* (New York: Random House, 2008), 124–125.

7. Madison in 1792 connected this hope to his own stark realism about the limited capacities of people, acting either alone or in groups, and the need to structure institutions to help citizens gather information, deliberate, and make wise decisions. "[M]ysteries belong to religion, not to government; to the ways of the Almighty, not to the works of man," he wrote. "And in religion itself there is nothing mysterious to its author; the mystery lies in the dimness of the human sight. So in the institutions of man let there be no mystery." (Madison, "Who Are the Best Keepers of the People's Liberties.")

8. Jefferson himself, in writing this statement, had consulted Milton and Locke. Kevin Hayes, *The Road to Monticello* (Oxford: Oxford University Press, 2008), 10, 204.

9. In 1774 Quakers and Baptists of Pennsylvania arraigned the Massachusetts delegation for prejudice and control of Baptists in Massachusetts. Bailyn, *The Ideological Origins of the American Revolution*, 268.

10. "There had been nothing before in America on such a scale quite like the evangelical defiance and democratic ferment of this Second Great Awakening." Wood, *The Radicalism of the American Revolution*, 332.

11. Nathan Hatch, *The Democratization of American Christianity* (New Haven, CT: Yale University Press, 1989), 11. These movements, Hatch wrote, "offered the humble a marvelous sense of individual potential and of collective aspiration" (ibid., 5). They also reinforced the increasingly radical democracy of the time, as "democratic values and varieties of evangelical Christianity were mutually reinforcing in the early republic" (ibid., 255, note 79).

12. Wood, *The Radicalism of the American Revolution*, 190. Or as Wood put in later, Americans of this age believed in "An approaching age of perfection—[BUT] a perfection that would be brought about, some said, 'Not by Miracles but by Means,' indeed, 'BY HUMAN EXERTIONS.'" Gordon Wood, *Empire of Liberty: A History of the Early Republic, 1789-1815* (Oxford: Oxford University Press, 2009), 618.

13. Perhaps not surprisingly, it was Whitman who most perfectly captured this balance between the worldly and the soul, writing in 1871: "I hail with joy the oceanic, variegated, intense practical energy, the demand for facts, even the business materialism of the current age, our States. But woe to the age or land in which these things, movements, stopping at themselves, do not tend to ideas. As fuel to flame, and flame to the heavens, so must wealth, science, materialism—even this democracy of which we make so much—unerringly feed the highest mind, the soul. Infinitude the flight: fathomless the mystery. Man, so diminutive, dilates beyond the sensible universe, competes with, outcopes space and time, meditating even one great idea" (Whitman, *Specimen Days and Collect*, 294).

14. George Fitzhugh, *Cannibals All: Or, Slaves Without Masters* (Cambridge, MA: Harvard University Press, 2006).

15. Du Bois, *Black Reconstruction*, 39, 631. And indeed, that indefatigable "sociologist" Fitzhugh led the way in the early years after the war in continuing to libel the political abilities of African Americans, whether they had ever been enslaved or not. (George Fitzhugh, "Camp Lee and the Freedmen's Bureau," *Debow's Review* 2, no. 4 [October 1866]: 346–355.)

16. "British railway engineer" quote from John White, "Andrew Carnegie and Herbert Spencer: A Special Relationship," *Journal of American Studies* 13, no. 1 (1979).

17. Spencer was anything but unique in such musings. The English writer Thomas Carlyle and the French philosopher Auguste Comte held similar views.

18. White, "Andrew Carnegie and Herbert Spencer," 63.

19. Jacob Davidson, "The 10 Richest People of All Time," *Money*, July 30, 2015.

20. Joseph Frazier Wall, *Andrew Carnegie* (New York: Oxford University Press, 1970), 382–383.

21. Barry Werth, *Banquet at Delmonico's* (New York: Random House, 2009); see also Wall, *Andrew Carnegie*, 386–387.

22. Wall, *Andrew Carnegie*, 365.

23. As White put it, "Such misunderstandings of or deviations from Spencerian theory prompt

the question of whether Carnegie (the most literate of millionaires) had actually read Spencer, or whether he had imbibed, possibly at second hand, certain key phrases and premises" (White, "Andrew Carnegie and Herbert Spencer," 67).

24. Karl Popper, in *Open Society and Its Enemies*, details how after the French Revolution had shattered most of the feudal autocratic societies of Europe, Prussia's King Frederick William III intentionally elevated the philosopher Georg Wilhelm Friedrich Hegel to the highest levels of power within the Prussian academy precisely in order to enthrone Hegel's deterministic vision of social and economic structures. The effort, Popper writes, essentially amounted to the installation of a new religious "ideology." Karl Popper, *The High Tide of Prophecy*, vol. 2 in *Open Society and Its Enemies: Hegel and Marx* (Princeton, NJ: Princeton University Press, 1971), 30.

25. Thorelli, *The Federal Antitrust Policy*, 116. Thorelli also makes clear where such thinking originated. "The emerging brand of economics has been variously labeled . . . [But] its representatives were all influenced by the revolution against English classical economics that was taking place in Germany" (ibid., 119).

26. Wall, *Andrew Carnegie*, 371.

27. Andrew Carnegie, "The Gospel of Wealth," in *The "Gospel of Wealth" Essays and Other Writings* (New York: Penguin, 2006), 3.

28. William James Ghent, *Our Benevolent Feudalism* (New York: Macmillan, 1902), 29.

29. La Follette, *Robert La Follette's Autobiography*, 294.

30. Croly, *The Promise of American Life*, 191.

31. Walter Bagehot, *Lombard Street: A Description of the Money Market* (London: John Murray, [1873] 1927), 104. See also Alexander Zevin, *Liberalism at Large: The World According to the Economist* (London: Verso, 2019).

32. Walter Bagehot, *Physics and Politics* (New York: Alfred Knopf, [1872] 1948), 10.

33. In the words of economic historian Duncan Foley, these economists "labored to create an axiomatized, mathematical political economy that could endow the social relations of capitalism with the aura of 'natural laws' that guaranteed the stability and rationality of economic life." Duncan Foley, *Adam's Fallacy: A Guide to Economic Theology* (Cambridge, MA: Harvard University Press, 2006), 157.

34. Leon Walras, *Elements of Pure Economics: Or the Theory of Social Wealth* (Abingdon, UK: Routledge, 2003), 71, emphasis added.

35. Foley writes: "The mathematical version tries to remove the question of morality altogether from economic life, which it represents as governed by objective laws which we have no choice but to follow exactly" (Foley, *Adam's Fallacy*, 158).

36. Jan Keppler, *Monopolistic Competition Theory: Origins, Results, and Implications* (Baltimore: Johns Hopkins University Press, 1994), 12.

37. As Keppler describes the efforts of Stigler and his allies, "Without presenting any conclusive theoretical or empirical evidence for their allegations, they managed to undermine the scientific credibility of the work undertaken in monopolistic competition theory." It was "more of a crusade than . . . an honest attempt to further economic science." Yet it worked, and it provided the budding neoliberal movement with its first great victory (ibid., 114, 119).

38. Karl Popper, *Open Society and Its Enemies: The Spell of Plato* (Princeton, NJ: Princeton University Press, 1971), 5, 199.

39. Du Bois, *Black Reconstruction*, 715.

40. Foley holds that "The history of economics . . . oscillates between these two poles" of "mathematical physics" and "evolutionary biology" (Foley, *Adam's Fallacy*, 157).

41. Ibid., 158.

42. One writer who came close was the sociologist Karl Polanyi, born in Austria three years after Schumpeter, and who was also deeply influenced by Marx. As Quinn Slobodian described Polanyi's writing in *Globalists*: "Polanyi's ideas provide an elegant parable whereby the capitalist world economy progressively eliminates barriers to its own functioning, to the point that it destroys its own capacity for self-reproduction. In this narrative, the market is omnivorous,

relentlessly transforming land, labor, and money into commodities, until the basis for social life has been destroyed" (Slobodian, *Globalists*, 16).

43. Joseph Schumpeter, *Capitalism, Socialism, and Democracy* (New York: Harper & Brothers, 1942), 83. In addition to adopting Carnegie's pet idea of biological determinism, Schumpeter also adopted Carnegie's idea of potential competition. For more on Carnegie's thinking on this, see Thorelli, *The Federal Antitrust Policy*, 116.

44. Thorelli, *The Federal Antitrust Policy*, 120.

45. Wilson, *The New Freedom*, 60.

46. Berk, *Louis D. Brandeis and the Making of Regulated Competition, 1900–1932*, 65.

47. Ibid., 46, 68.

48. Ibid., 68, 79–81.

49. Schlesinger, *The Politics of Upheaval*, 650.

50. Binyamin Appelbaum, *The Economists' Hour: False Prophets, Free Markets, and the Fracture of Society* (New York: Little, Brown, 2019).

51. Richard Posner, *Economic Analysis of Law*, 3rd ed. (Boston: Little, Brown, 1986), 23.

52. Ibid., 24, emphasis added.

53. Ibid., 23.

54. Ibid., xix, 24, emphasis added.

55. Ibid., 26.

56. Ibid., 25, emphasis added.

57. Ibid., 25, emphasis added.

58. Ibid., 23.

59. Ibid., xix.

60. Marc Allen Eisner, *Antitrust and the Triumph of Economics: Institutions, Expertise, & Policy Change* (Chapel Hill: University of North Carolina, 1991), 138.

61. Ibid., 189.

62. Ibid., 190.

63. Eisner adds, "Economic expertise was given an organizational presence at each stage of the policy process, creating an institutional transmission belt." Ibid., 188.

64. Ibid., 191.

65. Ibid.

66. John Eggerton, "FCC Economics Office's First Conclusion: Office Is Justified," *Broadcasting + Cable*, April 5, 2019.

67. Paul Krugman, "Why We're in a New Gilded Age," *New York Review of Books*, May 8, 2014.

68. Okrent, *The Guarded Gate*, 208–209.

69. Thomas Piketty, *Capital in the Twenty-First Century* (Cambridge, MA: Harvard University Press, 2014).

70. For Piketty's warning about relying on "purely economic mechanisms," see ibid., 20. Yet on his first page, describing his central thesis, Piketty writes, "When the rate of return on capital exceeds the rate of growth of output and income . . . capitalism automatically generates arbitrary and unsustainable inequalities that radically undermine the meritocratic values on which democratic societies are based" (ibid., 1). For the article on Piketty's determinism, see Rana Foroohar, "Thomas Piketty: Marx 2.0," *Time Magazine*, May 8, 2014.

71. Piketty, *Capital*, 573–574.

72. Piketty defines "political economics" as the effort to study "rationally, systematically, and methodically, the ideal role of the state in the economic and social organization of a country" (ibid., 574). For the comment on Slim and Gates see ibid., 444.

73. Ibid., 575.

74. Ibid., 30.

75. Ibid., 515.

76. Ibid., 31.

77. Ibid., 32, 574.
78. Ibid., 32, emphasis added.

CHAPTER NINE
1. Alex Zucker, a physicist, was the first person I found to have used this phrase, in 1988, when he was acting director of Oak Ridge National Laboratory. Alex Zucker, "Toward a Technological Commons," *Oak Ridge National Laboratory Review*, vol. 21, no. 1 (1988): 2.
2. Reed Hundt, *A Crisis Wasted: Barack Obama's Defining Decisions* (New York: Simon & Schuster, 2019).
3. Amos 3:10.
4. As Gordon Wood said of the revolutionaries, "There is simply too much fanatical and millennial thinking" to be able to characterize these people "as peculiarly rational and legalistic." Gordon Wood, "Rhetoric and Reality in the American Revolution," *William and Mary Quarterly*, 3rd series, 23 (1966): 2.
5. Sacvan Bercovitch wrote that, the jeremiad "marked the colonists' first literary innovation and their most enduring social legacy." The jeremiad offered "a promise of threat, doomsday, and millennium entwined—that vision of America as an unfolding prophecy." Sacvan Bercovitch, *The American Jeremiad* (Madison: University of Wisconsin Press, 2012), xii, xiii. See also James Darsey, *The Prophetic Tradition and Radical Rhetoric in America* (New York: New York University Press, 1997).
6. Or as Abraham Heschel put it, "Their words are onslaughts, scuttling illusions of false security, challenging evasions, calling faith to account, questioning prudence and impartiality." Abraham Heschel, *The Prophets* (Peabody, MA: Prince Press, 1999), xi.
7. John Milton, "Areopagitica," in *John Milton Prose*, 209.
8. Numbers 11:29.
9. Bercovitch, *The American Jeremiad*, 9.
10. King, *Where Do We Go from Here?*, 181.

INDEX